# MARITAL THERAPY

## INTEGRATING THEORY AND TECHNIQUE

**LEN SPERRY**
MEDICAL COLLEGE OF WISCONSIN

**JON CARLSON**
GOVERNORS STATE UNIVERSITY, ILLINOIS

D0188212

LP

**LOVE PUBLISHING COMPANY**
Denver, Colorado 80222

# *Dedication*

**T**his book is lovingly dedicated to our spouses, Patricia Sperry and Laura Carlson, and our children: Tracey, Christen, Tim, Jon, and Stevie Sperry; and Kirstin, Matthew, Karin, Benjamin, and Kali Carlson.

# Contents

# Preface

The field of marital therapy is in the midst of tremendous growth and ferment. To begin with, the fields of psychotherapy, including marital therapy, are undergoing a major paradigm shift. The initial paradigm and the first-knowledge explosion in psychotherapy were basically therapist-focused—which is to say that developments in theory and technique emphasized the training of competent therapists to deal with therapeutic issues. And that was how it should have been at that time. Now a paradigm shift is occurring following a second knowledge explosion in the field. The new paradigm emphasizes treatment tailored to the individual's needs, styles, and expectations. It also will focus on early interventions such as prevention and enrichment, rather than on just pathology.

Why is this shift occurring now? It is happening because of theoretical breakthroughs and because of clinical necessity and policy changes. Significant theoretical and clinical research advances have given rise to more specialized and effective treatment modalities. In the past "traditional" couples seeking therapy tended to be younger middle-class individuals who had relatively focused concerns. Today, more and more nontraditional couples are in need of professional treatment. These couples are of varying ages—many are older—and socioeconomic classes, and they present a wider variety of difficult and pervasive issues including medical and psychiatric concerns. Furthermore, in our clinical practice we regularly work with couples who have terminated with other therapists because of an incompatibility between their needs, style, expectations, and the previous therapist's approach. Despite increased therapeutic know-how, clients' and couples' concerns likewise have become increasingly more complex.

Another important reason for this paradigm shift involves changes in health care policy. Health care personnel are under tremendous pressure today to justify the need for treatment and to be accountable for effective treatment outcomes. Just as with the practice of individual therapy, those preparing to practice marital therapy must be thoroughly trained in the use of several different modalities for assessment and treatment, in order to effectively tailor treatment to a wide variety of couples and their concerns.

What makes this book different from others is that it describes and illustrates such a couples-centered tailored focus. Today, individuals who are training to do marital therapy need strong grounding in the traditional subject matter of the field, and an orientation and training experiences that will prepare them for tomorrow's anticipated changes in the kind of therapeutic services that will be marketable and in the nontraditional settings in which these services will be situated. The therapist will be challenged to think integratively and comprehensively—that is, in terms of the biological as well as the psychological and systems perspective—and to match or tailor treatment. In short, then, this book is oriented to training creative and flexible therapists who can accommodate to the changing needs of the marketplace and provide competent and accountability-based treatment.

Designed as a primary textbook for marital therapy courses in counseling or clinical psychology, social work, and nursing programs, this book also can be effectively incorporated into psychiatry and family medicine residency training programs. And it can serve as a library or desk reference for practicing professionals who want to develop further skills in tailoring treatments and work from a more integrative and preventive-enrichment orientation.

The text is arranged in four sections. The first overviews pertinent psychological and sociocultural factors affecting contemporary marriages. It also characterizes the relational skills and attitudes of high-functioning as compared with low-functioning or dysfunctional couples. A chapter on health factors in marriage is one of the unique aspects of this text.

The second section focuses on the dominant models of marital therapy in contemporary practice. Separate chapters are included on psychoanalytic, behavioral, and systems approaches, as well as extensive coverage of the integrative approaches to marriage and marital therapy. Another unique feature of this book is the section in the psychoanalytic chapter on the self-psychology approach.

Chapters in the third section describe and illustrate the practice of marital therapy, covering the process of treatment from initial contact through termination. A detailed chapter on assessment offers a comprehensive approach to couple evaluation and treatment planning and includes reviews of several assessment devices. Chapters on effective treatment intervention techniques and special treatment issues complete this section.

The last section presents separate chapters on professional concerns and research issues in marital therapy. A full-length case study exemplifies the integrative and tailored approach to treatment that is the basic theme of the text.

We wish to acknowledge several individuals who have helped transform a number of clinical experiences, lunch discussions, and rough drafts into a coherent finished product. We are especially grateful to our teachers, Rudolf Dreikurs, Don Dinkmeyer, Bernard Shulman, Robert Powers, Harold Mosak, Mim Pew, and Gerald Mozdzierz. Editorial support and typing thanks go to Candace Ward Howell, Kim James, and Dawn Stalbaum. We additionally would like to thank our reviewers, Dr. Robert Smith and Dr. Margaret Emerson, who provided helpful feedback on earlier versions of the manuscript.

Finally, we would like to thank our friend and publisher, Stan Love. His flexibility and understanding of the professional field has made collaboration both possible and enjoyable.

*Len Sperry*
*Jon Carlson*

# 1

# Psychosocial Factors in Marital Functioning

**M**arital therapy typically begins with a phone call such as this one: "Hi, I'm Janet Johnson. We got your name from the Simpsons. I'd like to make an appointment. I think my husband and I need some help with our marriage."

Marital problems are the most common reason for the referral of clients to mental health professionals. Indeed, 50% of individuals presenting to psychiatrists complain of marital difficulties (Sager, Gundlach, & Kremmer, 1968). Sholevar (1985) estimated that 75% of individuals entering psychotherapy do so because of marital disorders or difficulties in addition to another presenting problem.

An examination of marital therapy best begins with a discussion of the larger contexts in which marriages exist and in which marital problems and issues arise. This chapter and the following two chapters provide this overview. Specifically, this chapter provides the reader with a panoramic view of the changing social and cultural trends that have and are influencing the institution of marriage. The chapter also provides a psychological perspective on the process of attraction, love, and the developmental phases of a marital relationship. Finally, we briefly describe the development of marital therapy as a professional discipline and profile the changing pattern of the clinical practice of marital therapy.

# SOCIAL AND CULTURAL INFLUENCES ON MARRIAGE

## The Traditional Model of Marriage

During the past several generations, the institution of marriage has undergone considerable change. For centuries marriages were arranged. They had culturally defined, prescribed, and nonnegotiable rules and duties. The purpose of this type of marriage—known as a *traditional marriage*—was for each spouse to fulfill expected role obligations. There was common cultural agreement about what husbands and wives "should" do. Marital rules were closely associated with sex role stereotypes, so that men were reluctant to perform women's duties and vice versa. The traditional male roles were husband, father, breadwinner, sexual aggressor, financial planner, household mechanic, and so on. Traditional female roles were wife, mother, homemaker, sexual recipient, child care provider, housemaid, and so on.

Two key concepts in the traditional marriage were *duty* and *responsibility*. Duty connoted a known set of role functions that each spouse accepted at marriage. If a person refused such role functions, he or she would not marry. Once married, each spouse was "responsible" for his or her role function. If love occurred at all in traditional marriages, it developed after the marriage was consummated. Basically, love was not a prerequisite in the decision to marry.

Traditionally, the marital agenda usually focused on the development of a family—children—and the acquisition of property—the home. Such an agenda implied a high degree of stability so that "roots" could be established. In the past, role conflict was less of a factor in marital strife than it is today because marital roles were relatively fixed by the state, religious teachings, and tradition. Also, there was little need to change role expectations because of the stability of the prevailing culture. Examples of the traditional marriage model can be seen today in the Old Order Amish and some of the conservative Mennonite sects. These groups follow the Bible literally and maintain stable relationships because of their fixed and socially supported devotion to biblical injunctions about the roles of husband and wife. When there is any doubt about what husband or wife should do, the family and group pressure combine to ensure that the couple capitulates to these roles.

Traditional marriages produced predictable marital problems. Because marital roles were prescribed and could not easily be changed, marital difficulty was usually related to role adaptation. This adaptational pathology took a few predictable patterns. The most common form of pathology was the *trapped wife syndrome*. Women were so constrained and bored by the repetitiveness and demands of childrearing and household duties that they often became resentful, depressed, angry, and unfulfilled. The most common clinical manifestation of this syndrome was depression, for which many sought the assistance of mental health professionals.

## The Modern, or Companionate, Marriage Model

A perceptible shift away from the traditional model of marriage started with the Industrial Revolution in the latter part of the 19th century. The emergence of the modern model did not become obvious until after World War II, however. In the modern, or *companionate*, style of marriage, roles are not prescribed; they evolve through negotiation and can be variable and vague. Therefore, communication and negotiation skills are vital in this process, as is enough maturity on the part of each spouse to know what he or she wants from the marriage.

Key concepts in the companionate marriage are *love* and *choice*. In this type of marriage, the woman and man want to be together because they love each other and expect to obtain fulfillment from their relationship. The potential for attaining this romantic ideal is a relatively recent phenomenon that implies a level of prosperity sufficient to extricate persons from a survival mode of living. This model also requires a degree of equality between the spouses that was not possible in times when life expectancy was short, when there was a lack of economic opportunity and education for women, and when adequate birth control means did not exist. The freedom of both spouses to choose marriage is a far cry from the arranged marriages of the past. This freedom appears to be an ongoing matter after marriage, because divorce is relatively easy to obtain. Now that women have joined the work force and are slowly beginning to achieve economic freedom, divorce is as much an option for them as it is for men.

The increasing status and freedom of women are recent trends that derive largely from increased employment rates among women, increased educational achievement (more than 50% of college enrollments in 1980 were women), fewer children per woman, childbearing at a later age, and increased utilization of day care facilities. With this increased status has come increased freedom of choice as well as increased marital stress, which has probably contributed to a higher divorce rate (Stewart, Bjorksten, & Glick, 1985).

In contrast to traditional marriages, companionate marriages lead to different kinds of marital issues and problems. Because companionate marriages focus on emotional fulfillment, role functions are not carefully considered during the courtship. Thus, marital difficulties manifest in terms of marital role definition and include role ambiguity, power struggles, communication problems, and unmet expectations. Of these, communication difficulties are the most common manifestation, but they are usually the symptom, not the cause, of more basic problems. Not surprisingly, communication difficulties are unique to companionate marriage because communication is the sine qua non of love and is required for role negotiation.

## THE CHANGING MARITAL SCENE

We have now broadly described the shift from the traditional model of marriage to the companionate model. This section further characterizes this shift with some specific statistics regarding the structure of the family, the style of marriage, divorce, remarriage, and childrearing practices. Then we can suggest some likely future trends of marriage and the family.

Today, there is no one form of marital and family living arrangement in the United States as there was at the end of the 1960s. The single-breadwinner, nuclear family that was the dominant form now comprises less than 10% of living arrangements. Today the most prevalent household composition is one in which people live in a child-free or post-childbearing marriage. This form comprises approximately 23% of the households and is followed by single, widowed, separated, or divorced persons, comprising approximately 21%; single-parent families, comprising 16%; and dual-breadwinner, nuclear families, comprising about 20%. Stepfamilies make up at least 15% of all households in the United States (Glick, Clarkin, & Kessler, 1988).

Although most Americans still marry prior to age 30, there has been a noticeable delay in marriage, with more marriages occurring when partners are between 25 and 44 years of age. At the end of the 1960s, the average age at which people got married was between 18 and 22 years.

A vast majority of women continue to become mothers, although increasingly large numbers of them delay childbearing and prefer to have fewer children. In 1900, the average female bore approximately six children, whereas today the average female bears one or two children.

Divorce rates have been rising in most developing countries since the mid-1970s. Today, approximately 50% of new marriages will end in divorce, usually within the first 2 years, although there have been some signs that divorce rates are leveling off. In 1979, 41.5% of all marriages involved at least one partner who had been previously married. In 1980, it was noted that following the first divorce, almost 80% of partners remarried. Following a second divorce, approximately 90% remarried (Stewart, Bjorksten, & Glick, 1985).

In short, current trends in the modern marriage include a longer wait before a women has children, fewer children per family, the use of alternative childrearing facilities such as day care centers, and high divorce rates. Do these statistics and trends suggest the demise of marriage and family life? A growing number of researchers say "no"; they feel that marriage and family are in fact evolving and developing. Men, women, and children have more options than their ancestors did. Individuals are no longer forced to work at an early age and can thus develop their creative potential. Men are no longer limited to the disciplining function in childrearing; they can also be involved in the nurturant function. The family itself has more choices.

Because our culture has moved to an extended kinship model—father, mother, grandparents, relatives, housekeepers, ex-spouses—each individual can support other family members in diverse ways. There may even be some advantages in one-parent families: Individual growth for both the child(ren) and the parent may be greater than in two-parent families. Researchers predict even more changes in lifestyle, peer and power relationships, social and intellectual competence, health patterns, and family values. They predict there will be an increase in dual-career and single-parent families in the future, and although there will be a leveling off of single-parent families, there will be more households headed by females (Bjorksten & Stewart, 1984).

So far we have described a number of social, political, and economic influences that have radically changed marriage as an institution in our society. The discussion now shifts to the psychological processes of attraction and mate selection and the developmental processes and phases of marriage.

# THE DEVELOPMENTAL PROCESSES IN MARRIAGE

This section describes how two individuals become attracted to one another, get married, and develop a life together. We will look at three components that are involved in this developmental process model of marriage: each spouse's personality and the influence of his or her family of origin, the attraction and mate selection process, and marital systems dimensions and the stages of marriage. See Figure 1.1 for a developmental model of this process.

## Family-of-Origin Influences

A basic tenet of marital and family theory is that an individual spouse's functioning in a marriage relationship is greatly influenced by his or her family of origin. The belief that a person can totally separate from the family of origin and become an autonomous individual is erroneous. The impact of a spouse's heritage and transgenerational background is strong. The influence is, however, not uniform from couple to couple. Some persons do replicate dysfunctional marital

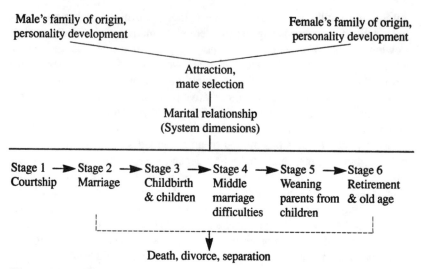

Male's family of origin,
personality development

Female's family of origin,
personality development

Attraction,
mate selection

Marital relationship
(System dimensions)

Stage 1 ⟶ Stage 2 ⟶ Stage 3 ⟶ Stage 4 ⟶ Stage 5 ⟶ Stage 6
Courtship   Marriage   Childbirth   Middle   Weaning   Retirement
                    & children   marriage   parents from   & old age
                                  difficulties   children

Death, divorce, separation

**Figure 1.1   A Developmental Model of Marriage**

patterns from their families of origin, whereas others from disturbed and inadequate families of origin manage to achieve adequately functional marriages. Similarly, some individuals whose parental marriages appear to be functional do not necessarily fare well in their own marriages. But, generally speaking, there is a reasonable degree of correspondence between the nature and strength of a person's own family of origin and his or her own marriage and family.

The influence of relatives on a marriage can range from subtle to obvious. If parents are alive, they may be involved very clearly and specifically in a new or ongoing marriage. They may take sides, comment on childrearing practices, or live in the flat upstairs. In healthy families, in-laws can provide a great deal of cohesion and emotional and financial support to make a new marriage function more efficiently. But in-laws can also be a destructive force. Even when the extended family is not physically present, the patterns experienced by the spouses in their families of origin inevitably influence their current marital and family interactions.

Another basic tenet of marital and family theory is the *multigenerational hypothesis* (Berman, Lief, & Williams, 1981), which holds that values, beliefs, behaviors, and symptoms may be passed down from one generation to the next through a complex chain of relatedness. In a sense this hypothesis is a restatement of the scripture maxim: The sins of one generation will be passed to the next (Exodus 20:5).

Boszormenyi-Nagy and Spark (1976) noted that the major connecting tie between generations can be called "invisible loyalties." They believe that loyalty and justice play a major role in determining family relations. They view parenting and "childing" as relationships in which certain "things," such as caretaking, are "owed." According to Boszormenyi-Nagy and Spark, families keep account ledgers of balance and imbalance concerning what is owed: indebtedness and reciprocity. An important task of adulthood is to balance loyalties to one's parents. This is most commonly done by becoming a parent oneself. In short, "invisible loyalties" guide adults in relating to spouses and children.

Often a person will attempt to live up to the normative value orientations of his or her family of origin and also try to get the spouse to do likewise. Even if the couple is able to make a reasonable attempt to balance old loyalties with new ones, problems come up in the marriage because each family of origin has its own type of accounting system. For example, the wife in a new marriage comes from a family in which affection is shown by the bestowing of large gifts, whereas the husband's family of origin does not use gifts as part of its accounting system but is affectionate and supportive. What does the couple owe to the latter family in response to affection and support? Boszormenyi-Nagy and Spark (1976) noted that unconscious attempts to maintain "invisible loyalty" to the family of origin by rejecting a spouse may actually underlie problems such as impotence, premature ejaculation, and anorgasmia.

**Personality Development**

A marriage is a union of two individuals with different families of origin, different loyalties, and different needs and expectations. Both individuals expect or "contract" that the marriage will in some way meet their needs. Why would one spouse want to change the terms of the marriage contract once it has been made? We turn to the research on adult development for some answers. This literature suggests that there are predictable changes in the needs and expectations of adults over time. Thus, the marital contract needs periodic restructuring if the spouses are to remain together.

Levinson, with Darrow, Klein, Levinson, and McKee (1978) described adult stages of development in terms of the "life structure" and its changes. Levinson's research was in large part informed by Erik Erikson's stages of psychosocial development. Levinson defined life structure as the "underlying pattern or design of a person's life at a given time" and included the individual's psychosocial matrix, values, ego functions, and participation in the world as part of the structure. Levinson viewed the person as an active agent creating his or her own life structure. He described each stage as a stable period of approximately 6 to 8 years in duration in which the individual's task is to form a stable life structure. He also described periods of 3 to 5 years between each stage in which the task is to review, examine, and revise the life structure.

Levinson describes the following periods in the life structure:

*Ages 22 to 40—Early Adulthood:* Forming an initial life structure; becoming an adult; "intimacy vs. isolation".
1. 20 to 28. "Getting into the adult world" and forming a provisional life structure.
2. 27 to 31. Age 30 transition—questioning one's initial life structure.
3. 32 to 38. "Settling in", becoming a full adult; the usual life structure includes marriage, children or occupation, or singlehood.

*Forty to 60—Mid-Adulthood:* "Generativity vs. Stagnation".
1. Age 40 transition, which may take much of the decade: reexamination of the past; issues of generativity, giving back to the community; life structure for the next half of life, reassessment and revision of life structure.
2. 50's transition. Questioning one's new life structure. May not be necessary if age 40 transition has been prolonged.
3. 50 to 60. "Settling down" into mid-adulthood.

*Sixty to 80—Later Adulthood:* "Integrity vs. Despair". Settling accounts with oneself, choosing a life structure for the remaining years.
1. 59 to 62. Age 60 transition—life review: summing up, finding new life structure and goals for remaining years.
2. 70 "Settling into older adulthood".
3. 70's "Old old" (issues of declining health are central).

Levinson viewed the period of the 40s as the most turbulent and confused. Here the individual has attained some measure of power and status but also must be content with the loss of youth, a changing body, and missed opportunities. Adult development research suggests that actual change in personality does occur as a person ages. Because marriage requires some shared goals and some shared perceptions of the spouse's personality, needs, and wishes, differing patterns and degrees of growth in each spouse can produce considerable marital disruption.

Marital stress is most likely to occur at transition points. During a transition phase, everything may feel awkward and "out of phase." During such times, disenchantment and serious questioning occur and a need for change is often deeply felt. Such transitions can be particularly stressful for already troubled relationships because marriages that have been difficult but bearable often tend to feel unbearable during a life review.

# ATTRACTION AND MATE SELECTION

We have already considered the questions of the impact of the family of origin and stage of personality development. We have seen how both dimensions influence spousal expectations for the marriage relationship. A related question is how do two individuals become attracted to one another and fall in love? There are two commonplace explanations of this phenomenon: "Birds of a feather flock together," and "opposites attract." Interesting research on the attraction process tends to focus on one or the other of these explanations. We will look at both.

## Birds of a Feather

Sternberg (1987) summarized research on the *similarities hypothesis* of interpersonal attraction. In essence, the similarities hypothesis states that the more similar two individuals are to one another, the more likely they are to be attracted to one another. Sternberg indicated that there are six components that affect the attraction of one person to another: physical attractiveness, arousal, proximity, reciprocity, similarity, and barriers.

### Physical Attractiveness

People look for partners whose level of physical attractiveness matches their own (Murstein, 1976). Sternberg's research revealed that men tend to place more value on a woman's physical attractiveness than women do on men. Yet, Sternberg contended that one individual's perception of another's attractiveness increases to the extent that one likes the other and decreases to the extent that one does not.

### Arousal

Sternberg's research (1988) showed that an individual is more likely to be attracted to another if he or she experiences some arousal. The arousal need not come from the other person; it may reflect the environment. An example of this might be taking a date to an exciting environment, such as a collegiate basketball game between two closely matched rivals. Later, generating excitement in a relationship helps keep the relationship going.

*Proximity*

Proximity may be the most important factor in determining whom an individual will meet. Individuals are most likely to meet persons who are in close physical proximity to them. For the average person, mate selection occurs based on contact and experience with fewer than 12 potential mates.

*Reciprocity*

People tend to like those who think like them. They are more likely to be attracted to a person who is willing to self-disclose if they believe in self-disclosure and sharing. The old saying "What you give is what you get" reflects this principle of reciprocity.

*Similarity*

Similarity is the heart of the birds of a feather explanation of the attraction process. In essence, the more similar one person is to another, the more likely he or she is to be attracted to that person. Similarities typically involve background, education, life experiences, hobbies, religious affiliation, professional training and experience, and interests. People who are similar in a variety of ways tend to respond to situations in an emotionally congruent manner. Thus, they become even more attractive to one another.

*Barriers*

Sternberg (1988) defined barriers as the "hard-to-get effect." Basically, most individuals tend to be attracted to those persons who are selective in whom they date. In other words, individuals are more attracted to persons who seem to be a challenge than to people who are not. Difficulty "getting" to the other person not only intensifies passion; it renews the person's attempt to attain the goal.

Sternberg concluded that unless a number of these factors are operational, it is unlikely the two individuals will reach the point of "falling in love." This birds of a feather perspective on interpersonal attraction is only one side of the coin. The other side is aptly described by the old adage "opposites attract."

**Opposites Attract**

Sperry (1978) contended that searching for similarities and commonalities is primarily a conscious process and follows the unconscious attraction of personalities. It is at this unconscious level that attraction of "opposites" or complementarity develops. From this perspective, there are three phases in the attraction process: "love at first sight," "checking each other out," and "formalizing the private pact."

## Love at First Sight

Within the first few moments of meeting—or even observing—another person, contact is made at a very deep unconscious level. An individual somehow senses whether another person has the capability of fulfilling his or her deepest needs. The "love at first sight" feeling that poets and novelists have described is none other than an exuberant recognition that the other person has the capacity to offer fulfillment.

This first phase can be likened to a radio or sonar transmission and reception. An individual's personality style is like a transmitter that is constantly beaming out a message on a particular frequency. The message contains the person's life story: who he or she is, how he or she sees the world and other people, and how he or she has decided to secure a sense of meaning and belonging in life. The message also contains a set of expectations for what the person will and will not do, how he or she expects to be treated, and how he or she will treat others. This message is beamed out constantly, and it does not change unless the personality structure changes. This message is primarily unconscious and thus is largely transmitted nonverbally. It shows as much in how an individual speaks as in what he or she says. This message goes unheeded by some but is received by others. Persons who are seeking a mate who can complement or fulfill their own unconscious personality needs and strivings will have their receivers tuned in to such a frequency. When the transmission is received "from across a crowded room," a recognition response is likely.

## Checking Each Other Out

Whether the relationship develops depends on phases two and three. In the second phase, prospective mates do what amounts to a credit check on each other that determines how closely the prospective mate resembles the consciously constructed picture of the "ideal" mate. This checking-out process, which also includes a scrutiny of the other person's background, interests, and values, may take 10 minutes or 10 months—or even longer.

## Formalizing the Private Pact

In phase three a mutual decision must be reached about the future of the relationship. The decision may be instant and idyllic or protracted and filled with turmoil. Relatives or friends may object. More often than not, the prospective mate will not match the culturally embodied stereotype of the ideal mate. Dissonance and confusion follow, often resulting in rationalization and unrealistic expectations for changing the prospective mate. This unconscious coupling of two personality styles ultimately can make or break a relationship.

This coupling does not mean a merging of the personality styles. On the contrary, opposites often attract because they complement one another. For example, an aggressive, determined person may want a spouse who is supportive and willing to be led, just as a passive, submissive person may seek a mate on whose strength he or she can rely. Or the person with a high need to please others and to be accepted may choose someone who demands, often in a selfish way, admiration and submission.

## The Loss of Attraction

Because these deeper personality needs and patterns do lead to strong attraction, how is it that two people who are strongly attracted to each other come to a point when they can no longer tolerate each other? Dreikurs (1946) was one of the first to observe that the qualities that initially attract two people to each other are basically the same factors that cause discord and divorce. Dreikurs noted that any human quality or trait can be perceived in a positive or a negative way. A person can be considered either kind or weak or strong or domineering, depending on point of view. Dreikurs suggested that one person does not like another for his or her virtues or dislike that person for his or her faults. Rather, an emphasis on a person's positive qualities grows out of affection for that person, just as an emphasis on weaknesses grows out of rejection. This emphasis on the individual's weakness or negative trait provides an excuse for having to communicate, to negotiate, and to resolve conflicts.

Typically, during a marital evaluation we will ask one spouse what attracted her to her mate. What did she see in this person that was different from others? Often physical attraction is mentioned first. But on further probing the woman may admit, "I like his gentleness. . . . I like the way he could get things done, how he could plan things out . . . how well he used money." Looking at her background, we might discover that she experienced less than gentle upbringing, that she had difficulty making plans and commitments, that she had trouble budgeting and using money and time wisely. These reflect her personality style and some of the specific need fulfillment she seeks.

In responding to the same question, the male will often give the culturally expected response of physical attractiveness. Then he might add, "I like her free spirit; she really knows how to have a good time. . . . She's the kind of individual who doesn't get bogged down into things. . . . She can be the life of the party . . . and she's a very generous and giving person." An investigation into his background and personality style will suggest how his unfulfilled needs could be complemented in relationship with such a person. Each of these persons actually has qualities that the other values, and thus they are attracted to each other.

Everything goes along smoothly until one or both are threatened, at which point courage begins to wane. When cooperation and courage decrease, defensiveness increases and the attracting qualities come to be perceived in a much more negative way. Whereas before she viewed him as gentle, now she describes him as weak and cowering. Whereas previously she perceived him as being able to plan and structure things, now she sees him as domineering and inflexible. Initially, he perceived her as free spirited, but now he views her as flighty, coquettish, and scatterbrained. Rather than generous and giving, she is now deemed a careless spendthrift.

As courage wanes, so does trust. The more two partners become defensive, the more they are likely to disown any responsibility for a problem and blame the other. This is the basis of most conflicts. What brings two people together can be the source of their separation. What unites two people actually creates a bond between two separate uniquenesses that can add a new dimension of strength and vitality to each other's life.

### Positive and Negative Cooperation

As Dreikurs (1946, 1968) noted, this process of relabeling—that is, of perceiving formerly "ideal" qualities as "despised" qualities—has much to do with cooperation. He stated that whatever two poeple do to and with each other is based on mutual agreement and full cooperation. No relationship is possible without both spouses communicating to each what they think and feel and without full cooperation, be it for the good or for the bad. Dreikurs noted that people are so accustomed to using the term *cooperation* for constructive interactions that they overlook that one person cannot even fight without the other's full cooperation. Cooperation is an orderly, harmonious working together toward a common objective. Positive cooperation is the expression of a sense of belonging together, a sense of self-confidence, a sense of confidence in the other, and the element of courage. Dreikurs believed that these four qualities are the sources of positive cooperative action, whereas hostility, distrust, inferiority feelings, and fear are the bases of negative cooperation (Dreikurs, 1946).

## Collusion and Projective Identification

This discussion of negative and positive cooperation is closely related to two concepts that have been particularly useful in understanding the intrapersonal as well as the interpersonal dimensions of marital relations: projective identification and collusion. *Projective identification* is the process of imaginatively splitting off part of one's self and attributing it to the spouse for the sake of controlling the spouse (St. Clair, 1986).

Projective identification requires reciprocity. A relationship does not result unless each spouse is willing at an unconscious level to accept and identify with the projective identifications from the other spouse. This willingness is called *collusion*, or a "secret pact" (Dreikurs, 1968; Sperry, 1978). Collusion can be described as an unspoken and basically unconscious alliance of two persons to fulfill each other's needs for completeness at any cost. Often this pact challenges logic and common sense. It may even require a distancing from other people for it to work. The lyrics of the song "You and Me Against The World," recorded by Helen Reddy, stated the basic attitude of such pacts. In the song two people have convinced themselves that even though they have very little to offer each other—besides the illusion of completeness—somehow magically and mysteriously everything will work out. The two hang tenaciously onto each other and their illusion as they scorn a world that tries to tell them they are irresponsible and deluded.

Various combinations of personality styles between spouses have been described (Sperry, 1978; Topf, 1984; Main & Oliver, 1988). Sperry (1978) posited a stage theory according to which the development of healthy intimate relationships proceeds through the stages of dependence, negative independence, positive independence, and interdependence. The early phases are related to negative cooperation; the later stages more closely approximate positive cooperation.

## Complementary, Symmetrical, or Parallel Relationships

These phases in the development of cooperation have been described by other authors and researchers in somewhat different terms. Relationships have been described as complementary, symmetrical, or parallel (Lederer & Jackson, 1968). A complementary relationship is based on a maximization of differences between spouses and on an exchange of behaviors that seem to fit together or complement one another. A symmetrical relationship is based on a minimization of differences between spouses and on an assumed equality in behavior. A parallel relationship is based on flexible and situationally appropriate interactions in which there is a blending of the complementary and symmetrical styles of relationships. Most agree that healthy relationships are parallel, or interdependent. Research supports the position that parallel, or interdependent, relationship styles lead to higher levels of marital adjustment and satisfaction than do either complementary or symmetrical relationship styles. Main and Oliver (1988) reported that personality styles and priorities that are both parallel and symmetrical are significant indicators and predictors of marital adjustment.

## THE TRIANGLE OF LOVE

According to Sternberg (1986, 1988), love has three components: intimacy, passion, and decision/commitment. Intimacy encompasses the feelings of closeness, connectedness, and bondedness. Passion encompasses the drive that leads to romance, physical attraction, and sexual consummation. Decision/commitment comprises a short-term decision to love one another and a long-term commitment to maintain that love.

Sternberg's research suggests that the amount of love one person experiences for another depends on the absolute strength of these three components. The kind of love an individual experiences depends on the strength of these components relative to each other. In their interactions, the three components give rise to a number of different kinds of loving experiences.

Sternberg (1986) and Goleman (1985) indicated that intimacy, passion, and commitment change in level or degree during the course of a long-term relationship. Figure 1.2 reflects these changes. The reader should note that intimacy and passion develop rapidly in conjunction with one another, but at a certain point in the relationship the level of commitment begins to rise and match the level of intimacy while the level of passion greatly drops off.

Conceptualization of love in terms of these three components and their changes is quite useful. Couples often complain that their "love has cooled" when in reality they are speaking about a change in the level of passion. If commitment and intimacy continue to be adequate, the relationship is not in jeopardy.

### Stages of Marital Development

So far we have described the potential spouses as two individuals who have developed through various stages and have unique needs and expectations for marriage based on their families of origin and cultural milieu. These two individuals become attracted to one another, develop a contract for their relationship, and marry. Let us complete our discussion of marital processes by examining the stages of marriage.

Milton Erickson viewed couples therapy from a developmental perspective. He believed that marital problems occur when couples have difficulty mastering the specific learning tasks required in each stage of the life cycle. Haley (1973) summarized Erickson's six phases of the marital life cycle and emphasized the transition points in marital relationships.

### Phase 1: The Courtship Period

This phase has two critical tasks for the couple to master. First, each member learns to deal with the opposite sex using socially appropriate behaviors. Second, each individual become sufficiently detached from his or her family of origin to establish intimate bonds outside the original family.

### Phase 2: Marriage and Its Consequences

A number of challenges follow the formal declaration of marriage. Whatever the couple's relationship before marriage, formal commitment can shift the nature of the relationship in unpredictable ways. After professing marriage vows, spouses are often relieved of the need to hold back from each other. This greater openness may be welcomed, but it may also generate stress in the relationship. This openness, along with unrealistic expectations for the other spouse, frequently results in disappointment, confusion, and conflict.

A number of agreements need to be worked out by the couple to live in harmony. Relationships with in-laws, friends, and associates, as well as leisure activities and household chores, become an arena for issues that were not worked out or even anticipated before marriage. Furthermore, as individual issues are worked out, spouses must devise ways to deal with disagreements. A great amount of effort, compromise, and negotiation is needed during this phase.

### Phase 3: Childbirth and Dealing with the Young

Even though an acceptable pattern of relating was achieved during the previous phase, many couples find that childbirth raises new issues and unsettles old ones. Couples who considered their marriage a trial arrangement now find separation and divorce a less acceptable option. Others who thought they were committed to each other find themselves feeling differently after the arrival of a child. With the birth of a child, a three-way sharing must be learned. Otherwise, one spouse may feel that the other spouse is more attached to the

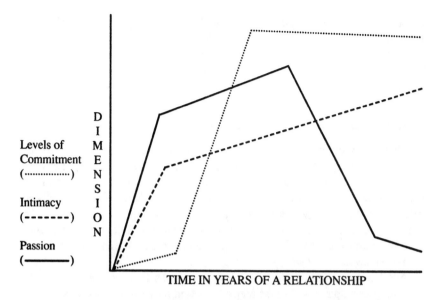

Levels of
Commitment
(················)

Intimacy
(- - - - - -)

Passion
(————)

D I M E N S I O N

TIME IN YEARS OF A RELATIONSHIP

**Figure 1.2   The Dimensions of Commitment, Intimacy, and Passion Over Time
in Long-Term Relationships**

child. The birth of a child also represents the coming together of two families and creates grandparents, aunts, uncles, and other relationships—in short, an extended family.

Unless the couple can negotiate an agreement amid pressures from kin, a complicated power struggle will ensue. A second potential period of crisis occurs when the child begins formal schooling. Conflicts between spouses about childrearing practices become painfully manifest when the child represents them in public. Finally, the act of sending children off to school can be a harbinger of the dread that parents are likely to experience when children ultimately leave home and the parents are a dyad again.

### Phase 4: Middle Marriage Difficulties

Being married for 10 to 15 years brings new challenges and transitions. Individually, spouses are at the midlife stage of development and must contend with their successes and failures and with issues of stagnation and generativity. Maritally, the couple has presumably worked out relatively stable patterns of interaction. But as children are home less often, the couple begins to realize that soon children will be leaving home. If the spouses have stayed together "because of the children," they are bound to experience conflict even before their adolescents have emancipated. As adolescents are experiencing their own turmoil and identity crises, struggles for power and control within the family can escalate. Struggles between adolescents and parents greatly impact the marital relationship unless the couple can effectively deal with power and boundary issues.

## Phase 5:  Weaning Parents from Children

The beginning of this phase is often a time of intense marital turmoil, which subsides as children leave and spouses work out new ways of relating as couples. Extreme difficulties in the marital relationship often arise because of the special importance children have had to the marriage. Spouses may have been able to communicate with each other only through or about their children. Or the couple's relationship may have been held together only by a common concern and care for the children. If this has been the case, the challenge is for the couple to develop new ways of relating.

Another transition of this phase involves the shift from being parents to becoming grandparents. A third major transition may involve spouses dealing with the loss of their own parents.

## Phase 6:  Retirement and Old Age

After spouses successfully negotiate the task of the weaning phase, they often experience a period of relative harmony until the time of retirement. Retirement is fraught with new problems and challenges primarily because the spouses face the prospect of spending 24 hours a day together. Resolution of issues related to the frequency and use of time together constitutes a major challenge for the marriage during this phase. In addition, issues of aging involving physical, psychological, and economic well-being must be faced and resolved. Eventually, one spouse dies and the relationship physically ceases. Issues involved with mourning and working through unfinished business regarding the deceased partner are important tasks for the widow or widower. Later, the establishing of a new lifestyle, which may include remarriage, is an additional challenge.

Obviously, Erickson's developmental schema assumes that the couple remains together without early death, separation, or divorce. Carter and McGoldrick (1980) and McGoldrick and Carter (1982) have described marriage and family life cycles for different family types, such as the single-parent family and the blended family, and for different ethnic groups. Berman and Lief (1975) and Nichols (1988) offered other schemes of the marital life cycle that integrate developmental stages with issues such as commitment, communication, power, intimacy, and boundaries.

The process of working out a satisfactory marital relationship involves shared agreements between the spouses. These agreements may consist of explicit rules, implicit rules, and rules that an observer would note but that the couple itself would probably deny. Often these shared agreements are largely undiscussed or involve areas of the relationship of which the couple may not be aware. Seen this way, conflicts in a marriage arise when there are disagreements about the rules of living together, about who sets the rules, and about who enforces them.

## SYSTEM DIMENSIONS: POWER, INTIMACY, BOUNDARIES

Another convenient way of understanding marital relationships is through three system dimensions: power, intimacy, and boundaries (Berman & Lief, 1975). The power dimension involves issues of competition and cooperation and focuses on who is in charge of the relationship and who takes responsibility for specific aspects of the relationship. The intimacy dimension involves the spouses' need for and fear of closeness and caring. The boundary dimension involves other influences that affect the marital system, such as relatives or other persons and time allocations for career, entertainment, and hobbies. (These dimensions are further elaborated in subsequent chapters.)

The way in which these dimensions are handled depends on each spouse's personality style, the marital pact, the relational style that has developed, and the stage or phase of the marriage itself at the time in question. Dysfunctional or negatively cooperative couples tend to be less flexible and more static and rigid; more functional couples can more easily adapt and change with new needs, demands, and circumstances.

Having now overviewed the sociocultural basis of the institution of marriage, the psychological factors involved in the process of attraction, and stages of the marriage relationship, we turn to other matters. This last section briefly describes the history of marital therapy as a profession and some of its present and future trends.

## THE HISTORY OF MARITAL THERAPY AS A PROFESSION

Marital therapy as a distinct mental health profession is only 60 years old. Initially, marriage counselors were physicians, lawyers, educators, and social workers who had little if any formal training but some degree of commitment to dealing with marital problems. Both clergy and physicians ordinarily had contact with family members at significant times in the life cycle: birth, marriage, illness, and death. Therefore, it was not uncommon or unreasonable for people to turn to ministers or physicians for help with many types of personal and family problems.

Marital therapy as a specialized body of knowledge and techniques dates back to the 1920s and the 1930s. Abraham and Hannah Stone began offering professional marriage counseling at the Community Church in New York City in 1929. Neither of the Stones was a member of the clergy, but the church sponsored their clinical work. Soon afterward, Paul Popenoe's American Institute of Family Relations in southern California and Emily Mudd's Marriage Counsel of Philadelphia were opened. Both centers offered counseling specifically for marital issues. As such, these centers were different from other family agencies of that time. The 1930s saw the establishment of what has become known as the Groves Conference on the Family and the National Council on Family Relations. Leaders from these two groups were among those who established the American Association of Marriage Counselors (AAMC) in New York City in 1942.

With the establishment of the AAMC, marital therapy became a distinct professional field. In subsequent years AAMC members began to conceptualize the marital relationship as an integral part of the family system. To reflect this trend, the AAMC changed its name and became the American Association of Marriage and Family Counselors (AAMFC). In 1963 the state of California became the first state to pass a licensure law for marriage and family counselors. With the enactment of this law the profession of marital therapy came of age (Broderick & Schrader, 1981). In 1978 the AAMFC became the American Association for Marriage and Family Therapy (AAMFT), thereby dropping the word *counselor* in favor of the more accurate and contemporary term *therapy*. Also in 1978, the U.S. commissioner of education designated the AAMFT's Commission on Accreditation for Marriage and Family Education to perform the task of accrediting training programs in marriage and family counseling.

## THE EXPANDING SCOPE OF MARITAL THERAPY

The most comfortable and easiest way to practice marital therapy is to view many, if not all, couples and their problems as basically similar and then apply a standard therapy or mix of therapies to these couples. Many therapists employ this strategy with some measure of success, particularly with the "traditional couple," who is a relatively young couple, married at least 2 but usually not more than 7 years, with a fairly focused set of concerns (Berman, Lief, & Williams, 1981). Such a strategy is misguided and deprives many couples of effective treatment. This is particularly apparent with the following types of couples who are being referred with increasing frequency for marital therapy:

- One or both spouses are at or are past midlife.
- One spouse has a recurrent psychiatric disorder such as panic attacks, agoraphobia, or depression.
- One spouse has an acute medical condition, such as recent recovery from a heart attack, and is fearful about returning to marital responsibilities.
- One spouse has a chronic health condition, such as hypertension or kidney dialysis, and it has become an issue in the marriage.
- One spouse is a mental patient who is noncompliant with sessions or medications.
- The progress of a client in a weight management or smoking cessation program appears to be impeded by his or her spouse.
- An apparently motivated couple has been in therapy for approximately 6 to 10 sessions and is making little to no progress (this is the most common situation).

Recently, there has been a tremendous growth in the field of marital therapy, which can be divided into two periods. In the first, the focus was on the therapist; developments in theory and technique emphasized the training of competent therapists to work with marital issues. The result was that marital therapy became therapist-centered. (This development was consistent with changes in other areas of the health and mental health fields.) We are now experiencing the beginnings of a second period in which the focus has shifted to the tailoring of treatment to the individual differences, needs, and styles of spouses and to the subsystem of marriage. This shift grows out of theoretical breakthroughs, recent research findings, and clinical necessity. In short, marital therapy is becoming more and more client-centered.

Marital therapy is also becoming more common in public and health care settings than in private practice settings. The client population is becoming older, more diverse, and more multisymptomatic, including health and medical factors. Of necessity, marital therapists will have to expand their repertoires of assessment and treatment modalities to adequately tailor their therapy to spouse and couple. In the process marital therapy will continue to become more client-centered.

## CONCLUDING NOTE

We have now reviewed some of the major social and cultural changes and trends that impact the institution of marriage as well as the psychological factors involved in attraction, love, and the developmental phases of a marriage relationship. We have also reviewed the development of marital therapy as a profession. In the process, we have briefly introduced the reader to some of the principal concepts and constructs in marital therapy and therapy: mate selection, marital pacts, cooperation and collusion, families of origin, and the system dimensions of boundaries, intimacy, and power. Finally, we have suggested that changes in the focus of treatment toward a more couple-centered marital therapy and the expanding varieties of couples as well as settings for marital therapy will all contribute to the further evolution of this relatively new profession.

## REFERENCES

Berman, E., & Lief, H. (1975). Marital therapy from a psychiatric perspective: An overview. *American Journal of Psychiatry, 132*, 583–591.

Berman, E., Lief, H., & Williams, A. (1981). A model of marital interaction. In G. Sholevar (Ed.), *The handbook of marriage and marital therapy*. New York: SP Medical and Scientific Books.

Bjorksten, O. J. W. & Stewart, T. J. (1984). Contemporary trends in American marriage. In C. C. Nadelson & O. C. Polonsky (Eds.), *Marriage and divorce: A contemporary perspective*. New York: Guilford Press.

Boszormenyi-Nagy, I., & Spark, G. (1976). *Invisible loyalties*. New York: Brunner/Mazel.

Broderick, C., & Schrader (1981). The history of professional marriage and family therapy. In A. Gurman & D. Kniskern (Eds.), *Handbook of family therapy*. New York: Brunner/Mazel.

Carter, E., & McGoldrick, M. (1980). The family life cycle: An overview. In E. Carter & M. McGoldrick (Eds.), *The family life cycle: A framework for family therapy*. New York: Gardiner Press.

Dreikurs, R. (1946). *The challenge of marriage*. New York: Duell, Sloan, and Pearce.

Dreikurs, R. (1968). Determinants of changing attitudes of marital partners toward each other. In S. Rosenbaum & I. Alger (Eds.), *The marriage relationship*. New York: Basic Books.

Glick, I., Clarkin, J., & Kessler, D. (1987). *Marital and family therapy* (3d ed.). New York: Grune & Stratton.

Goleman, D. (1985, September 10). Patterns of love charted. *The New York Times*.

Haley, J. (1973). *Uncommon therapy: The psychiatric techniques of Milton H. Erickson*. New York: Norton.

Lederer, W., & Jackson, D. (1968). *The mirages of marriage*. New York: Norton.

Levinson, D. (1978). *The seasons of a man's life*. Boston: Little, Brown.

Main, F., & Oliver, R. (1988). Complementary, symmetrical, and parallel personality priorities as indicators of marital adjustment. *Individual Psychology, 44*(3), 324–332.

McGoldrick, M., & Carter, E. (1982). The family life cycle. In F. Walsh (Ed.), *Normal family processes*. New York: Guilford Press.

Murstein, B. (1976). *Who will marry whom?* New York: Springer.

Nichols, W. (1988). *Marital therapy: An integrative approach*. New York: Guilford Press.

Sager, C. J., Gundlach, R., & Kremmer, M. (1968). The married in treatment. *Archives of General Psychiatry 19*, 205–217.

Sholevar, G. (1985). Marital therapy. In H. Kaplan & B. Sadock (Eds.), *Comprehensive textbook of psychiatry IV* (Vol. 2). Baltimore: Williams and Wilkins.

Sperry, L. (1978). *The together experience: Getting, growing and staying together in marriage*. San Diego, CA: Beta Books.

St. Clair, M. (1986). *Object relations and self psychology: An introduction*. Monterey, CA: Brooks/Cole.

Sternberg, R. (1986). A triangular theory of love. *Psychological Reviews, 93*(2), 119–135.

Sternberg, R. (1987). *The triangle of love: Intimacy, passion, commitment*. New York: Basic Books.

Stewart, T., Bjorksten, O., & Glick, I. (1985). Sociodemographics of contemporary American marriage. In O. Bjorksten (Ed.), *New clinical concepts in marital therapy*. Washington, DC: American Psychiatric Press.

Topf, D. (1984). *Personality priorities and marriage adjustment*. Unpublished doctoral dissertation, University of South Dakota.

# 2

# Health and Marital Functioning

**D**oes the stress of separation or divorce make an individual more susceptible to cancer or early death? Can a spouse's prescription medication affect the marriage? What about diet? Do marriages in which one spouse
works swing shifts have more conflict and health problems? Can drugs cause
sexual dysfunction?

Each of these questions reflects very real concerns that are affecting more
couples than ever before. Surprisingly, interest among medical researchers in
these concerns is growing. Nevertheless, it is the rare therapist who is informed and conversant on these topics, even though they have immediate,
practical interest for marriage therapy. Why is this? This chapter offers some
answers to the question and then reviews a number of pertinent biological correlates that impact marital satisfaction and functioning. The final section of
this chapter discusses the practice of marital therapy in a relatively new treatment setting: medical hospitals and outpatient clinics.

Because marital therapy is usually associated with the social and psychological sciences, the notion of associating biological factors with marital functioning may at first appear odd, and, in fact, influential writers in the field
such as Haley (1973) have repudiated biological influences on system functioning. Marital therapy, until recently, has usually been practiced by nonmedical therapists with traditional couples. For the most part these couples
have been seen conjointly in private practice settings, or treatment of marital
issues has occurred in the context of treatment of their children in child guidance and community mental health clinics.

But these circumstances are changing. Researchers predict that in the near future the majority of marital and family therapy will be practiced in a variety of treatment settings with more diverse age groups. These new treatment settings will include medical inpatient and outpatient settings, schools, and juvenile corrections centers (Berger & Jurkovic, 1984). At the same time, because the population is getting older, health problems will become more prominent in the lives of couples and thus will affect marital functioning. To adequately understand a couple's concerns and effectively treat them, marital therapists will probably have to consider biological as well as psychological and social factors, an approach that is currently utilized primarily by psychiatrists who do marital and family therapy (Beavers, 1985).

As marital therapy matures, many, if not most, marital therapists will likely begin to conceptualize marital functioning in a more holistic and integrative fashion, meaning that biological factors as well as the psychological and social will be considered. There is a developing literature on the health status correlates of marital harmony and discord. Even though most of this information is not readily available to the nonmedical marital therapist, much of it is potentially useful in clinical practice. Such information can be critically important in dealing with treatment impasses, in breaking through what might at first appear to be "resistance," and in educating couples.

## THE IMPACT OF BIOLOGICAL FACTORS ON MARRIAGE

Let us now turn to some of the biological correlates of marital functioning. We review longevity and health status, medication side effects, biological rhythms, nutrition, psychosomatic illness, and common medical and surgical conditions.

### Health and Longevity

Epidemiological data on physical and mental health show that marriage has a positive effect on individuals. But this relative health advantage appears to be more pronounced for men than for women. In the United States, and with only a few exceptions, married men consistently have the lowest death rates for reported cases. Among widowed and divorced white males, suicide rates are more than four and three times higher, respectively, than for married men, as are accident rates. Among black men, death rates from cirrhosis of the liver are four times higher for divorced and three times higher for widowed than married men. For the most part, married women have the lowest reported death rates among the most common causes of death (Bjorksten & Steward, 1985).

In terms of physical well-being, there are a number of interesting correlates of marital disruption. First, married persons have substantially fewer physician visits per year than do never-married individuals. Unmarried persons are likely to smoke more, drink more, and have more risk factors for illness or accidents—for example, they are less likely to wear seat belts—than their married counterparts. Never-married persons report being ill more often than married individuals do. Those who are separated report being sick more often and having more physician visits than the married or the never married. Similarly, the divorced and widowed are overrepresented among both inpatient and outpatient psychiatric populations (Bjorksten & Steward, 1985).

In short, divorced and separated people have the worst health status of all marital groups. They have the highest rates of acute and chronic medical conditions, suffer the most partial work disability, take the most disability days per condition, and have the highest average physician utilization rate and the longest hospital stays. Widowed persons rank second worst for overall health status. Individuals who are married have the best overall health status. They have the fewest acute and chronic medical conditions as well as conditions that produce work disability (Bjorksten & Steward, 1985).

What effect does remarriage have on health status? Persons who had divorced and remarried successfully are less susceptible to health problems than are people who remain in an unhappy marriage. Remarriage appears to provide men, but not necessarily women, with increased resources for dealing with life stresses as well as with increased survival and mental health (Renne, 1971).

What is the impact of dual careers and working women on marital well-being? Working married women report fewer physical and psychosomatic symptoms than either single working women or married women who work at home. Even though work may have its liabilities for married women, the benefits outweigh the liabilities. Employment's benefits do not necessarily extend to the husband, however; a wife's work reportedly can increase strain and illness for the husband because of reduced attention from his spouse and greater demands for sharing duties. It appears that changes in the wife's employment—entering or leaving the work force or gaining a promotion—rather than employment per se are related to the husband's strain or illness (Booth, 1977).

### Marriage as Protection

The most likely explanation for changes in physical well-being and longevity or life span of married persons is that marriage somehow protects spouses from stress. Routine habits, adequate nutrition, social support, intimacy, and possession of a reason for living are factors that confer this protection. Marital disruption implies that when this protection is removed, individuals are exposed to the full impact of life stressors (Jemmott & Locke, 1984).

In a review of nearly 28,000 cancer cases, Goodwin, Hunt, Key, and Samet (1987) noted that cancer patients who were married had a 23% higher survival rate than did unmarried patients. These researchers attributed this increased longevity to the emotional protection provided by marriage. Also noted was that married persons tended to get diagnosed at an earlier stage of the disease and that married cancer patients more frequently received a definitive or potentially curative treatment than did their unmarried counterparts. (Unfortunately, these researchers did not account for the economic factors that greatly influenced utilization of medical services.)  Goodwin et al. also confirmed that divorced cancer patients had a greater risk of death from cancer than did those who were widowed or separated. Lynch (1977) noted a similar finding in his classic work: *The Broken Heart: Medical Consequences of Loneliness.*

Lifestyle changes secondary to marital disruption often result in psychosocial stresses that can have severe consequences. Some of these consequences are clinical depression, substance abuse, cardiovascular disease, and alterations in immune system functioning. Decreased immune functioning probably accounts for the known increases in the rates of death due to infections and cancers among the bereaved and divorced population (Kiecolt-Glaser & Glaser, 1986).

What impact can marital discord have on immunity?  Researchers such as Kiecolt-Glaser et al. (1987) studied the impact of marital discord on immunity.  They concluded that mental health affects physical health by altering the immune system, which provides the body's defenses against illness. Specifically, they found that women in unhappy marriages had decreased immunity. Research of recently separated or divorced men showed that both groups were less capable of fighting two common herpes virus infections, which suggested immunosuppression difficulties (Glaser, Kiecolt-Glaser, Speicher et al., 1985).

## Medication Side Effects

Spousal use of prescription medications is so commonplace, particularly among the middle aged and elderly, that the therapist should have some familiarity with the behavioral and psychological effects of the more common medications. Often a primary care physician will prescribe an antianxiety or antidepressant drug, but more likely a spouse will be taking medication for a common medical condition, such as hypertension or for contraceptive purposes. Such medications have a host of side effects ranging from the psychic—dysphoria, irritability, or anxiety—to the somatic—fatigue, loss of libido, or impotence. The spouse will seldom report these side effects to the marital therapist; in fact, the spouse may not connect such side effects to the medication and instead may attribute them to psychological or interpersonal difficulties. This is particularly the case with drug-induced sexual dysfunction.

Here are some of the most often reported side effects related to commonly prescribed medications: Dysphoria or depressive-like features can be noted in individuals taking cardiac and hypertensive medications such as Inderal, Digoxin, Minipress, Aldomet, and Lidocaine. Depressive symptoms are also common with Tagamet, which is prescribed for peptic ulcer disease.

Anxiety and insomnia are commonly seen with Inderal, Theodur, and other bronchodilators as well as with diet pills containing amphetamines. A number of over-the-counter decongestants as well as excessive intake of caffeine—more than four cups of coffee or 48 ounces of caffeinated soft drinks—can also cause such symptoms.

Sedation, or fatigue (as it is commonly called), can be due to sedative-hypnotics or sleeping pills such as Dalmane, Halcion, Serax, or Seconal. Fatigue is also quite common with the use of antianxiety agents such as Valium, Librium, Ativan, and Tranxene and antidepressants such as Elavil and Sinequan (Abramowicz, 1983).

## Medication and Sexual Functioning

The problem of sexual dysfunction is widespread. Researchers have reported that 75% of couples seeking marital therapy had a significant sexual complaint in addition to their presenting psychological concern. Usually the sexual problem was an unreported concern (Berg & Snyder, 1980). For example, a 42-year-old male who was becoming more disenchanted with his marriage of 12 years had recently been started on Inderal by his physician for control of a high blood pressure problem. The physician had failed to mention that impotence was a common side effect of that medication. A week later the man began having difficulty maintaining an erection and assumed that this was due to increased marital discord. Soon after the physician changed the medication the impotence disappeared, although strained communications and discord continued.

Such situations point up the value of taking a brief drug and health history as part of the initial assessment. When routine screening for sexual dysfunction of nearly 1,200 males at a large outpatient medical clinic was done, 34% were found to be impotent. Of these cases, 86% were diagnosed as related to prescription medication or medical conditions such as diabetes mellitus or neurological disorders (Slag et al., 1983). For both sexes, the most common cause of drug-induced sexual dysfunction are antihypertensive drugs such as Diuril, Dyazide, Aldomet, Catapres, Tenormin, and Apresoline. Inderal is also reported to decrease sexual desire. Antidepressants such as Nardil, Tofranil, and Norpramin have been reported to inhibit or cause painful orgasm. High doses of antianxiety drugs and sedative-hypnotics can also decrease sexual desire and impair orgasm, as can recreational drugs such as alcohol, marijuana, and cocaine. Ascendin, however, can have an aphrodisiac effect on some females (Abramowicz, 1983).

### Biological Rhythms

Research data are now confirming the clinical speculation that conflict is nearly inevitable between a "night" spouse and a "day" spouse. Psychologists doing research on biological rhythms have found that being out of sync with one's biological cycle can significantly affect human behavior and performance on the job and at home (Folkhard, 1983). Research data indicate that there are some basic metabolic and physiological differences between day people, or "larks," and night people, or "owls." Larks tend to be more physical, spend more time outdoors, optimize their energy, and have better job performance if they work during the day. Owls tend toward more nonphysical activities, have greater social involvements, tend to be more sexually active, and prefer lovemaking later in the day.

Mismatches in a marriage between a lark and an owl can increase the stress in a relationship. Out-of-phase couples, as they are called, tend to engage in less serious conversations and fewer shared activities, such as sex. Some research has shown that these couples tend to face more unmanaged conflicts, which can increase the likelihood of divorce. Out-of-phase couples who can productively cope with these stressors, however, tend to show more flexibility and adaptability than do in-phase couples (Sperry, 1978).

Even when the couple is in-phase, external factors such as shift work (working evenings or night) may adversely affect the relationship. Approximately 20% of the work force is currently involved in shift work. Studies of self, health, and family problems point to shift work as a stressor that can exacerbate an existing, previously minor problem. Shift workers average 7 hours less sleep per week than others do. Not surprisingly, shift workers have increased morbidity or health problems/concerns (Monk & Folkhard, 1983).

Such research confirms clinical observations that shift work seems to set the stage for a unique set of potential conflicts that in-phase couples may never face. One of the most common occurs as a result of the shift worker's need for peace and quiet while spouse and family are awakening and beginning normal morning activities, which are often noisy and can disrupt the shift worker's sleep. The female shift worker is often expected to attend to house-keeping responsibilities in addition to her job, thus adding to her sleep deficit. In addition, spouses of shift workers are confronted with other dilemmas: They see their spouses less frequently, may have less time for shared enter-tainment than their in-phase social friends do, and may of necessity have to assume more childrearing responsibilities than they desire. Shift workers at greatest risk for physical and marital dysfunction are those who rotate shifts, such as nurses, police, other emergency personnel, and factory employees who work alternating shifts. The biological clocks of such workers get out of phase, and they resemble individuals suffering from jet lag, except that the sit-uation is chronic (Whybrow & Bahr, 1988).

## Nutrition

A recent surgeon general's report on nutrition and health (Koop, 1988) left lit-tle doubt about the impact of diet on health. The surgeon general noted that nearly 75% of all deaths are associated with poor dietary habits. Of the 2.1 million Americans who died in 1987, nearly 1.5 million succumbed to dis-eases connected with diet, such as heart disease, stroke, diabetes, some can-cers, and alcohol-consumption-related illnesses. It may be that the old apho-rism "You are what you eat" has more to say about marital harmony than most would have imagined.

One of the first hints that there was an intimate connection between diet and marital harmony came from Jackson and Lederer (1968). These writer-researchers studied 278 young and middle-aged married couples. Among this group, troubled marriages had a higher incidence of *fatigue-irritability-irra-tional behavior syndrome*. It appeared that biological imbalances brought about negative, irrational behavioral exchanges that blurred the individual's perceptions and subsequently affected the marital relationship. Commonly experienced symptoms included fatigue, depression, angry outbursts, insom-nia, headaches, indigestion, and sensitivity to light and noise. For the majority of couples this was a subclinical condition rather than a full-blown, well-defined medical event. Lederer (1981) reported that when the biological caus-es of such symptoms were eliminated, marital therapy tended to proceed more efficaciously. In some cases, little or no therapy was needed. Lederer conclud-ed that biochemical imbalances such as under- and over-nutrition, food sensitivities, and environmental toxins accounted for the fatigue-irritability-irrational behavior syndrome.

Statistics from Lederer's and two other well-known marital therapy clinics indicated that 50–90% of couples were diagnosed as having some biochemical or nutritional problems that were causally related or that exacerbated marital conflict. (Because these statistics may reflect a self-selection of couples to these clinics or therapists who were sensitized to such biological factors, a replication of these studies is needed.)

A related research project was reported by Kitner, Bass, and Johnson, 1981. Results from the initial phase of a longitudinal study on diet and marital-family behavior provided some corroboration of Lederer's hypothesis as well as Minuchin's hypothesis that the cause of anorexia nervosa lies within the family system (Minuchin, Rosman, & Baker, 1978). Families with poor diets had higher levels of conflict than did those with adequate diets. Dysfunctional relational patterns also correlated with eating behavior. These researchers noted that dependent or controlled wives tended to have poorer nutritional habits, whereas independent wives tended to have much better ones. In families with high degrees of cohesion, wives had diets with more protein, calcium, iron, vitamin A, and riboflavin. Husbands in families with high conflict had lower quality diets.

### Psychosomatic Illnesses

Minuchin, Rosman, and Baker (1978) have identified a number of preconditions for the development of psychosomatic illness in families. According to their research, psychosomatic symptoms arise in the family member who is physiologically vulnerable and has a belief system that encourages somatic expression of distress and conflict. The family or marital system that is most likely to support and elicit psychosomatic illness tends to be enmeshed, overprotective, rigid, and without appropriate conflict resolution skills. The particular illness and symptoms serve the function of diffusing conflict and maintaining homeostasis. By therapeutically challenging the rigid, overprotective structure, Minuchin found that dramatic improvement in the symptom carrier was likely. These researchers studied psychosomatic symptoms such as diabetes, asthma, sickle cell anemia, and anorexia nervosa. Other researchers have noted that eating disorders such as obesity, bulimia, and anorexia are closely related to maladaptive marital conflict resolution (Casper & Zachary, 1984).

Pratt (1976) studied healthy families without psychosomatic features and found that they differed markedly from psychosomatic families. The transactional styles of these marriages and families were characterized by varied and frequent intrafamily autonomy, established communication ties, creative problem solving of conflicts and differences, and the ability to adjust to role changes within the marriage or family.

## Common Medical and Surgical Conditions

A number of common medical conditions have psychiatric manifestations. We are all familiar with the depressive-like features that accompany the common cold and flu. We may not be familiar with how often clinical depression occurs among spouses recovering from heart attack, stroke, cardiac bypass surgery, breast removal, and pancreatic cancer. Depression, anxiety, and self-deprecation have also been noted with the onset of menopause (Dickes, 1980). Diabetes mellitus affects potency in men and often results in a reduction in sexual desire and a loss of orgasmic pleasure in women as the disease progresses.

A heart attack or cardiac bypass surgery can profoundly affect a marriage relationship. Many spouses believe that sexual relations during recovery from the heart attack or surgery are taxing and dangerous to the healing heart. Actually, the risk is no different than that of the progressive exercise prescribed in the patient's cardiac rehabilitation program. Similarly, the spouse who leaves the cardiac unit may fear that the exertion of returning to work or household duties will result in sudden cardiac death. Needless to say, anxiety and depressive symptoms are common in the cardiac patient. One researcher has noted, however, that the noncardiac spouse also experiences these symptoms (Carter, 1984). When the couple's anxiety and concerns cannot easily be allayed by reassurance, a few couples sessions are usually indicated.

Depression is noted in 45% of individuals recovering from a stroke. As with recovery from a heart attack or open heart surgery, there may be a shift in marital roles that is often as unsettling to the well spouse as it is to the affected spouse. Carter (1984) has described four patterns of conflict resolution for couples after a heart attack. Clearly, psychotherapeutic intervention is indicated with some couples, and brief marital therapy is often the treatment of choice.

Given that 40% of adult Americans are overweight, weight issues often influence marital functioning. For the morbidly obese (100 pounds more than 100% of ideal weight) who have not been able to control their weight, gastric bypass surgery is one (radical) option when major health concerns or fear of premature death is present. Research indicates that morbidly obese patients tend to have a very high presurgery divorce rate, which remains higher after surgery among those patients reporting marital difficulties prior to surgery. Surgery only occasionally precipitates marital problems. Most marriages, however, improve following surgery, although some do experience social discomfort and interpersonal strain (Rand & Kuldau, 1983).

## MARITAL THERAPY IN HEALTH CARE SETTINGS

Marital therapy is increasingly considered a necessary part of the multimodal treatment plans implemented by multidisciplinary staffs in medical hospitals and outpatient clinics. Although usually provided by a psychologist or clinical social worker, marital therapy is also being provided by nurses and nurse practitioners.

The delivery and marketing of this type of therapy in a medical setting tend to be different from those in psychiatric and other nonmedical settings. First, marital therapy is indicated when the behavior of one or both spouses interferes with the principal medical treatment. Thus, marital therapy is usually prescribed or suggested by health care staff rather than sought out by the couple. Second, marital therapy tends to be shorter in duration and more focused and structured than in a mental health private practice or agency setting. Third, marital therapy usually has a strong educational component related to the particular medical problem. Fourth, because marital therapy is one part of a multifaceted treatment program, the therapist has to function as a treatment team member. Initially, traditionally trained marital therapists find this role sharing different and difficult. Fifth, marital therapy in a medical setting places additional demands and expectations on the therapist. The therapist must have proficiency in marital therapy as well as a working knowledge of basic biological processes.

At a local general hospital familiar to the authors, marital therapy is routinely available, and in one instance required, in several inpatient and outpatient medical programs, including the Cardiac Rehabilitation Program, the Weight Management Program, and the Geriatric Institute. In addition, marital therapy is provided in the hospital's traditional inpatient and outpatient psychiatry programs.

The Chronic Pain Management Program requires marital therapy for all married patients in addition to individual and group therapy. (The staff had observed that until there were changes in the marital system, the prognosis for change in the chronic pain patient was very guarded.) In the other programs couples therapy is prescribed on a case-by-case basis. For instance, in the Weight Management Program marital therapy is often indicated when treatment compliance is an issue. When the person in treatment is not able to stay on a diet regimen or change eating behaviors, spousal behavior is often implicated. The spouse may either send subtle mixed messages to his or her mate or overtly sabotage the change efforts. Short-term couples sessions in such instances are often structured and task-oriented. The patient's spouse is enlisted as a "collaborator" or "coach" for the weight management program rather than as a patient. When framed in this manner, changes in the couple's role structure and expectations and thus in boundaries, power, and intimacy issues are usually forthcoming.

This process is quite similar to the spouses group in the hospital's Phobia Clinic and Mood Disorders Clinic. Because panic disorders and agoraphobia usually have a biological substrate, medication is initially prescribed while individual and couples group therapy focuses on the psychological treatment of the anticipatory anxiety component of the disorder. When spouses are approached about serving as coaches for their afflicted mates, they find participating in a structured spouses group much less threatening than if they were told that they needed marital therapy.

Soon after its inception, the Mood Disorders Clinic recognized the contribution of marital therapy to the treatment of depression. Often, treatment of only the biological component led to only partial remission of depressive features. But when the interpersonal context among depressed patients who were married was also addressed, outcomes were greatly improved. Coyne (1987) has clearly articulated the challenges that a depressed spouse presents for the therapist regarding refusal to participate in treatment, goal setting, and compliance. He has also pointed out how conjoint interviews and enactment can prove to be counterproductive measures with such couples.

## CONCLUDING NOTE

We have now reviewed several dimensions of health and physical well-being as they affect and are affected by marital functioning and dysfunctioning. As we stated at outset of this chapter, the impact of health factors on marital functioning is significant. Health concerns have merited increased attention by those practicing couples therapy not just because the profession is maturing and becoming more comprehensive and integrative but also because the scope of marital therapy has widened to include nontraditional couples, especially those who are older and more likely to have concurrent medical and health concerns.

## REFERENCES

Abramowicz, M. (1983). Drugs that cause sexual dysfunction. *The Medical Letter on Drugs and Therapeutics, 25*(641), 73–76.

Beavers, W. (1985). *Successful marriage: A family systems approach to couples therapy.* New York: Norton.

Berg, P., & Snyder, D. (1980). Differential diagnosis of marital and sexual distress. *Journal of Sexual and Marital Therapy, 7,* 290–295.

Berger, M., & Jurkovic, G. (1984). *Practicing family therapy in diverse settings.* San Francisco: Jossey-Bass.

Bjorksten, O., & Steward T. (1985). Marital status and health. In O. Bjorksten (Ed.), *New clinical concepts in marital therapy.* Washington, DC: American Psychiatric Press.

Booth, A. (1977). Wife's employment and husband's stress: A replication and refutation. *Journal of Marriage and Family, 39*, 301–313.

Carter, R. (1984). Family reactions and reorganization patterns in myocardial infarctions. *Family Stress Medicine, 2*, 55–64.

Casper, D., & Zachary, D. (1984). The eating disorders as a maladaptive conflict resolution. *Individual Psychology, 40*, 445–452.

Coyne, J. (1987). Depression, biology, marriage and marital therapy. *Journal of Marital and Family Therapy, 13*, 393–407.

Dickes, R. (1980). Surgery, medicine, drugs and sexuality and the physician's role in sex education. In G. Kaplan, M. Freedman, & L. Saddock (Eds.), *The comprehensive textbook of psychiatry: III*, Vol. 2. Baltimore, MD: Williams and Wilkins.

Folkhard, S. (1983). Impotence in medical clinic outpatients. *Journal of the American Medical Association, 249*, 1736–1740.

Glaser, R., Kiecolt–Glaser, J., Speicher, C. et al. (1985). Stress, loneliness, and changes in herpes virus latency. *Journal of Behavioral Medicine, 8*, 249–260.

Goodwin, J.S., Hunt, W. C., Key, C. R., & Samet, J. M. (1987). The effect of marital status on stage, treatment and survival of cancer patients. *Journal of American Medical Association, 258*, 3125–3130.

Haley, J. (1980). *Leaving home.* New York: McGraw-Hill.

Jackson, D., & Lederer, W. (1968). *The mirages of marriage.* New York: Norton.

Jemmott, J., & Locke, S. (1984). Psychosocial factors, immunologic mediation and human susceptibility to infectious disease: How much do we know? *Psychological Bulletin, 95*, 78–108.

Kiecolt-Glaser, J., Fisher, L., Ogrocki, P., Stout, T., Speicher, C., & Glaser, R. (1987). Marital quality, marital disruption and immune function. *Psychosomatic Medicine, 49*, 13–34.

Kiecolt-Glaser, J. & Glaser, R. (1986). Psychological influences on immunity, *Psychosomatics, 27*(9), 621–624.

Koop, C. (1988). *The surgeon general's report on nutrition and health.* Washington, DC: U.S. Department of Health and Human Services.

Lederer, W. (1981). *Marital choices: Forecasting, assessing, and improving a relationship.* New York: Norton.

Minuchin, S., Rosman, B., & Baker, L. (1978). *Psychosomatic families: Anorexia in context.* Cambridge, MA: Harvard University Press.

Monk, T., & Folkhard, S. (1983). Circadian rhythms and shift work. In R. Hockey (Ed.), *Stress and fatigue in human performance.* New York: Wiley.

Pratt, L. (1976). *Family structure and effective health behavior.* Boston: Houghton Mifflin.

Rand, C., & Kuldau, J. (1983). Psychiatric aspects of surgery for morbid obesity. In S. Akhtar (Ed.), *New psychiatric syndromes: DSM-III and beyond.* New York: Jason Aronson.

Renne, K. (1971). Health and marital experience in an urban population. *Journal of Marriage and the Family, 39*, 301–313.

Slag, M., Morley, J., Elson, M., Trence, D., Nelson, C., Nelson, A., Kinlaw, W., Beyer, S., Nuttal, F., & Shafer, K. (1983). Impotence in medical clinic outpatients. *Journal of the American Medical Association, 249*, 1736–1740.

Sperry, L. (1978). *The together experience: Getting, growing and staying together in marriage*. San Diego: Beta Books.

# 3

# *The Nature of Functional and Dysfunctional Marriages*

**M**arriage has been, at least up to now, an important institution in every culture. There is no element in social history more pervasive than this basic unit of the family. It creates the universal environment in which human beings learn to eat, walk, speak, and acquire their sense of identity and modes of behavior. Every culture that we know of, past or present, has included the marital unit as a necessity for survival and a common denominator of the society.

In the past, marriage was defined in functional terms in that each person was expected to fulfill role obligations. Marital failure or dysfunction was easily determined, as it was synonymous with role failure. Likewise, success of a marriage was easy to determine. The successful marriage was one in which the couple owned its own home and was able to produce children. The objective criteria, therefore, for whether a marriage was successful were easy enough for everyone to see.

## PATHOLOGY IN THE TRADITIONAL MARRIAGE

In the traditional marital model, roles were prescribed and could not easily be changed; therefore, marital pathology was usually related to role adaptation. The trapped wife syndrome was one of the more common forms of marital pathology. One of the most common aspects of this syndrome was an increasing discrepancy between a woman's professional development and that of her partner. The most common clinical manifestation of the trapped wife syndrome was depression.

Rebelliousness was another form of role adaptation pathology. In this, the partner defied the prescribed rules, much like a rebellious adolescent would. This role identity problem led to difficulties in accepting the marital role that were characterized by blatant breaking of the marital rules or by covert cheating on marital responsibilities.

Role incompetence was another difficulty. In this problem, the partner, for whatever reason (mental illness or inadequate preparation, for example), was incapable of performing his or her marital role functions. Treatment for these problems usually took the form of individual psychotherapy aimed at helping the identified patient adapt and learn to accept the prescribed roles.

## PATHOLOGY IN THE COMPANIONATE MARRIAGE

Today's companionate marriages with their process orientation lead to different kinds of problems. Because the focus is on emotional fulfillment, role functions are not carefully considered in the courtship and are often ambiguous, which results in power struggles, communication problems, and disappointed expectations. Even though marital partners are free to determine their own style of marriage and to determine who does what in a relationship, few partners have had training in how to make decisions. Thus, marriages are often troubled by a role ambiguity in which partners are not sure just what their roles are.

### Power Struggles

Because roles are not clearly defined, each partner must fend for him- or herself, which leads to power struggles. These conflicts determine which partner's preference will prevail. To negotiate effectively requires a degree of maturity, tolerance, fairness, good faith, and clarity about one's own desires. Many partners, however, develop a win-at-any-cost mentality, leaving one partner a winner and the other a loser; when one partner loses in a relationship, both lose. Partners often feel insecure and afraid that losing or giving in on one count will mean a lifetime of subjugation. This results in an adversarial stance with little trust and little respect for one another; in the process, the common goals of marriage are lost.

According to Glick, Clarkin, and Kessler (1987), this power competition is not new. "In Teutonic marriages in the Middle Ages, each partner attempted to place his or her hand on top when asked to join hands during the marriage ceremony. Occasionally this led to such turmoil that the minister had to settle it, usually by putting the man's hand on top, thus symbolizing his supremacy in the marriage" (p. 38). Although the struggle for power may have always occurred in the past, there was little doubt about who or what was right or wrong. Today there is little consensus about who should be dominant, and most people advocate either equality or parity, equality being a symmetrical relationship and parity suggesting equivalent power but in different areas.

Communication problems are one of the most common manifestations of a variety of marital problems. In today's marriage in which couples are struggling to negotiate power problems, communication failure is very costly. It is difficult, if not impossible to have a successful relationship with ineffective communication skills. When communication fails, partners view their marriage as routine and problematic.

### Bases of Happiness or Distress

The modern marriage is characterized by four features, which are at the heart of either marital happiness or marital distress. First, each partner can choose to marry whomever he or she wants, although some prohibitions are still attached to this freedom. Second, there is an equality of the sexes; in terms of the vows of marriage, men and women begin their union as equals. Third, each individual can develop his or her own marriage contract. Fourth, there is an increased emphasis on intimacy.

According to Goleman (1985), commitment, intimacy, and passion change over time in a long-term relationship. Commitment starts slowly and develops gradually. Intimacy develops throughout the relationship. Passion rises quickly and then begins to drop. The range of intimacy varies from couple to couple. There is no absolute best level of intimacy. Indeed, intimacy is a flexible state in which couples are close at one time and further apart at other times.

### An Integrative Approach to Marital Discord

Each approach to or theory of marital therapy has its explanation as to why marriages become conflicted, dissatisfying, and painful. In this book, we are endorsing an integrative point of view and therefore need to take into account all of the various explanations. According to Glick, Clarkin, and Kessler (1987), the following are the major explanations:

(1) Distressed couples engage in fewer rewarding (positive reinforcement) exchanges and more punishing (negative reinforcement) exchanges than nondistressed couples.

(2) Distressed couples are more likely to reciprocate the partner's use of negative reinforcement. These individuals are immediately reactive to the negative (actual or perceived) stimuli of the partner and respond in kind.

(3) Distressed couples are likely to attempt to control the behavior of one another through negative communication and the withholding of positive communication. Unhappy couples tend to strive for behavior change in the other by aversive control tactics, that is, by strategically presenting punishment and withholding rewards.

(4) Distressed systems are characterized by intense, binding coalitions, e.g., mother and child are close at father's expense.

(5) Covert coalitions often exist that cross generational lines.

(6) Third parties are used to interfere and deflect conflict or closeness between marital pairs.

(7) Individuals who need assistance with marital conflicts seem to have a rigidity in their personalities that forces them to deny or be blind to the existence of certain aspects of themselves. If they are confronted with a similar aspect of the partner's personality, this would be ignored or not accepted.

(8) Many tensions and misunderstandings between partners seem to result from the disappointment that one or both feel and resent when the other fails to play the role of spouse after the manner of a preconceived model or figure in their fantasy world.

(9) Individuals may persecute tendencies in their spouses that originally caused attraction. The partner is perceived unconsciously as a symbol of "lost," that is, repressed aspects of the subject's own personality.

(10) The preponderance of secure, loving outcomes of reality testing and conflict resolution in early developmental years creates a reservoir of relational potential that is brought to the marriage. In less fortunate cases, however, there will remain unresolved needs and demands on parent figures invested with deeply ambivalent feelings of love and hate.

(11) In the process of mate selection, the partner is attracted because he or she promises a rediscovery of an important lost aspect of the subject's own personality which owing to earlier conditioning has been recast as an object for attack or denial. (pp. 267–268)

A further explanation for dysfunction might be if one spouse had a serious disorder such as depression, mania, phobias, alcoholism, or schizophrenia. This disorder would put an undesirable strain on the marital relationship. Although some theories contend that marital interaction causes problems such as these, by itself the disorder cannot account for marital discord. It is likely that all of these explanations have some validity, and as we move forward in this text, we will apply this understanding to the development of a comprehensive approach to treating couples.

## QUALITIES OF THE HEALTHY COUPLE

Couples who have been successful in maintaining satisfying relationships for many years possess certain characteristics. According to Beavers (1985), healthy couples have beliefs that include the following:

1. Relative rather than absolute truth. Successful couples believe that people are limited and finite and therefore never possess the unchallengeable truth.
2. Subjective reality. These couples realize that individuals can see the same events differently.
3. The basic neutrality or benignity of people's motives. Successful couples have a fundamental belief that people close to them have decent and healthy motives.
4. Human encounter as rewarding. These couples believe that even miserable situations will get better.
5. A systems point of view. Successful couples assume that any individual needs a group, a human system, for individual definition, coherence, and satisfaction; causes and effects are interchangeable; any human behavior is the result of many variables; because humans are limited and finite, a social role of absolute power or helplessness prohibits many of the needed satisfactions to be found in human encounters.
6. Value and meaning in the human enterprise. Healthy marital partners have a belief in something that is larger than themselves. It may be provided by conventional religion or by a commitment to some passionate cause. The content seems unimportant; having a belief that directs energy and provides community with others outside the family is vital.

Beavers (1985) also maintained that observable patterns differentiate healthy from unhealthy couples. These patterns include a modest, overt power difference, the capacity for establishing clear boundaries, operation mainly in the present, respect for individual choice, skill in negotiating, and the sharing of positive feelings.

## HEALTHY, FUNCTIONAL MARRIAGES

Stinnet and DeFrain (1985) completed extensive research to identify the qualities of strong families/couples. Their research showed that families with healthy relationships have commitment, appreciation for one another, and good communication; spend time with one another; are spiritually well; and have good coping abilities. We feel that it is important for a therapist to know what is involved in creating and keeping a good marriage going. Professionals are often trained to identify and treat pathology, not to promote a successful and satisfying marriage. A marital therapist cannot articulate treatment goals that ensure a long-term relationship if he or she does not clearly understand the components of effective relationships. The remainder of this chapter focuses on the skills needed to make a marriage successful rather than on the problems that stand in the way. It is our belief that problems occur when skills are absent and that problems are resolved as skills are developed.

## SKILLS OF MARRIAGE*

The following principles are fundamental to skill-based marital interventions.

1. Developing and maintaining a good marital relationship require a time commitment. For any marriage to succeed, it must be made an important priority. Each couple determines how that priority is defined and established. For some marriages, priority means a large quantity of time spent together. In another relationship, a large portion of quality time is necessary. At different stages in the marital relationship (early marriage, family, empty nest) more time or less time is available.

2. The specific skills that are essential to a healthy marriage can be learned. Once a couple can understand how a marriage works and how to build a successful marriage, the partners can develop the skills that create a positive, rewarding relationship. The variable, as in most learning situations, is how long such skill acquisition takes, not if acquisition is possible. Some couples can acquire skills very quickly; others take a bit longer. But all couples can learn and grow.

3. Each partner has a responsibility to change. The first step in modifying a marriage involves creating a commitment to change. Each partner needs to understand what his or her role is in the marriage and what he or she needs to do to make it different. Patience and allowance for different rates of change are helpful. Each partner often has difficulty seeing just how he or she is involved in creating a less than satisfying relationship but often has no difficulty identifying what the other partner is or is not doing.

4. Feelings of love and caring that had decreased or disappeared often return once behavior changes. Romantic feelings, intimacy, and love often diminish in a marriage relationship. When feelings change, many couples believe that the relationship is over. This need not be the case. A change in

---

*The material in this section has been adapted from Don Dinkmeyer and Jon Carlson's *TIME* (Training in Marriage Enrichment) program and book *Time for a Better Marriage* (Circle Pines, MN: American Guidance Service), 1984.

feelings usually means that the partners are not being reinforced in the marriage and that the relationship deserves a higher priority. It is important at such time that they act as if all were well, and by acting as if their relationship is the intimate, satisfying relationship they desire, new behaviors and feelings can be established.

5. Small changes are very important in bringing about big changes. A happier relationship results from many small changes during a period of time. Often people attempt to bring about a change by focusing on a large task or a major accomplishment. Although this may help, it is often not necessary. Small changes will produce just as big a result. In any given day, there are hundreds of possible choices that can create small changes in a relationship.

The skills necessary for creating and sustaining an effective marriage are learned. A couple begins marriage with an assortment of skills, some effective and some ineffective. The skills needed to enrich a marriage can be expressed in simple terms. In exciting, satisfying marriages, partners relate in the following ways:

1. They individually accept responsibility for their behavior and self-esteem.
2. They identify and align their personal and marital goals.
3. They choose to encourage each other.
4. They communicate their feelings with honesty and openness.
5. They listen empathically when feelings are expressed.
6. They seek to understand the factors that influence their relationship.
7. They demonstrate that they accept and value each other.
8. They choose thoughts, words, and actions that support the positive goals of their marriage.
9. They solve marital conflicts together.
10. They commit themselves to the ongoing process of maintaining an equal marriage.

## Responsibility

Each partner plays an important role in creating an atmosphere of love and support or in sustaining marital conflict. If either partner changes to a more effective pattern of behavior, the other partner has to respond differently. An important step, and often the first step, in creating an effective marriage occurs when a partner takes responsibility for his or her own behavior. This involves spending less time blaming the other partner for failures in the marriage and more time choosing new behaviors and actions to improve the relationship. In a healthy marriage, partners take responsibility for their actions and do not blame each other. They have the courage to be imperfect and to make mistakes. This requires self-discipline.

In an enriched marriage relationship, couples choose to act in ways that nourish the sense of belonging that each partner desires. Rather than acting solely out of self-interest, the couple chooses behaviors that support positive goals of marriage. There are four positive goals that foster a good marriage relationship: to accept responsibility for individual behavior, to cooperate, to contribute to the relationship, and to encourage each other.

A healthy, satisfying marriage relationship is never accidental. Basic to the process of building a stronger, happier marriage is a commitment to spend time together learning and applying relationship skills. If a relationship is not working, it is necessary to change habitual ways of being together.

Instead of spending leftover time together, both partners can learn to plan so that they have the time together to build a better marriage. Planning can help identify ways to change day-to-day routines so that they move toward agreed-on marital goals. Couples with effective marriages plan together and use time management strategies.

*Daily Dialogue.* Putting planning and time management skills to work can be accomplished by meeting each day for daily dialogue. Daily dialogue involves a daily sharing time in which each partner says what is going on with him or her right then. This takes 10 minutes per day, allowing 5 minutes for each partner to talk uninterruptedly while the other listens. It is a time for sharing feelings, not facts. When couples share their real feelings, they share their real selves. They share hopes and fears, excitement and anxiety, joy and sorrow, pride and embarrassment, apprehension, feelings of inadequacy, feelings of anger—in short, all the important feelings that are rarely shared but that are essential information for people who are in love with each other.

### Encouragement

Encouragement is the force that builds a happy marital relationship. Characteristics of encouragement are:

1. Acceptance. This acceptance is complete and unconditional, which gives partners the freedom to grow or to stay put. Given this option, most individuals choose to move ahead.
2. Faith. Partners have confidence in one another. They choose to believe in each other, even though at times there may be little or no concrete evidence to support such faith. Faith can be expressed aloud by saying,

"I know you are doing your best" or "I believe in you" or silently by not pointing out a partner's faults or limitations.

3. Recognition of effort. Encouragement is further communicated by recognizing and commenting on a partner's effort and improvement. Encouragement recognizes not only superior accomplishment but any kind of positive movement.

4. A focus on strengths. Encouragement can help an individual become aware of strengths and resources. As a partner communicates the strengths he or she observes, the other partner becomes more aware of personal assets. If one partner feels unable to recognize and affirm the other's strengths, it may be a reflection of his or her own feeling of inadequacy.

Although encouragement sounds easy and good intentions are many, frequently one partner's behavior toward the other has a discouraging effect. Four common methods of discouragement are as follows:

1. Subtle domination. Sometimes one partner feels that his or her way is the best and only way of accomplishing something. In order to have the job done right, he or she chooses to take over a job rather than be satisfied with the partner's progress.

2. Intimidation. If one partner continually expects the other to be more and do more, the latter realizes that no matter what is accomplished, it will not be "enough."

3. Oversensitivity. A partner operates from the faulty assumption that he or she must be better than others to be "someone." That partner may feel the need to attack any perceived threat to his or her imagined superiority.

4. Failure to acknowledge progress. By failing to recognize progress, one partner prevents the other from getting the positive feedback that could provide the motivation to keep trying. Like subtle domination, failure to recognize progress communicates rejection.

Encouragement can be provided in a marriage relationship by practicing the following skills:

- Listening. An encouraging partner hears not only the words but also the feelings behind the words. To listen effectively means being totally in the present, focusing attention on what is being said, and not allowing distractions.
- Responding with empathy. Empathy is the ability to enter another person's world and understand how that person feels. A partner's empathic response demonstrates understanding of, but not necessarily agreement about, the feelings and themes being expressed.

- Communicating respect. By respecting a partner's unique and irreplace-able value as a human being, the individual provides support and hope that help build self-esteem. Communicating respect, one partner says to the other, "I know you have the ability to handle this situation," "I know you will make good decisions," "I trust you," "I have faith in you."
- Being enthusiastic and hopeful. Enthusiasm raises the spirits of others and transmits positive energy. Enthusiasm begins with identification of what is positive in the marriage relationship, which enables a partner to become aware of what he or she wants to change.
- Creating positive meanings and alternatives. There are many ways to view any given situation. Although each partner understands the situation from his or her point of view, it is always possible to choose another viewpoint. Often situations in marriage that a partner considers negative can be viewed positively. Positive meanings and alternatives can be created.
- Encouraging self. By encouraging self, a partner increases personal worth. In order to be a resource to others, it is important to develop self-esteem. A partner's self-esteem will grow as he or she learns to identify, verbalize, and claim personal strengths.

*The Encouragement Meeting.* There are unlimited opportunities for encour-aging each other. As partners practice the skills of encouragement, they identi-fy numerous opportunities. Encouragement meetings provide a regular, sys-tematic way to strengthen a marriage by focusing on what is positive. An encouragement meeting two or three times a week is helpful. Some couples so enjoy the process that they schedule daily meetings. The purpose of an encour-agement meeting is to allow each person to share the positive things he or she is seeing in the other and in the relationship. Encouragement meetings have the following guidelines:

1. Meet in a place and at a time that are quiet and free of interruption.
2. Sit facing each other close enough to hold hands comfortably.
3. One partner begins by saying, "The most positive things that happened today were . . ." Then the partner continues by saying, "Something that I appreciated about you today was . . ." The other partner just listens and makes no comments. Then the partners switch roles.

### Understanding the Marriage Relationship

A person's marriage is his or her most important relationship. Many couples do not get the most from it, however, because they do not understand what factors influence the relationship. Like all relationships, marriage is a system. The marriage system reflects individual goals, beliefs, and priorities as well as the goals, priorities, and beliefs two people share as a couple. If goals and priorities are aligned, the system functions smoothly. Once an understanding is developed of the marriage system, partners can learn to relate in an increasingly positive manner and assure that goals and priorities are in harmony.

What people initially know about how to relate was learned from their family. Individuals observe cooperation, quarrels, revenge, love, and many other interactions. Observation of a parents' marriage may not always be the best training for relating in a person's own marriage. Even though both partners may have come from healthy, happy home environments, the systems operating in their respective homes may have been quite different. Many individuals try, consciously or unconsciously, to replicate the kind of environment with which they are familiar.

When individuals come together in marriage, they struggle for control. Often they focus on personal gain, rather than on the growth of the relationship. To reach their goals, they adopt sophisticated, patterned maneuvers that are in fact destructive games. When marriage partners become aware of the nonconstructive games they use, they can choose to develop a game-free, honest relationship.

Marriage requires continual dialogue to keep partners in tune with each other. Through dialogue, partners share hopes, plans, and dreams. When communication is ineffective, the results may be misunderstanding, alienation, and loneliness—the enemies of marriage. By examining the way they communicate, partners can learn to avoid games. Regular encouragement meetings create the opportunity to develop understanding and to align goals. The game-free relationship is characterized by flexibility and empathy. There is less emphasis on power, control, and winning. Game-free relationships produce less stress, and although winning is not emphasized, both partners feel like winners. It is important for individuals to unlearn less effective habits of relating. The following guidelines can help to focus on behaviors that help create a loving relationship.

1. Know and accept self.
2. Remember that you create your own happiness. Neither your partner nor your marriage can make you happy. Stop demanding, blaming, and accusing.
3. Share your life with your partner whenever possible, but feel secure when you are not with your partner.
4. Share your deepest feelings with your partner.
5. Ask for what you want; enjoy what you get.

6. Appreciate your partner, and help your partner to feel lovable.
7. Enjoy the unity in your relationship.

## Honesty and Openness: Being Congruent

To be congruent is to express the feelings and experience of the moment. In a congruent relationship, partners can be who they really are and say what they really think and feel. When couples openly and honestly express thoughts and feelings, true intimacy grows and grievances can be revealed and resolved. Couples practice congruency by expressing what they are feeling and experiencing at the moment and by encouraging partners' feedback on what is heard and experienced. To be congruent requires courage, especially sufficient courage to risk rejection. In a congruent relationship, the partners individually practice self-acceptance, accept responsibility for thoughts and feelings, cooperate willingly, and communicate clearly. Any style of communication can be adapted to create a more congruent relationship. In a congruent marriage, communication allows each partner to know what the other is feeling without guessing. "I" messages help each partner to express his or her thoughts and feelings without placing the blame on the other. In an "I" message, a partner says, "When you _____, I feel _____ because I _____." The following guidelines can be used for being more congruent.

1. Be courageous. Take risks in things that matter.
2. Be self-accepting. Value yourself and have the courage to be imperfect.
3. Communicate clearly. Seek feedback to clarify how you are being heard.
4. Communicate your thoughts and feelings openly.
5. Accept change as a way of life and learn to welcome it.
6. Have a positive purpose. Be involved in what you do.
7. Focus on the potential and resources in your relationship, instead of on the limitations.
8. When sharing your feelings, be empathic and sensitive to how your partner feels.

## Communication

Communication is one of the most powerful factors influencing the quality of a relationship. When effective communication is developed in a marriage, the couple is able to solve problems, and sharing, empathy, and understanding increase. Therefore, intimacy increases as well. It is through communication that the relationship either grows or is destroyed. The way in which a person communicates in his or her marriage is greatly influenced by family background. What a person consciously or unconsciously chooses to model from family background influences marriage communication. If, for example, an individual's family expressed negative feelings frequently and loudly, he or she may assume it is the way to talk things out and may resent a partner's unwillingness to argue.

## Birth Order

In addition to the psychological atmosphere in which an individual was raised, his or her birth order position also influences the marriage relationship and communication. The oldest child in a family is accustomed to being first and dominant. Because oldest children are accustomed to telling others what to do and in getting their way, oldest children may find it difficult to compromise. When two oldest children marry, they may both struggle to be in charge and control decisions. Second children tend to be rebellious. If both partners are second children, they may continually rebel against each other. Youngest children are often used to having things done for them. If two youngest children marry, each may expect the other to carry out major responsibilities.

Middle children have often learned to compromise and be aware of the needs of others. The marriage of two middle children may reap the benefits of give and take. An oldest child married to a youngest child is often initially a compatible relationship. One may be accustomed to controlling, and the other expects to have decisions made. Eventually the relationship may become a power struggle. An only child may be either very dependent or extremely responsible.

Although birth order alone does not determine a person's perception of human relationships, birth order does have an influence. The way in which an individual interprets his or her role in the family, however, has an even greater influence than the actual birth order position.

## Beliefs

Beliefs and assumptions affect communication. Positive beliefs about self and partner will help a person improve his or her communication. The following attitudes block communication and cause conflict or interfere with problem solving:

1. "I'm right." "I don't need to hear what you have to say." "I'm just that way." "You know how I am."
2. "It's your problem." "Don't expect me to bail you out." "Take care of it yourself." "They are your relatives." "If you had only listened to me in the first place, this wouldn't have happened."
3. "You should anticipate my desires and feelings." "By now you should

know me." "Why do we have to discuss it?" "Can't you guess what I'm feeling?"

4. "If we really love each other, why do we have to talk about this?" "Love should conquer all."

Great progress can be made when both partners are willing to work on their communication. If one partner is resistant, the task is more difficult, but it is not the job of one partner to change the other. As a person changes, he or she influences a partner. If one partner is more empathic and understanding, the other partner may also choose to communicate with greater understanding.

Level communication allows openness, flexibility, honesty, and genuineness. Communication on a level, equal plane demonstrates that a person accepts responsibility for his or her behavior and is sensitive to the partner's feelings. A level communicator observes and shares opinions; understands, negotiates, and commits; encourages and discloses feelings openly.

In summary, the following guidelines can be used for improving communication in the marriage:

1. Be aware of the feelings being shared.
2. Be aware of the intentions being shared.
3. Be aware of the beliefs being shared.
4. Strive for level, equal communication.
5. Be empathic. Hear, identify, and verbalize the other person's feelings.
6. Be responsible for your feelings.
7. Free each other to be; encourage uniqueness.

## Communication Skills

Partners with effective communication use seven sets of skills. First, they are aware of their true feelings and thoughts and share their awareness. They are sensitive to what they are experiencing so that they are able to share perceptions, ideas, intentions, and feelings.

Second, they share feelings in an open, caring way by stating what they feel without blaming. Their inner emotional experiences are communicated to their partners. Sharing feelings makes it possible to work on solutions to problems in the relationship.

Third, they share meanings to be sure they understand each other. Because a person interprets another's message in light of his or her own experiences, to understand what is communicated he or she must continually clarify personal meanings and share another person's messages.

Fourth, they share intentions. This means letting their partners know what they want for themselves in the relationship. Intentions can be expressed by making "I" statements, such as "I want," "I prefer," "I'd like to," "I will be," "I intend."

Fifth, they affirm positive feelings by expressing ways they accept and value each other. By affirming what they see as positive about their partners in marriage, they communicate acceptance and love. Positive statements provide feedback that builds self-esteem.

Sixth, they give positive feedback. When they state what they are experiencing without making a demand for change, they create greater certainty in marriage. Feedback can be pleasant or unpleasant. The challenge is to let their partners know what they are experiencing without judging, criticizing, or complaining.

Seventh, they communicate negative thoughts and feelings in a caring manner. By sharing feelings, ideas, and beliefs, they are attentive, respectful, and accepting. By listening attentively in order to understand a partner's frame of reference, sensitivity is demonstrated.

*Marriage Meeting.* A marriage meeting provides an opportunity to put communication skills into practice in a systematic and caring way. It emphasizes equal participation and responsibility and provides a time and a place for a couple to make decisions and solve problems. The meeting provides a setting for putting into action the marriage skills. When couples regularly schedule marriage meetings, they make a strong commitment about the importance of their marriage. In a marriage meeting, couples meet on a regular basis where they will not be interrupted for a minimum of 40 minutes. An agenda is prepared for each meeting. Each partner lists items for discussion. An agenda is posted prior to the meeting.

## Choices

A current marriage relationship reflects the choices that have been made since the marriage began. Through choices the couple created and maintained the desired marriage relationship. The marriage relationship is the way the couple really wants it to be, or it is what the couple has settled for. Regardless of whether a couple is satisfied with the marriage, both partners have chosen the quality of their relationship through their past decisions. Therefore, it is vital to understand the process of choosing.

In a marriage relationship, partners have the power to make harmful choices that restrict the marriage or helpful choices that encourage the development of a better relationship. Harmful choices include not listening, disregarding or breaking agreements, and abusing each other physically or verbally. Helpful choices include encouraging, helping with a chore, or demonstrating affection. It is important to increase the frequency of helpful choices and to elimi-nate harmful choices. Partners can enrich the marriage by choosing to show love and concern, by choosing to be assertive, by choosing to have fun, by choosing to be challenged, and by choosing to be congruent. Couples who make helpful marriage choices use the following skills.

1. They have learned to identify the instant when they have the possibility to choose.
2. They have clearly identified what they want to achieve.
3. They have identified their alternatives and assessed the potential gains and drawbacks of each. They ask themselves, What are our options? Are there any choices we might have overlooked? If somebody offered us $100,000 to discover another solution, could we?
4. They make choices that allow them maximum use of their strengths and abilities.
5. They are aware of how their choices will affect themselves and others.
6. They make a choice and then assume responsibility for making that choice work.
7. They are always aware that any choice can be changed.

### Conflict Resolution

Although there is no area of married life in which spouses are immune from potential conflict, marital conflict centers mostly on the issues of money, sex, work, children, in-laws, religion, friends, alcohol and drug usage, and recre-ation. The way a couple deals with a conflict determines whether the conflict will be harmful to the marriage. Failure to deal with conflict constructively is the most powerful force in dampening marital satisfaction. When conflict occurs, it tends to be repeated. Thus, it is important to learn how to handle conflict appropriately. Conflicts inevitably occur in all marriages. The follow-ing steps can be used to find effective solutions to marital conflict.

*Step 1:* Show mutual respect. Rather than the issue itself, the attitude of one or both of the partners is often at the heart of the conflict. In a relationship with mutual respect, each partner seeks to understand and respect the other's point of view.

*Step 2:* Pinpoint the real issue. Most couples have difficulty identifying the real issue. Who does what around the house, how money is spent, or whether to have sex usually is not the real issue. These disagreements do have to be resolved, of course, but the purpose or goal the partner is trying to achieve is the real issue. Once the real issue is identified, resolution of surface disagreements becomes easier.

*Step 3:* Seek areas of agreement. In a conflict situation, the most comfortable solution that comes to a person's mind is to suggest how the partner could change to alleviate the problem. A more effective approach is for the person to ask what he or she can do to change the relationship. This creates an atmosphere in which agreement can be reached. Although the ultimate solution to conflict involves mutual change of behavior, the desire and decision to change are the responsibility of each individual. By agreeing to cooperate rather than bicker, a couple sets the stage for discovering what both partners can do to resolve the conflict.

*Step 4:* Mutually participate in decisions. As partners work at a problem and the issue becomes clear, either may propose a tentative solution. A partner may respond by accepting the proposed solution, modifying it, or making a countersuggestion. An atmosphere of give and take is most effective. When agreement is reached, clarification of the role of each partner in carrying out the decision and specification of what should be done if either partner does not follow through are necessary.

In resolving conflict, a couple can use the following guidelines:

1. Be specific.
2. Be present and future oriented.
3. Use active listening.
4. Use "I" messages.
5. Avoid absolutes.
6. Do not attempt to determine who was right and who was wrong.
7. Remember that solutions are not forever.
8. Solve one problem at a time.
9. Affirm that understanding is the goal.
10. Know that your attitude determines the meaning you give to the facts.
11. Watch for fouls and low blows.
12. Do it now.
13. Optimize the conditions.
14. Learn to recognize normal developmental crises.
15. Say what you are thinking and feeling.
16. Learn to change habitual responses.
17. Set a limit on time spent discussing the problem.
18. Allow time to change.
19. Ask yourself a new question when you cannot find a solution.
20. Accept responsibility.

## Dealing with Anger

Anger is often triggered by fear, frustration, lowered self-esteem, and hurt feelings. Partners have a great deal at stake in their marriage. They mean more to each other and therefore have the potential for hurting each other more deeply. They interact in more facets of each other's life than in any other relationship. In short, marriage partners have the opportunity and the potential to evoke feelings of frustration, fear, and lowered self-esteem in each other, feelings that may result in anger. To allow anger to be a constructive force in the marriage relationship it is necessary to learn a process for dealing with it when it occurs. When a partner is experiencing anger, he or she can vent feelings, or suppress them, or process them with the other partner. The following seven-step process is effective in processing anger.

*Step 1:* Cool down from the heavy anger. This may require taking a time-out and physically separating. When both of you are calm, the process can begin.

*Step 2:* Define the anger, but agree not to attack, blame, or provoke.

*Step 3:* Communicate with each other by using "I" messages and tentative guesses. Do not use accusing messages.

*Step 4:* Prepare a separate written (oral, if possible) statement in which you both put the other's point of view into words.

*Step 5:* Exchange and correct, if necessary, each other's statement.

*Step 6:* List all available options and all courses of action to be taken.

*Step 7:* Together choose the option on which you both agree.

## Marriage Maintenance

No marriage can be totally divorce-proof. There is sometimes a fine line between the things that make a marriage work and those that break it up. Equal marriage has no room for complacency. It requires both partners to take risks. The following skills are helpful, however, in divorce-proofing a marriage.

Encourage each other often. Make it a practice to encourage your partner daily. Nobody ever gets enough positive feedback. Encouraging each other seems simple. Nevertheless, one of the most common complaints of partners is that they are not appreciated. In lasting relationships, partners make an effort to value and encourage one another. Encouragement can be incidental and spontaneous or planned. A partner who receives encouragement is more likely to give encouragement.

Communicate openly and honestly with one another. Be open and willing to share your thoughts and feelings as well as to listen to your partner. Do not clam up or walk out on opportunities to grow and learn. Certain times are more appropriate than others for sharing. Sometimes it is wise to postpone a discussion.

Deal with conflict. Life involves conflict. In healthy marriages couples manage and respond to conflict in effective ways. Believe you can work out your problems together, and take the time to do it. Use the conflict solution process.

Develop the courage to be imperfect. Be willing to apologize. The forgiveness process should not dwell on past grievances; it should set the stage for greater harmony. "Where do we go from here?" is the question to ask after an apology. There is no need to keep the conflict going or to try proving a point at this time. Accepting that mistakes and problems are the normal part of married life can speed the transition to a satisfying marriage.

Support each other fully. Provide consistent and dependable support. Learn to suspend judgment and provide encouragement, even when your partner's goals temporarily conflict with your own best interests.

Develop regular time for fun each week. Schedule time to be alone with each other. Fun should be a weekly, maybe even a daily, activity.

Choose to create a more satisfying relationship. You are not a victim; you always have a choice.

Develop shared dreams, goals, and interests. Shared dreams and interests provide opportunities for conversation and mutual enjoyment. Couples with shared goals are less disturbed by minor or major crisis.

Be self-accepting. The more you accept yourself, the more you will accept your partner. Mutual self-acceptance promotes both personal growth and growth of the relationship.

Adopt realistic expectations. Society fosters unrealistic, romantic expectations of marriage. Even in the best relationships, some dreams and expectations are unfulfilled. Be honest and realistic when assessing your relationship.

## CONCLUDING NOTE

The characteristics, skills, and roles of functional and dysfunctional marriages have been presented. Writers have traditionally focused on pathology and its removal and have had very little understanding of what makes an effective marriage relationship. Effective therapists, however, have a clear idea of what behaviors, attitudes, and expectations constitute a healthy marriage. The process involves building on existing strengths and developing skills to produce functional marriages. We now turn to an examination of the various approaches to marital therapy. We have highlighted psychoanalytic, cognitive-behavioral, and systems theories and pulled them together in our own integrative approach.

## REFERENCES

Beavers, W. R. (1985). *Successful marriage: A family systems approach to couples therapy.* New York: Norton.

Dinkmeyer, D., & Carlson, J. (1984). *Time for a better marriage.* Circle Pines, MN: American Guidance Service.

Dinkmeyer, D., & Carlson, J. (1984). *Training in marriage enrichment.* Circle Pines, MN: American Guidance Service.

Glick, I. D., Clarkin, J. F., & Kessler, D. R. (1987). *Marital and family therapy* (3d ed.). Orlando, FL: Grune & Stratton.

Goleman, D. (1985, September 10). Patterns of love charted. *The New York Times.*

Stinnet, N., & DeFrain, J. (1985). *Secrets of strong families.* Boston: Little, Brown.

# 4

# *Psychoanalytic Approaches to Marital Therapy*

A lthough it is among the oldest psychotherapeutic systems, psychoanaly-sis has shown relatively little interest in the treatment of marital discord. Yet, psychoanalysis is the only major orientation that stresses the impact of individual personality forces on marital dysfunction. This chapter focuses on psychoanalytic approaches to the treatment of this discord. (Subsequent chapters describe the behavioral, systemic, and integrative approaches.)

Teaching and learning about the psychoanalytic perspective are probably more difficult and challenging than they are for any other psychotherapy system. Thus, even though this chapter contains basic concepts and principles, mastery of this information requires considerable effort and study. Someone has said that clinicians might utilize the psychoanalytic approach more if only they could understand it! So given this caveat, let us proceed.

We begin by clarifying the meaning of the terms *psychodynamic* and *psychoanalytic,* which are erroneously used synonymously. Psychodynamic refers to a broad range of theories of human behavior that commonly assume that a person's thoughts, feelings, and behaviors are a function of the complex inter-action of mind, body, and external environment. In addition, psychodynamic theories contend that human behavior can best be understood and predicted with specific constructs, two of which are the unconscious motivation of be-havior and the influence of early life experiences (Paolino & McCrady 1978). Psychoanalytic refers to constructs and principles of psychic functioning derived from Freud and his followers and to a set of techniques for treatment and for scholarly investigation. More specifically, psychoanalytic theories and approaches are a subset of psychodynamic thinking.

## DIFFERING PSYCHOANALYTIC PERSPECTIVES

There is no *one* psychoanalytic approach to marital discord because a unified psychoanalytic theory does not exist. Rather, there is a continuum of analytic views with varying theoretical differences. At one end is the orthodox analyst who believes that marital discord is merely a presenting symptom that reflects individual psychopathology in one or both spouses. Therefore, the orthodox analyst treats one of the spouses in an individual therapy format and forgoes any contact with the other spouse or family member. Treatment involves interpretation of transference issues between the analyst and the patient, and insight is expected to result in a cure.

At the other end of the continuum is the contemporary analytic marital therapist who regards the marital relationship as the basic unit of observation and treatment. The couple undergoes conjoint therapy. This therapist is more concerned with transference issues between the spouses and is more likely to utilize communication and skill training, behavioral methods, and systemic interventions as adjuncts to interpretation. Between these extremes is a variety of analytic perspectives. Three representative perspectives (Bellak, 1983) with applications to marital treatment that span the continuum from the orthodox to the contemporary are classical, object relations, and self-psychology. Those approaches closer to the contemporary end of the continuum are less purely psychoanalytic and begin to resemble the concepts and methods of the other major theoretical orientations.

## COMMON PSYCHOANALYTIC PERSPECTIVES

Despite these differences, there are some essential characteristics that all analytic perspectives share. Offenkrantz and Tobin (1975) suggested four such characteristics. First, the analytic mode represents a strictly deterministic view of human behavior. Second, this determination is manifested by the effects that early experiences exert on adult behavior, attitudes, and feelings. Third, unconscious mental activity can be inferred from current thoughts, dreams, feelings, behaviors, and the like. Fourth, insight or consciousness produces cure.

Segraves (1982) noted that there is a treatment orientation regarding marital discord that can be identified as psychoanalytic. Segraves indicated that all analytic perspectives emphasize that psychopathology resides in the individual spouse and that the past determines current difficulties. Specifically, marital discord is a function of a misperception of a spouse's character and actual behavior. The significance of mate selection is highlighted in all perspectives, albeit differently, as a causal factor in marital discord. Finally, insight is presumed to be the curative factor in marital treatment.

## THE CLASSICAL PSYCHOANALYTIC PERSPECTIVE

### Key Concepts

Although its influence is waning, classical analytic theory continues to be the dominant analytic approach in this country (Bellak, 1983). As previously noted, this approach views marital difficulties as the result of psychopathology in one or both spouses. Marital discord is considered an *acting out* of internal conflicts within an interpersonal context. These conflicts are the result of developmental events within the spouse's early childhood.

In analytic terms conflict has three elements: the defense, the anxiety, and the hidden impulse (Malan, 1976). The aim of analytic treatment is to clarify each of these elements. The defense and the anxiety are interpreted first, which facilitates conscious recognition of the hidden and feared impulse. Because the conscious experience of impulses can be frightening or threatening, the individual employs defense mechanisms to avoid such an experience. Because they are socially unacceptable, anger and sexual impulses are highly defended (Offenkrantz & Tobin, 1975).

These elements are recognizable in three types of interpersonal relationships: the marriage, the therapeutic context, and the distant past (the original relationship, usually between the individual and his or her parents, in which the conflict initially arose). Presumably, a sequence of behaviors recurs predictably, and the intrapsychic roots of these *repetition compulsions* can be analyzed. As a result, through analytic treatment the individual should be able to understand and experience these three relationships so that he or she can recognize and self-correct these forces after treatment is terminated. In short, analytic treatment enables the individual to consciously experience his or her conflicts.

### Treatment Process

For the classical analyst the treatment unit involves only one of the spouses, and the two basic treatment strategies are the therapeutic alliance and the interpretation of transferences and resistances (Nemiah, 1975). The *therapeutic alliance* is the working relationship between the individual spouse and the therapist. The purpose of the alliance is to aid the individual in allying himself or herself with the analyst so that the individual can better understand the conflicts that inevitably impact on the marriage relationship. Treatment progress occurs only when the individual can identify with the logic of the analyst, which allows the individual's circumstances to be appropriately analyzed.

*Interpretation* is the form of communication the analyst uses to elucidate the unconscious meaning in dreams, resistances, transferences, and other intrapsychic phenomena. The purpose of interpretation is to make the unconscious conscious, which is called insight. Interpretation is the chief tool of the analyst and the primary activity in the course of treatment.

Dream work is an important means of interpreting unconscious material. Analysts describe dreams as having two levels of content/meaning: manifest and latent. *Manifest content* is the dream as it appears to the individual. *Latent content* is the disguised and symbolic aspect of the dream, which, because such content can be painful and threatening, is transformed into the more acceptable manifest content. The analyst works to uncover the latent content by analyzing and interpreting the manifest content.

In the treatment context, *transference* refers to the individual's misperceptions of the therapist's motives and feelings. Similar misperceptions were previously attributed to parental figures and often are presently attributed to the other spouse. A basic element in classical therapy is to allow the transference to the therapist to develop fully. This is called the *transference neurosis*. The clarification and understanding of the transference by both therapist and individual permit the individual to avoid the repetition compulsions manifested in the marital discord. *Countertransference* is the analyst's unconscious response to the individual's transference. *Resistance* refers to the individual's efforts to obstruct the aims and process of therapy. Resistance is not so much an obstacle to treatment as it is a way in which the individual reveals the nature of his or her difficulties and conflicts.

### Key Figures

Bernard Greene (1960) and Peter Giovacchini (1965) are two of the rather small number of analysts who have written about marital therapy from the classical perspective. There are, however, a number of psychoanalytically oriented marital therapists who have made some modifications in the classical model. Perhaps the most obvious modification has been a shift from individual treatment to conjoint sessions. Through conjoint work the transference occurs mainly between the spouses rather than between one spouse and the therapist.

The approach of Christopher Dare (1986) is fairly representative. Dare, a British child psychiatrist, describes a conjoint approach in which interpretation is used to neutralize and integrate aggressive and libidinal needs so that behavior can be motivated more by service of the ego and less by impulse and intrapsychic conflict. Nevertheless, like a number of analytic marital therapists who work with couples, Dare utilizes a number of interventions from other orientations. In the early stages of treatment he focuses on communication training and problem-solving interventions.

## THE OBJECT RELATIONS PERSPECTIVE

### Key Concepts

Whereas in classical analysis the basic motivation is drive reduction, the basic motivation in the object relations perspective is object seeking. It may be helpful to review some basic terminology before we describe the object relations approach. *Self* refers to the individual, and *object* refers to some aspect or quality of another person that has been *introjected*—that is, symbolically absorbed within the individual. Thus, *object relations* refers to the introjected representation of a previous interpersonal relationship. Object relations can be further described as the emotional bonds between one individual and another. As such, the term suggests the individual's capacity for loving and relating appropriately to others. Each object relation has a *self-representation*, an *object representation*, and an *affective component*. Furthermore, object relations become incorporated as a part of the developing ego (Kernberg, 1976).

The first object relationship—between mother and child—shapes the pattern of later interpersonal relationships, including that with the spouse. Object relations theory holds that the infant is primarily seeking a relationship with the mother rather than seeking only instinctual gratification (Fairbairn, 1952). This early bond is important because if "good enough mothering"—the mother adapting to the child's need without smothering or withdrawing from the child—is lacking, subsequent personality development will be impaired (Winnicott, 1965).

The formation of original ties is marked by varying degrees of ambivalence as the mother attempts to provide for the child's needs for food, protection, emotional nurturance and love, and discipline. Initially, the child perceives all objects as either "all good" or "all bad" as he or she cannot emotionally or conceptually experience them as some combination of good and bad. Normally, this evolves toward an integration of ambivalence such that the child can experience an object as having good and bad features. As this can be tolerated in the self and with others, the child can forgo the primitive splitting of object components into opposing parts or representations.

When perceived negative experiences can be tolerated and mastered, the child is said to have developed internalized object consistency (Mahler, Pine, & Bergman, 1975).

## Marital Choice

The object relations therapist understands interpersonal relations, including marriage, as efforts by the individual to seek out and become emotionally attached to people and things outside himself or herself. Basic to marital satisfaction is the spouse's acceptance of the needs of his or her partner because he or she can projectively identify or tolerate these needs as a good parent does. Mate selection theory—the reasons marital partners are chosen and the relationship of these reasons to marital discord—is perhaps the most important legacy from the psychoanalytic orientation.

According to classical psychoanalytic view, need represents a form of idealization wherein the object becomes a substitute for an unattained ego ideal. So, for example, the spouse with strong needs to dominate would be expected to select a mate with strong needs to submit. Unfortunately, the classical view cannot adequately explain mate selection as a mutual exchange, which object relations theory does.

The object relations view of mate selection is based on the constructs of projective identification and collusion. *Projective identification* is an interactional style between the spouses that represents a reenactment of earlier relationships. A child handles conflicts with his or her parents by introjecting (symbolically absorbing) the parental relationship, including both sides of the conflict. In projective identifications, some introjected parts of the self are split off or disavowed and then projected onto the spouse, who complies with the split. In other words, a deep unconscious "idea" is arranged in which the fixed view that each spouse has for the other is swapped—for example, "I will regard you as nonsexual as long as you see me as nondemanding." For projective identification to occur and continue, the object must periodically exhibit the behavior projected on him or her by the subject. In other words, the relationship cannot continue unless each spouse is willing at the unconscious level to accept and identify with the projective identification. In neurotic couples, mate selection is based on projective identification. As Skynner (1976) noted, "Couples are usually attracted by shared developmental failures."

*Collusion* (Dicks, 1967) is the unspoken process by which such mate selection arrangements are upheld in relationship. There is an interesting paradoxical element to this unconscious agreement: Each spouse holds out the promise that he or she will help the other work through early life conflicts and hurts while at the same time guaranteeing that such conflicts will not be worked through and that nothing will change (Dicks, 1967).

Furthermore, this contract relieves both of responsibility for "growing up" and facing the requisite anxiety and effort needed for change and development. In short, collusion is a collaboration in which spouses do not merely choose the other but enter into an implicit agreement that they will meet the unfulfilled needs of the other. Another feature of this implicit agreement is that each spouse will support and maintain the other's self-perception, even in the face of conflict. It has been said that choosing a spouse is more a matter of refinding an old love object than finding a new one (Friedman, 1980). So from an objective relations perspective there is more than a kernel of truth to the lyric "I want to marry a man just like dear ol' dad."

*Marital Discord*

A rather high level of maturity is required to sustain a love relationship. According to Kernberg (1976), staying in love requires the spouses to establish a total object relation rather than a partial one. Marital satisfaction results when both spouses have adequately differentiated object relations. This kind of maturity is a function of clear sex roles, effective communication and responsible behavior when dealing with issues, and the ability to work together with mutual satisfaction. For most couples, such maturity results from a considerable expenditure of time and effort, a large part of it involving a change in the original collusion. Discord and dissatisfaction usually bring the honeymoon experience to an end. For the first time, each spouse begins to see glimpses of the other as he or she really is. Marital discord and marital dissatisfaction suggest maladaptive object internalizations (Meissner, 1978). From an analytic perspective, marital discord results from inappropriate needs and unconscious expectations combined with an inability to cope with disappointment and disillusion.

Paradoxically, the very traits that initially attracted the partners to each other become the focus for their discord. For example, a wife may have been initially attracted to her husband because she perceived him as "having it all together and knowing where his life was going." She was in awe of these qualities as she did not possess them herself. So the relationship developed based on the somewhat irrational notion that she could somehow share those admired qualities just by being around him. But, as conflict and dissatisfaction mounted in the marriage, she began to perceive the negative aspects of those once-attractive qualities. Now she considers him overbearing, overcontrolling, and narrow-minded.

As long as the other spouse was unconsciously idealized, any ambivalent feelings for that spouse were repressed. But as the idealized image of the love object became tarnished, ambivalent feelings welled up, resulting not only in interpersonal conflict but also in intrapersonal conflict. In short, what became problematic was not the husband's inability to meet the wife's needs but the ambivalence and contradictions within the wife's intrapsychic structure. These contradictions rendered it impossible for the wife's needs to be met (Gurman, 1978), and marital dissatisfaction and discord grew.

## Treatment Process

### Goals and Roles

Because object relations theory considers marital discord the result of a break-down in the mutual gratification of conscious and unconscious needs, the major goal of object relations marital therapy is the restructuring of the couple's perceptions and expectations so that they are more reality-based. An increase in intrapsychic awareness and growth on the part of each spouse is prerequisite to improved marital functioning.

The couple is usually seen conjointly, although individual sessions may also be arranged, particularly during the assessment phase. The therapist's role is to clarify and interpret the dysfunctional nature of the spouse's object relations. This occurs through the therapist's function as a transference object in which conflicts are reexperienced, reenacted, and then resolved. The spouses also function as transference objects for each other, with the therapist supplying clarification and interpretation.

### Treatment Stages

Four stages of analytic treatment have been described by Nadelson (1978). Her approach to structuring the treatment process is in some ways similar to the structure of treatment in the other major orientations.

Stage one is called *contract negotiation,* and during this phase administrative and therapeutic issues are discussed. In addition to agreement on fees and appointment times, the therapist assesses the couple's goals for treatment, the spouses' motivations, and the likelihood both partners can profit from analytic treatment.

Stage two is the *initial phase* of treatment. It primarily concerns the assessment of intrapsychic and interpersonal factors and the development of the therapeutic alliance. Treatment at this stage emphasizes that each spouse has brought a unique set of needs, perceptions, and experiences to the marriage.

Stage three is the *middle stage* of therapy. The therapist facilitates the spouses in strengthening their alliances with one another by exploring their past perceptions and experiences. This usually results in increased empathy and a strengthening of their commitment to each other. Interpretation of unconscious material is the major intervention strategy. Transference interpretations at several levels are made by the therapist.

Stage four is the *termination phase*. The main object at this stage is to decrease the spouses' ambivalence about separating from the therapist and help them become comfortable with their ability to be their own therapists. The end point of therapy comes when each spouse can accept and understand the other and when both have learned more appropriate means of resolving conflict.

## Assessment Strategy

There are many ways in which analytic marital therapists can gather and organize information on a couple. Martin (1976) has outlined a three-step procedure for doing so that consists of opening presentation, individual history of each spouse, and history of the marital relationship.

In the opening presentation the therapist examines the major complaints of each spouse, which usually include children, finances, sex, and in-laws. The question "What needs to be increased, and what needs to be decreased in your relationship?" is a central theme. The therapist attempts to articulate the positive as well as the negative forces that were involved in mate selection and that still affect marital satisfaction and discord.

The therapist then begins the assessment of the individual life history of each spouse in five areas: earliest memories, later childhood and adolescent memories, current and recurrent dreams, fantasies and daydreams, and medical history (which should differentiate psychological from physical problems that result in physical symptoms). Using the spouses' individual histories as a basis for understanding, the therapist begins the assessment of the couple's relationship. The specifics of the first encounter, the conscious and unconscious forces of attraction, and the marriage contract (the expressed and unexpressed expectations and beliefs about each spouse's obligations to and benefits from the relationship) are explored. Developmental factors relating to stages of the marriage (the marital life cycle) are investigated in relation to the marital discord. A detailed sexual history is then taken to clarify the extent to which sexual problems mask individual and relationship issues.

A discussion of the therapeutic contract concludes the assessment phase. According to Martin, just as a marital contract has its conscious and unconscious aspects, so does the therapeutic contract the couple makes with the therapist. Therefore, the therapist needs to elicit both spouses' beliefs and expectations about treatment outcomes as well as their perceived role in the treatment process. The specifics of a treatment agreement can then be negotiated. Not only does this process of clarifying a treatment contract help the therapist in understanding the couple and in guiding treatment; it also serves as a role model for the couple to follow in developing a workable marital contract.

## Intervention Strategies

Object relations marital therapists employ the same psychoanalytic methods described in the previous section: development of the therapeutic alliance, dream work, and the analysis/interpretation of resistances and transferences. In conjoint therapy, application of some of these strategies does differ, particularly with the interpretation of resistances and transferences.

Resistances represent the spouses' defense against anxiety in their daily lives. Resistances are also a maneuver that interferes with the spouses' ability to experience satisfaction in their marriage relationship. Resistance operates in marital therapy by preventing the couple and therapist from gaining access to painful and anxiety-provoking unconscious thoughts. By interpreting and working through resistances, both spouses gain insight, alleviate the maladaptive behaviors, and increase marital satisfaction.

Analyzing and interpreting transference are particularly important for the object relations marital therapist. When negative images and thoughts are projected onto one spouse, that spouse is likely to respond in a distorted manner stemming from early internalized objects. This results in an unconscious collusion that can maintain dysfunctional marital discord indefinitely. By understanding and interpreting this collusive process, the therapist aids the spouses in achieving insight into their own intrapsychic conflicts. In this process, the couple begins to understand how past internalized objects influence present functioning. Furthermore, this type of interpretation helps the couple work through early life maladaptive patterns that prevent satisfaction in the marriage. Sager (1976) noted that interpretation gives the couple a means of understanding its irrational behavior. Because of this, each spouse is often relieved of the guilt, confusion, or frustration that resulted from self-blame for the other's response.

## Adjunctive Techniques

Object relations marital therapists also utilize methods from other therapeutic orientations because, according to Gurman (1978), "there exists [in the psychoanalytic tradition] but a paucity of marital therapy interventions derived from such an orientation and most influential psychoanalytically oriented marital therapists, in fact, appear to be closet 'technical eclectics.'" (p. 479) Dare (1986) noted that analytic marital therapy "cannot be as exclusively interpretive as a psychoanalysis seems to be" (p. 24). A perusal of the writings of object relations marital therapists strongly suggests that these therapists are quite analytic in their formulation of the nature of a couple's marital discord but rather behavioral, strategic, and systemic in their descriptions of therapeutic interventions.

## Key Figures

H. V. Dicks, a British psychiatrist, has probably been the most influential in adapting object relations theory to marital discord and the practice of marital therapy. His book *Marital Tensions*, published in 1967, is a classic in the field. His writing was based on his experience at the famed Tavistock Clinic in London. Basically, Dicks expanded the formulations of the early object relations analysts, particularly Fairbairn and Winnicott, to include the interaction between spouses.

James Framo (1982), an American psychologist, has been an ardent advocate of the object relations approach to marital work. Based in large part on Dick's work, Framo's main contribution has been his process of guiding a couple through three treatment stages: couples therapy, couples group therapy, and intergenerational conferences in which family-of-origin issues are the treatment focus.

In the first stage, the therapist works with the couple to establish a therapeutic relationship with each spouse based on mutual trust. Then the therapist works to defuse conflict. Basic interventions such as communication skills training and negotiation training are utilized. Next the therapist begins the process of educating the couple about object relations theory and how issues that have been long unresolved in the family of origin may be responsible for present difficulties (Framo, 1981).

In the second stage, Framo shifts to the couples group format. The couples group is usually composed of three couples. The group helps the spouses further understand their own relationships and how to improve them. The group creates a sense of community in which the couples support each other in their attempts to recognize and confront unresolved issues from their families of origin that are affecting current relationships.

In the third stage, Framo shifts the treatment focus to a family-of-origin format. These sessions are held without the other spouse. The purpose of these sessions is for the individual to make contact with his or her own family and have a "corrective emotional experience" with the family (Framo, 1981).

In short, Framo's approach is an active and directive approach to resolving current issues rooted in the family of origin. This approach is not for every couple, and Framo (1981) acknowledges the limitations of his approach. Specifically, family-of-origin work is not necessary or appropriate for couples with relatively minor marital difficulties.

Clifford Sager (1976, 1983), an American psychiatrist, has advanced a unique approach to marital therapy that combines an object relations perspective with some systems and some behavioral exchange theory. Needless to say his treatment approach is eclectic. He refers to his approach as "marriage contract couples therapy." He proposes that the marriage contract is a metaphor for each spouse's expectations of the other in the marriage. The contract exists on three levels: consciously verbalized, conscious but not verbalized, and unconscious. He believes that the third level, which involves transference issues, accounts for most chronic marital discord. During the course of therapy, Sager helps the couple negotiate a new common contract. Interpretation of transference distortions is only one of a number of therapeutic interventions. He has also applied this approach to remarried couples (Sager et al., 1983).

## THE SELF-PSYCHOLOGY PERSPECTIVE

Recently, there has been growing interest among marital and family therapists in the self-psychology perspective (Feldman, 1982; Brighton-Cleghorn, 1987). Actually, self-psychology is a relatively new perspective within the psychoanalytic tradition, heralded and pioneered by Kohut (1971). In many respects self-psychology is a refinement of the object relations perspective, but there are some differences. For one, object relations is based on the philosophical tradition of positivism, whereas self-psychology is based on the symbolic-experientialist tradition. Practically speaking, this means that the vantage point for assessment in the self-psychology approach is that of the experiencing insider. The therapist becomes a part of the equation of observation and evaluation. In contrast, the object relations therapist is an outside observer in true scientific-positivist fashion (Brighton-Cleghorn, 1987). Kohut considers "empathy" as the experiencing insider's basic tool of analysis.

### Key Concepts

The basic concept in self-psychology is the *self-object*. From his or her earliest moments the child experiences certain individuals, particularly the mother, as part of the self. They are so intimately entwined in the child's mind that self and object are one, merged into a self-object. The child's experience during this early stage determines to a large extent whether the child's self will emerge as relatively healthy or dysfunctional.

There are three functions and qualities of self-objects (Kohut, 1977). The first is the "mirroring self-object." This is somewhat like the proud parent who builds up the child's sense of control, energy, and achievement (self-esteem) through encouragement and praise. The second is the "idealized parent imago." This refers to the calm, self-assured presence the parent provides the child. The child's sense of the world as basically predictable and secure develops from this parental imago. The third is the "alter-ego/twinship" function, which is characterized by the statement "Be just like me and let me be just like you in the sharing of our common skills and abilities." Persons, usually the parents, who perform these functions for the child are self-objects. The unique contribution of self-psychology to object relations thinking is Kohut's systematic description of these functional qualities and processes that regulate and control self-states (Brighton-Cleghorn, 1987). Kohut suggested that the basic motivating force is not object seeking but "structure seeking," by which he meant the drive to organize self-experiences in a cohesive manner throughout life. This is in contrast to the loss of a sense of cohesion of the self that is termed *fragmentation.*

To the extent that the parents have firmly grounded and independent selves, they are able to provide the child with "mirroring," empathic nurturance, and a cohesive environment in which to grow and develop. This type of experience allows the child to exhibit a pride and exhibitionism that the parents can accept. As a result, the child is able to develop a secure, vigorous, and cohesive sense of self.

When the parents possess fragile or insecurely established selves, however, the self-object experience of the child tends to be distorted. Habitually ignoring or refusing to encourage the child's accomplishments may bolster the parents' flagging self-esteem, but at the expense of the child developing a healthy and coherent sense of self. Where there is a significant failure in achieving or maintaining cohesion, vigor, and harmony, the possibility of "self disorders," particularly narcissistic or borderline personality disorders, is high (Kohut, 1977). As a result of distorted experiences in early self-object relations, the developing self tends to be extremely susceptible to fragmentation in the face of threats to self-esteem, called "narcissistic injury."

## Marital Conflict

The key to an understanding of dysfunctional marital conflict is the concept of *narcissistic vulnerability,* which is a weakness or deficiency in the structured cohesiveness of the self-presentation. Narcissistic vulnerability results from the relative weakness of approving and/or admiring introjects (Kohut, 1971) and promotes dysfunctional marital conflict through hypersensitivity, irrational narcissistic expectations, and deficient empathy. Dysfunctional conflicts occur when one spouse overreacts (hypersensitivity) to the other's criticism or rejection, when one spouse unconsciously expects the other to totally gratify (narcissistic expectations) narcissistic needs, and/or when one spouse provides the other with little or no empathic response (deficient empathy). The result of such dysfunctional conflict between the spouses is narcissistic rage, projective identification, and cognitive distortion.

## Mirror and Idealizing Transferences

Kohut (1971) described narcissistic needs in terms of the mirror and the idealizing transferences. In a *mirror transference* the individual's sense of self is maintained by an idealized or grandiose self that requires another person to be consistently and totally admiring. In an *idealizing transference* the individual's sense of self is maintained by means of an idealized image of the other (the idealized parent imago), with the idealized other being totally and consistently attentive. Kohut noted that the individual with mirroring expectations tends to be hypersensitive to actual or imagined instances of disapproval and criticism, whereas the individual with idealizing expectations tends to be hypersensitive to instances of inattention or neglect.

In conflicted marriages, the husband tends to relate primarily from mirroring expectations while the wife relates primarily from idealizing expectations (Feldman, 1982). To the extent that this occurs, there is little sense of each spouse being a separate individual with independent needs and feelings. To the extent that one spouse is invested in maintaining his or her own precarious sense of self, he or she tends to be insensitive to the needs and wishes of the other spouse.

## Narcissistic Rage and Anxiety

This lack of empathy generates narcissistic rage and anxiety. Narcissistic rage (Kohut, 1972) involves intense hostility, revenge, and an extreme lack of empathy toward the offending individual. Narcissistic rage also leads to narcissistic anxiety, which is a fear of repressed negative self-images, and then to projective identification. Two steps characterize the projective identification defense. The first involves a splitting or dividing of the intrapsychic self and other representation into two separate representations: "all bad" or "all good."

The second involves the projection of one or more of these split representations or images onto one or more external others.

Projective identification in conflicted marriages shows itself as the narcissistically injured spouse projecting "all bad" self and other representations onto the other spouse, who is then experienced as totally rejecting, harsh, or critical. The narcissistically injured spouse is then able to retain "all good" representations while maintaining the belief that he or she has been victimized by the "all bad" spouse. This perception is further reinforced as he or she projects the "all good" representation onto a fantasized other whom he or she believes could be an ideal mate.

*Overgeneralization and Denial*

As projective identification is mobilized, cognitive distortions are likely, particularly as a result of such processes as overgeneralization and denial. Whereas an accurate perception might be, "My husband sometimes criticizes me," the overgeneralized distortion becomes, "My husband is always criticizing me." Likewise, denial distorts perception. For example, when a husband ignores the occasional accepting behaviors of his wife, he reinforces a perception of his wife as totally rejecting. Feldman (1982) concluded that dysfunctional marital conflict behavior by one spouse stimulates narcissistic rage and anxiety, projective identification, and cognitive distortions in the other, leading to an escalation of dysfunctional behavior in which physical injury, separation, or divorce can ensue. Figure 4.1 summarizes this description of marital discord.

**Treatment Process**

The self-psychology model, particularly as described by Feldman (1982) of the Family Institute of Chicago, lends itself to systematic treatment of conflicted couples. The basic goal of treatment is to lessen narcissistic injury and cognitive distortion while increasing empathic understanding between spouses. As with other psychoanalytic approaches, both individual interviews and conjoint interviews are utilized.

*Assessment*

The initial assessment focuses on narcissistic vulnerabilities and expectations, cognitive distortions, and the specific nature of conflicted marital behavior. A detailed description of the couple's dysfunctional conflictural behavior focuses on precipitating events and each spouse's cognitions and feelings toward the

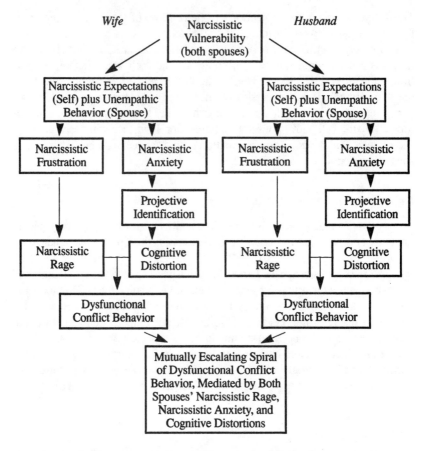

**Figure 4.1   Dysfunctional Marital Conflict: An Integrative Interpersonal-Intrapsychic Model**

*Source:* Feldman (1982), p. 421. Reprinted from Volume 8, Number 4 of the *Journal of Marital and Family Therapy*, Copyright 1982, American Association for Marriage and Family Therapy. Reprinted by permission.

other's behavior. As with the object relations approaches to marital therapy, a detailed family-of-origin history of each spouse is obtained. Finally, each spouse is required to record his or her dreams during the assessment phase.

### Treatment Intervention

As with other psychoanalytical approaches to marital therapy, therapeutic intervention tends to include systemic and behavioral techniques and methods. Feldman (1982) was one of the first to describe a self-psychology–oriented marital therapy. Interventions are planned and directed toward each element of the assessment process.

Initially the goal of treatment is to heighten each spouse's awareness of his or her feelings of narcissistic vulnerability. Later the goal is to reduce the narcissistic vulnerability while increasing each spouse's empathic skills. The therapist prescribes that each spouse attend to his or her feelings at the onset of a dysfunctional conflict, especially the hurt feelings preceding anger. These are then explored in therapy where connections between hurt-producing interactions in the present are made to those in the families of origin. Free association, dream work, and role playing are useful methods in dealing with narcissistic vulnerability. Increased empathic understanding is accomplished through modeling and empathy training. Throughout the course of treatment, the therapist models empathic listening and communication. Standard empathy training exercises are utilized to interrupt the couple's cycle of mutual blaming. Cognitive awareness training (Novaco, 1978) is used to moderate narcissistic expectations and reduce cognitive distortions. Self-instruction training (Novaco, 1978) teaches each spouse to make anger-controlling self-statements when he or she experiences his or her anger as becoming uncontrolled. This is one of a number of approaches to the reduction of narcissistic rage. Feldman (1982) utilizes problem-solving training and behavioral contracting (Jacobson & Margolin, 1979) to decrease the frequency and intensity of dysfunctional behavior while increasing positive and constructive intimacy-producing behavior.

### Key Figures

As mentioned earlier, the self-psychology approach to marital therapy is the most recent and least developed area of the psychoanalytic perspective; only Larry Feldman (1982) has published on self-psychology and marital therapy. Janet Brighton-Cleghorn (1987) has described the application of self-psychology to family therapy.

## CONCLUDING NOTE

Even as recently as 20 years ago, theorists speculated that the growth of marital and family therapy would be stunted if it were to be prematurely integrated with psychoanalytic thinking. In fact, with marital and family therapy's maturation have come developments in psychoanalysis aimed at integrating the psychoanalytic and systems models. This chapter has examined basic psychoanalytic concepts in the classical, object relations, and self-psychology approaches and described their corresponding treatment methods and processes. The object relations approach was detailed because it has been more developed, disseminated, and better integrated with the systems perspective than either the classical or self-psychology approach has been. Chapter 6 details the systems perspective, which should further clarify the differences between these two perspectives.

## REFERENCES

Bellak, L. (1983). Psychoanalysis in the 1980's. *American Journal of Psychotherapy, 37,* 476–492.

Brighton-Cleghorn, J. (1987). Formulations of self and family systems. *Family Process, 26,* 185–201.

Dare, C. (1986). Psychoanalytic marital therapy. In N. Jacobsen & A. Gurman (Eds.), *Clinical handbook of marital therapy.* New York: Guilford Press.

Dicks, H. 1967). *Marital tensions.* London: Routledge and Kegan Paul.

Dicks, H. 1976). *Marital tensions.* New York: Basic Books.

Fairbairn, W. (1952). *An object-relations theory of personality.* New York: Basic Books.

Feldman, L. (1982). Dysfunctional marital conflict: An integrative interpersonal-intrapsychic model. *Journal of Marital and Family Therapy, 8,:* 417–428.

Friedman, L. (1980). Integrating psychoanalytic object-relations understandings with family systems interventions in couples therapy. In J. Pearce and L. Friedman (Eds.), *Family therapy.* New York: Grune and Stratton.

Giovacchini, P. (1965). Treatment of marital disharmonies: The classical approach. In B. Greene (Ed.), *The psychotherapies of marital disharmony.* New York: Free Press.

Greene, B. (1960). Marital disharmony: Concurrent analysis of husband and wife. *Diseases of the Nervous System, 21,* 1–6.

Gurman, A. (1978). Contemporary marital therapies: A critique and comprehensive analysis of psychoanalytic, behavioral and systems approach. In T. Paolino & B. McCrady (Eds.), *Marriage and marital therapy.* New York: Brunner/Mazel.

Jacobsen, N., & Marolin, G. (1979). *Marital therapy: Strategies based on social learning and behavior exchange principles.* New York: Brunner/Mazel.

Kernberg, O. (1976). *Object-relations theory and clinical psychoanalysis.* New York: Jason Aronson.

Kohut, H. 1971). *The analysis of the self.* New York: International Universities Press.

Kohut, H. (1972). Thoughts on narcissism and narcissistic rage. *Psychoanalytic Study of the Child, 27,* 360–400.

Kohut, H. (1977). *The restoration of the self.* New York: International Universities Press.

Mahler, M., Pine, F., and Bergman, A. (1975). *The psychological birth of the human infant.* New York: Basic Books.

Malan, D. (1976). *The frontier of brief psychotherapy.* New York: Plenum Press.

Martin, P. (1976). *A marital therapy manual.* New York: Brunner/Mazel.

Meissner, W. (1978). The conceptualization of marriage and family dynamics from a psychoanalytical perspective. In T. Paolino & B. McCrady (Eds.), *Marriage and family therapy.* New York: Brunner/Mazel.

Nadelson, C. (1978). Marital therapy from a psychoanalytic perspective. In T. Paolino & B. McCrady (Eds.), *Marriage and marital therapy.* New York: Brunner/ Mazel.

Nemiah, J. (1975). Classical psychoanalysis. In D. Freedman and J. Dyrud (Eds.), *American handbook of psychiatry* (Vol. 5). New York: Basic Books.

Novaco, R. (1978). Anger and coping with stress: Cognitive behavioral interventions. In J. Foreyt & D. Rathjen (Eds.), *Cognitive behavioral therapy.* New York: Plenum Press.

Sager, C. (1976). *Marriage contracts and couples therapy: Hidden forces in intimate relationships.* New York: Brunner/Mazel.

Sager, C.J., Brown, H.S., Crohn, H., Engel, T., Rodstein, R., & Walker, L. (1983). *Treating the remarried family.* New York: Brunner/Mazel.

Segraves, R. (1982). *Marital therapy: A combined psychodynamic-behavioral approach.* New York: Plenum Press.

Skynner, A. (1976). *Systems of family and marital psychotherapy.* New York: Brunner/Mazel.

Winnicott, D. (1965). *The maturational processes and the facilitating environment.* New York: International Universities Press.

# 5

# Cognitive-
# Behavioral
# Approaches to
# Marital Therapy

C ognitive-behavioral approaches, which embody the principles of cognitive mediation, behavior modification, and social learning, are used by all marriage therapists. These approaches consider intrapsychic processes and the environment to be major influences on the marital relationship. In the cognitive-behavioral view, marital function/dysfunction is an interaction of two individuals' behavioral and cognitive responses. Consequently, treatment involves an integration of behavioral and cognitive techniques. (A purely behavioral view would focus on environmental determinants of an individual's responses, whereas a psychodynamic view would emphasize internal personality factors.)

A behavioral model of marital interaction (Stuart, 1980; Falloon, 1988) views marital satisfaction as a function of ratios of positive to negative behaviors exchanged between spouses. Behaviorists have traditionally focused on overt behaviors exchanged by spouses, although in recent years behaviorists have moved toward a cognitive/behavioral model that takes into account the unique cognitive appraisals spouses make of each other's behaviors. Whether one partner experiences his or her partner's behavior as positive or negative depends on the particular meaning that he or she attaches to that behavior. Spouses attach meaning to each other's behavior through an active process of cognitive appraisal. That appraisal in turn influences both the behavior and emotional responses of the person to the partner (Beck, 1988).

Cognitive-behavioral approaches also differ from psychodynamic approaches. Psychodynamic views of marital interactions stress two complementary and dysfunctional interpsychic processes that when combined lead to dysfunction in the relationship. According to this model, individuals form marriages that recreate unresolved conflicts from earlier (family-of-origin) relationships. In this sense, each partner's historical material rather than current interaction is the primary focus of treatment. In contrast, several foci are important for the cognitive behaviorist. Historical (family-of-origin) material, experiences in past intimate relationships (friendships and romances), general thinking style, beliefs about relationships engendered by the culture as a whole, and the nature of the current interactions between the partners are all important targets of assessment and treatment (Schlesinger & Epstein, 1986).

Cognitive-behavioral approaches to marital dysfunction use both behavioral interventions and cognitive restructuring techniques to change behaviors and cognitions. Changes in behavior are used to facilitate cognitive changes and vice versa. To the behavior exchange paradigm are added the intervening cognitive processes. Figure 5.1 illustrates such an interactive model in which two sets of processes are important. The first, depicted by the solid arrows, concerns interactions between the two partners. The second, depicted by the broken arrows, focuses on internal feedback loops within each partner. Interpersonally, each spouse's emotional and behavioral responses simultaneously result from his or her own cognitive appraisals of the partner's responses and in turn serve as stimuli that will be appraised by the partner. Intrapersonally, each partner's emotions, behavior, and cognitions interact. A person appraises his or her own emotions and behaviors as well as those of a partner. In this process, cognitions, emotions, and behaviors can be altered independently of

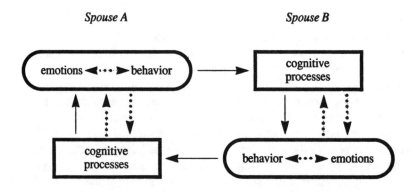

**Figure 5.1    Cognitive Mediation Model of Dyadic Relationships**

*Source:* Epstein, Schlesinger, and Dryden (1988), p. 15.

any interaction with the partner. These intrapersonal feedback loops have an important impact on marital interactions.

The cognitive-behavioral model identifies two categories of factors that influence marital interactions and therefore can be targets for treatment: overt behavioral and internal cognitive factors. This chapter describes each of the categories of factors, discusses ways of assessing them, and presents strategies for modifying them.

## OVERT BEHAVIORAL FACTORS

At a general level, in contrast to psychodynamic therapeutic approaches that focus on modifying underlying internal processes such as conflicts and motives, behavioral approaches are intended to change problematic behaviors by creating specific environmental conditions for new learning. Behaviorally oriented marital therapists identify both behavioral deficits and behavioral excesses that influence marital adjustment (Jacobson, 1981). On the one hand, deficits in basic skills such as communication, problem solving, assertiveness, and negotiation limit the extent to which spouses can make their needs known to one another and resolve any conflicts that may develop between them. On the other hand, there is substantial research evidence to support clinical observations that distressed couples use an inordinate amount of aversive stimulation such as criticism and threats in their attempts to influence each other and that such excesses are common targets for modification in therapy. Behavioral marital therapy consists of a variety of learning-based procedures for building relationship skills and decreasing the rate of aversive exchanges between spouses. Goldenberg (1983) identified 10 underlying assumptions of behavior therapy that help to define important terms:

1. All behavior, normal and abnormal, is acquired and maintained in identical ways—that is, according to the same principles of learning.
2. Behavior disorders represent learned maladaptive patterns that need not imply some underlying cause or unseen motive.
3. Maladaptive behaviors such as symptoms are themselves the disorder rather than a manifestation of a more basic underlying disorder or disease process.
4. It is not essential to discover the exact situation or set of circumstances in which the disorder was learned. These circumstances are usually irretrievable in any case. Rather, the focus should be on assessing the current determinants that support and maintain the undesired behavior.

5. Maladaptive behavior, having been learned, can be extinguished (that is, unlearned) and replaced by new behavior patterns.
6. Treatment involves the application of experimental findings of scientific psychology with an emphasis on developing a methodology that is precisely specified, objectively evaluated, and easily replicated.
7. Assessment is an ongoing part of treatment, as the effectiveness of treatment is continually evaluated and specific intervention techniques are individually tailored to specific problems.
8. Behavior therapy concentrates on here-and-now problems, rather than on uncovering or attempting to reconstruct the past. The therapist is interested in helping a client identify and change current environmental stimuli and reinforce the desired behavior.
9. Treatment outcomes are evaluated in terms of measurable behavioral changes.
10. Research and scientific validation for specific therapeutic techniques have been carried out continually by behavior therapists.

Behaviorists strive for precision in identifying a problem, employ quantification to measure change, and conduct further research to validate their results. They design programs that emphasize assessment (the behavioral analysis of the couple's difficulties), along with a number of direct and pragmatic treatment techniques to alleviate symptoms and teach the couple to improve its skills in communication and self-management. The behavior therapist is interested in increasing positive interaction between partners, altering the environmental conditions that oppose or impede such interaction, and training couples to maintain the improved behavior. No effort is made to infer motives, uncover unconscious conflict, hypothesize needs and drives, or diagnose interpathological conditions producing the undesired behavior. The partner(s) is not necessarily helped to gain insight into the origin of the current problems. Instead, emphasis is placed on the environmental, situational, and social determinants that influence behavior. Because almost all behavior is learned rather than innate, behavior can be altered by new learning. Thus, behavior therapists attempt to train a person's behavior rather than probe those dimensions of personality that according to other models underlie behavior. The following is a description of the major behavioral factors that have been implicated in marital distress and that have become the foci of treatment.

## Communication Problems

Couples often lack the skills necessary for communicating thoughts and feelings to one another. These deficits involve both problems in sending and in receiving messages. Therapists often use specific programs that teach spouses expressive skills and empathic listening skills (Guerney, 1977; Gottman, Notarius, Gonso, & Markman, 1976; Stuart, 1980). In these programs the therapist identifies the spouse's inability to communicate in clear, specific, and brief messages. The couples are taught how to send congruent messages and how to listen reflectively, which involves each partner paraphrasing what the other said before making a response. The therapist is always looking for communication patterns that might interfere with the effective transfer of information and specifically targets skill training in these areas.

The therapist teaches the specific skills of systematic human relations training (Carkhuff, 1969; Egan, 1986; Gazda, 1973; Ivey, 1971; Rogers, 1961). Often therapists discover that individuals have good communication skills but do not practice these skills with each other. When this is the case, the therapist must discover why these skills are not used within the marital relationship and change the reinforcement hierarchies in order to make it a bigger payoff to communicate effectively than to not communicate effectively with a partner.

### Assertiveness Problems

Often spouses have difficulty in assertively expressing their wishes or preferences. Sometimes assertiveness becomes a problem in the area of giving and receiving compliments. Problems with assertiveness often have their root in cognitive factors and beliefs about what the potentially negative consequences would be for acting assertively and in a confusion of assertiveness with aggression. Behavioral therapists will often teach partners how to effectively phrase requests, refusals, and compliments using "I" messages (Gordon, 1970).

### Problem Solving

A number of writers (Jacobson & Margolin, 1979; Stuart, 1980) have identified specific procedures for couples to use in solving problems. These specific steps include defining the problem, developing a list of potential solutions, evaluating the pluses and minuses of each possible solution, selecting a mutually acceptable solution, and monitoring each partner's performance of his or her role in the solution. All couples do have problems; yet few have a systematic way of resolving their conflicts. Training in a specific approach not only reduces conflict; it also increases marital satisfaction.

## Negotiation Problems

Problem solving often reaches an impasse when compromise or acceptance of one partner's plan is necessary. Negotiating and bargaining skills are helpful in generating creative and mutually acceptable solutions. The process involves learning how to develop solutions in which both partners feel like winners. Many individuals are good problem solvers at work or in community organizations but have difficulty in applying these processes to their marriages.

## Excessive Aversive Behavior Problems

Thomas (1977) provided a detailed description of how a variety of excesses and deficits in verbal communication can be problematic. Examples of behavioral excesses that are either distracting or distressing include provision of too much or redundant information, excessive agreement or disagreement, excessive questioning, negative talk, surfeit (such as frequent negative evaluation of others, the world, and events), topic content persistence, and disagreement about details. It is difficult to apply a fixed standard of normality in judging how much of any behavior constitutes an excess for a particular couple. Such a conclusion must be based on an assessment of the consequences that certain rates of behaviors have for that pair. Treatment often involves having one couple doing less and another couple developing more. Treatment also involves the increasing use of constructive skills and the decreasing frequency of behaviors that impede conflict resolution and create marital distress.

# INTERNAL COGNITIVE FACTORS

Three major cognitive factors are routinely considered in the assessment of marital dysfunction: *beliefs* each partner has about the relationship, *attributions* made about the causes of relationship problems, and *expectancies* about the likelihood that certain events will occur.

## Beliefs

Beliefs can originate from a number of sources. Sometimes beliefs are based on experiences in the family of origin or in other past relationships. Or an individual may model the relationships that he or she found desirable in the family, former romantic relationships, or friendships. Therefore, a person whose parents seemed inseparable and very happy may develop a belief that in a good relationship the partners should share in all of each other's interests and activities. Or an individual may set up standards to avoid what he or she perceived as undesirable aspects of past relationships. For example, a person who experienced turbulent arguments in a past relationship may develop a belief that a good relationship is free of any conflict. Other beliefs may be based on popular representations of family lives in movies, books, songs, and other media.

Burns (1985), Beck (1976, 1988), and Ellis (1962) have emphasized how an individual's dysfunctional emotional and behavioral responses to life events are commonly tied to basic underlying beliefs and assumptions that he or she holds about the world and his or her place in it. These beliefs, which generally take the form of "should" statements, are usually learned early in life, particularly in the family of origin, but they may also come from sources such as the mass media. Such beliefs become standards by which a person judges many aspects of life. With regard to marital relationships, people's faulty beliefs generally include ideas about role performance ("A good husband should . . . "), qualities of love ("Being in love feels like . . . "), and qualities of good marital interaction ("The way to communicate is . . . "). When a person's basic beliefs about an aspect of life are mistaken, extreme, or unrealistic, they cause distress.

### Attributions

Partners tend to make inferences about the possible causes of pleasant and unpleasant events that occur in their interpersonal relationships. Recent research studies have indicated that members of distressed couples are more likely than nondistressed spouses to attribute negative actions of their partners to global, stable characteristics such as negative personality traits ("She is selfish") or negative intent ("He was trying to hurt me").

In contrast, when spouses make causal attributions for pleasant events that occur between them, the opposite of the preceding pattern holds. Distressed individuals are more likely than nondistressed individuals to discount their partners' positive acts by attributing them to specific, unstable characteristics that are not predictive of future pleasant marital interactions, such as, "She was nice to me because she was glad to be on vacation." Nondistressed individuals are more likely to attribute such behaviors to stable, global characteristics and positive intent.

These inferences about determinants of positive and negative interactions can serve several functions. They can help a person understand intimacies, predict events in his or her relationships, and control outcomes in those relationships. Baucom (1987) further indicated that by attributing positive outcomes to himself or herself and negative outcomes to other sources, an individual can bolster self-esteem.

### Expectancies

Distorted expectancies can produce inappropriate responses in relationships. Based on past experiences with his or her partner, the individual develops estimates of the probabilities that the partner will respond in particular ways in specific situations. Expectancies can be either positive or negative, and they can vary in their accuracy. Those that are based on accurate observations of past marital interaction patterns can help partners anticipate the consequences of their behaviors and thereby enhance cooperation in conflict resolution. Distorted expectancies can inhibit a person from taking constructive action or can lead to defensiveness or aggression in anticipation of a negative response.

Therefore, based on a combination of general beliefs about relationships and a set of specific expectancies developed within the current relationship, marital partners approach their interactions with preconceived notions about what should occur and what will occur. The cognitive template is likely to serve as a set of standards for evaluating marital interaction, a filter that produces selective attention to behaviors that are relevant to the individual's beliefs and expectancies and inattention to other behaviors, and a guide for the individual's response to his or her spouse. For example, assume Mr. Jones believes that a good relationship is characterized by uncensored expression of needs and feelings, but he expects that Mrs. Jones will not communicate all her feelings to him. When he greets her at the end of a work day, he may try to coerce her to share all the experiences of her day. Unfortunately, his coercive style may lead her to be defensive and to withhold information, thereby creating a self-fulfilling prophecy consistent with Mr. Jones's initial cognitive set.

## ASSESSMENT

Assessment of cognitive and behavioral factors in marriage is still in its infancy, but there are a number of instruments that have proven reliable for clinical practice. The major methods for assessing the variables are self-report questionnaires, clinical interviews, and systematic observation and coding of behavior.

## Questionnaires, Interviews, and Observation

In general, the self-report questionnaires are simplest to administer. Although many are valid measures of the constructs they were designed to assess, they can be subject to response biases and should be interpreted with caution. Interviews permit more flexibility in data gathering because the clinician can inquire about a wide range of topics, tailor the inquiry to the particular characteristics and presenting problems of the couple, and follow up on "leads," such as a spouse's parenthetical remarks, that point to additional relevant information. The interview shares with the questionnaire the potential for bias in the respondent's reports.

In contrast to questionnaires and interviews, behavioral observation procedures potentially provide an objective view of marital interaction through the use of trained coders. This reduces the difficulty that spouses face when asked to be participant/observers of their own relationships. Behavioral observations are necessarily restricted, however, to small samples of a couple's interactions collected in an office, laboratory, or home. Such a sample may not be representative of the range of interactions that a couple has at other times, and the process of being observed may influence the spouses' behaviors. Nevertheless, research studies have demonstrated that behavioral observation systems reliably discriminate distressed from nondistressed couples and are sensitive to changes in their behavior due to therapy.

Although the coding systems used by researchers often will be too time consuming and expensive for clinicians, much can be gained from careful observation of behavioral interactions recorded on videotape. Not only can the clinician identify specific behaviors that impede communication and conflict resolution; he or she can also use videotape or audiotape feedback to illustrate to the couple what behavior should be targeted for change. Tapes of marital interaction are also useful for demonstrating circular causality to spouses who tend to attribute responsibility for problems to unidirectional causality (Schlesinger & Epstein, 1986).

## Cognitive Assessment Scales

To assess cognitive factors, scales have been developed that can identify extreme beliefs that might pose problems for spouses. These extreme beliefs cause spouses to set unrealistic standards and thereby reduce the hope for change (Jones, 1968; Eidelson & Epstein, 1982). A number of self-report scales have been developed to assess couples' causal attributions about positive and negative events in their marriages (Baucom, Bell, & Duhe, 1982;

Fincham & O'Leary, 1983). In these scales, a hypothetical event is presented, the individual is asked to imagine that the event has actually taken place, and the individual rates its perceived causes on a scale. A different scale by Pertzer, Fleming, and Epstein (1983) asks the individual to report causes of actual problems in his or her marriage. All of these attribution scales are easy to administer and score, and they have consistently been demonstrated to measure cognitions associated with marital distress. When used in clinical practice, these scales can stimulate productive discussion with spouses on an item-by-item basis, in addition to providing scores that can be compared to norms.

## Cognitive Therapy Interview Procedures

Clinical interviews are another source of information about spouses' beliefs, expectations, and attributions. Basic cognitive therapy interview procedures (Beck, 1979) can be used to probe for the "automatic thoughts" that occur when a spouse becomes upset with his or her partner. The task of the clinician is to observe changes in the spouse's emotions and behaviors and then inquire about the thoughts that were occurring when those shifts took place. Some clients initially will not be skilled at monitoring their cognitions, but with practice most can report relevant thoughts linked to dysfunctional marital interactions.

The covert nature of cognitions necessitates that assessment rely heavily on self-report methods, but a potentially less reactive way of eliciting spouses' cognitions about one another is to have them interact in an open-ended way, with or without the clinician present. When spouses are taped while discussing their relationship, they often forget that they are being observed and become quite involved in their interaction. The content of their communication in such a situation can reveal a great deal about their attributions and beliefs.

Self-report interviews and behavioral observation are widely used in assessing behavioral interactions. Questionnaires in which spouses report the quality and quantity of behaviors exchanged between them are often used. These instruments identify the extent of pleasing and displeasing behaviors that each partner encounters in a given day. Behavioral marital therapists rely heavily on clinical interviews to collect detailed reports about marital interactions. The goal of these interviews is to create a "functional analysis" in which both the antecedent stimuli and the consequences of any problematic behavior are identified. The result of this analysis reveals how each person's behaviors stimulate and reinforce or punish the other's behaviors and how this pattern involves circular causality. It is crucial, however, that this analysis be restricted to concrete, observable behaviors. Behaviorists have developed many reliable coding systems that trained observers can use to categorize both positive and negative behaviors in spouses (Weiss, Hops, & Patterson, 1973; Gottman et al., 1976; Raush, Barry, Hertel, & Swain, 1974).

## TREATMENT PROCESS

Following a thorough assessment, a cognitive-behavioral therapist begins treatment. The four basic techniques of treatment are discrimination training, communication and assertiveness training, problem-solving training, and cognitive restructuring. These procedures are not mutually exclusive, and marital treatment usually involves combining these into a treatment regimen.

### Discrimination Training

Discrimination training is a technique used to help couples monitor their behavior, both positive and negative, and their observations of each other, both objective and subjective, as a way of evaluating the accuracy of the appraisals and attributions they make regarding each other's behaviors. Distressed partners usually monitor the spouse's negative behaviors and form negative impressions of each other based upon these untested assumptions. These negative impressions and attributions lead to an almost exclusive focus on the partner's negative behavior. Initial observations are sometimes influenced by a partner's emotional state and are usually generalized beyond their applicability. Overgeneralization obscures the couple's ability to see appropriately the links between behaviors and their consequences and to highlight the cause/effect relationships between the behaviors both spouses exhibit. Monitoring frequently helps couples counteract distorted observations by bringing to bear collected and balanced data.

Homework assignments are the typical form for monitoring. Homework typically consists of maintaining a journal in which observations about the other's behavior and attributions about the other's intent are made. Journal instructions provide for the recording of both positive and negative events and for an assessment of how each journal entry improves or detracts from the couple's marital satisfaction. Spouses can then ask each other to increase the number of specific, satisfying behaviors, which in turn begins to quickly increase the amount of satisfaction in the marriage. The difficulty that negative attributions and beliefs cause throughout treatment is that they interfere with the spouses' rational ability to evaluate their observations of each other.

Negative attributions frequently constitute shorthand descriptions of untested and faulty conclusions. Even when such beliefs reflect some degree of truth, they often are so extreme as to preclude any perceived potential for change.

## Communication and Assertiveness Training

Treatment usually begins with the therapist helping couples develop expressive and listening skills. Techniques described in detail by Gottman et al. (1976) and Guerney (1977, 1983) are used. Once these procedures are developed, assertiveness training skills are introduced. Assertiveness training techniques teach couples to speak directly to each other in a brief and direct manner. Assertiveness training techniques help couples simplify their communication and speak congruently. Couples are taught a specific model of assertiveness such as that described by Guerney (1977, 1983), Schlesinger and Epstein (1986), or Gottman et al. (1976). Once the partners understand how to become more assertive, they engage in a number of exercises to illustrate its application. The exercises are most fruitful when they focus on recent incidents or current concerns. Opportunities are provided to apply and rehearse specific skills and to develop new ways of talking to one another and receiving feedback from the therapist. Role-play reenactments of prior incidents are often used.

Additionally, couples are taught to identify specific ideographic communication problems. These include interrupting each other, diverting conversations in unproductive directions, reading the other's mind, and predicting that communication efforts will be fruitless. Couples practice identifying and avoiding these communication pitfalls.

## Problem-Solving Training

Dysfunctional couples seldom have an appropriate model for solving problems. Cognitive behaviorists teach a three-step model that helps couples solve problems. In step one partners clearly define their problems. In step two they brainstorm for possible solutions. In step three the partners choose an agreed-upon solution.

## Cognitive Restructuring

The techniques used in cognitive restructuring apply to marital treatment in the same way they do to individual treatment. In many ways they are identical. It is often necessary for spouses to define individual cognitive processes as they bear on relationships. Therapists help to identify cognitions that have a direct effect upon relationships. Restructuring techniques emphasize cognitive rather than behavioral interventions and focus on two general areas: beliefs each partner has about the marriage and beliefs each has about the nature of relationships generally. Dysfunctional couples frequently have erroneous or extreme beliefs. These beliefs are attacked using specific procedures as described by Burns (1985), Beck (1988), and McMullin (1986).

## KEY FIGURES

The cognitive-behavioral approach to marital therapy is gaining in terms of supporters. The initial leaders were the initial founders of the different schools. Aaron Beck, Albert Ellis, Neil Jacobson, Richard Stuart, John Gottman, Bernard Guerney, Jr., Norman B. Epstein, David Burns, Gerald Patterson, and Stephen Schlesinger are among those key figures in this rapidly growing field. Although many of the leaders have identified with either a cognitive or a behavioral approach to improve marriage, many are now adopting the combined approach.

## CONCLUDING NOTE

In a cognitive-behavioral approach to marital therapy, the therapist serves as a consultant as the couple generates and either accepts or rejects new cognitions and behavior based upon a rational evaluation of the evidence. The focus of treatment is on those faulty cognitions and behaviors that are impeding the marital relationship. This form of therapy focuses primarily on the present and assumes that insight and reality testing are necessary for effective change. The therapist does an accurate and thorough assessment and then applies the appropriate intervention strategies in both cognitive and behavioral domains.

## REFERENCES

Baucom, D. H., Bell, W. G., & Duhe, A. D. (1982). *The measurement of couples' attributions of positive and negative dyadic interactions.* Paper presented at the annual meeting of the Association for the Advancement of Behavior Therapy, Los Angeles.

Beck, A. T. (1976). *Cognitive therapy and the emotional disorders.* New York: International Universities Press.

Beck, A. T. (1988). *Love is never enough.* New York: Harper & Row.

Burns, D. (1985). *Intimate connections*. New York: William Morrow.

Carkhuff, R. R. (1969). *Helping in human relationships* (2 vols). New York: Holt, Rinehart, and Winston.

Egan, G. (1986). *The skilled helper: A systematic approach to effective helping*. Monterey, CA: Brooks/Cole.

Eidelson, R. J., & Epstein, N. (1982). Cognitions and relationship maladjustment: Development of a measure of dysfunctional relationship beliefs. *Journal of Consulting and Clinical Psychology, 50*, 715–720.

Ellis, A. (1962). *Reason and emotion in psychotherapy*. New York: Lyle Stuart.

Epstein, N., Schlesinger, S. E., & Dryden, W. (1988). *Cognitive-behavioral therapy with families*. New York: Brunner/Mazel.

Falloon, I. R. H. (1988). *Handbook of behavioral family therapy*. New York: Guilford Press.

Gazda, G. M. (1973). *Human relations development: A manual for educators*. Boston: Allyn & Bacon.

Goldenberg, H. (1983). *Contemporary clinical psychology* (2d ed.). Monterey, CA: Brooks/Cole.

Gordon, T. (1970). *Parent effectiveness training*. New York: Wyden.

Gottman, J., Notarius, C., Gonso, J., & Markman, H. (1976). *A couple's guide to communication*. Champaign, IL: Research Press.

Guerney, B. G., Jr. (1977). *Relationship enhancement*. San Francisco: Jossey-Bass.

Guerney, B. G., Jr. (1983). Marital and family relationship enhancement therapy. In P. A. Keller & L. G. Ritt (Eds.), *Innovations in clinical practice: A sourcebook* (Vol. 2). Sarasota, FL: Professional Resource Exchange.

Ivey, A. E. (1971). *Micro-counseling: Innovations in interviewing training*. Springfield, IL: Charles C. Thomas.

Jacobson, N. S., & Margolin, G. (1979). *Marital therapy: Strategies based on social learning and behavior exchange principles*. New York: Brunner/Mazel.

Jones, R. G. (1968). *A factored measure of Ellis' irrational beliefs system with personality and maladjustment correlates*. Unpublished doctoral dissertation, Texas Technical College.

McMullin, R. E. (1986). *Handbook of cognitive therapy techniques*. New York: Norton.

Raush, H. L., Barry, W. A., Hertel, R. K., & Swain, M. A. (1974). *Communication, conflict, and marriage*. San Francisco: Jossey-Bass.

Rogers, C. R. (1961). *On becoming a person*. Boston: Houghton Mifflin.

Schlesinger, S.E., & Epstein, N. (1986). Cognitive-behavioral techniques in marital therapy. In P. Keller & L. Ritt (Eds.), *Innovations in clinical practice: A sourcebook* (Vol. 5). Sarasota, FL: Professional Resource Exchange.

Stuart, R. B. (1980). *Helping couples change: A social learning approach to marital therapy*. New York: Guilford Press.

Thomas, E. J. (1977). *Marital communication and decision-making: Analysis, assessment, and change*. New York: Free Press.

Weiss, R. L., Hops, H., & Patterson, G. R. (1973). A framework for conceptualizing marital conflict, a technology for altering it, some data for evaluating it. In L. A. Hamerlynk, L. C. Handy, & E. J. Mash (Eds.), *Behavioral change: Methodology, concepts, and practice*. Champaign, IL: Research Press.

# 6

# *Strategic, Structural, and Systemic Approaches to Marital Therapy*

I n 1982, epistemology, particularly constructivism, forcefully entered the consciousness of rank-and-file marital and family therapists. That year, the March issue of *Family Process* featured a series of articles about the "epistemological errors and assumptions" of practicing marital and family therapists. Disquieting questions were raised about the very legitimacy of the psychotherapeutic process: What gave therapists the right to direct other persons' lives? What was the basis of a therapist's authority? Could therapy really be value-free?

Epistemology is the study of knowledge. The predominant epistemology of most current therapy systems is the "objective viewpoint," which assumes that truth is primarily a neutral value with observable referents. When truth is discovered in the process of treatment and is properly revealed, the outcome should be increased psychological health. This epistemology is well represented by the more classical psychoanalytic approaches.

The epistemological viewpoint known as constructivism maintains that objective reality does not exist apart from the perceiver's construction of it. Constructivism holds that all human undertakings are value-laden. The heart of this viewpoint is the recognition that a person's hypotheses about the world cannot be directly proved. This does not mean that there is no place for science or that there is no scientific basis for marital therapy. Rather, the constructivist holds that scientific hypotheses exist for two reasons: first, because they are useful in clinical work, and second, because they have yet to be disproved or replaced by an alternative hypothesis. Scientific hypotheses are constructions that have utility in that they help portray reality. More specifically, therapists can never be objective observers because they cannot be disentangled from the observations they make.

In addition, everything derives its meaning from its context. Removing something from its context changes or even nullifies its meaning, whereas placing something in a new context gives it new meaning. Psychological problems and marital issues are not merely symptomatic expressions or actions occurring in isolation. They are attributions of meanings that have arisen within a particular context.

Constructivists place certain restrictions on how therapy is to be conceived. Issues of power and authority become obvious. The responsibilities of both couple and therapist must be considered and clarified, as must the consequences of any actions involved in the therapy process. Thus, therapy becomes essentially a collaborative enterprise.

More specifically, the constructivist therapist conceptualizes and responds to a wife's complaint that her husband is no longer romantic in a very different fashion than does an objective therapist. Indirect methods and techniques such as reframing and paradox are more consistent with constructivist thinking. Active and more directive techniques are more compatible with predictive, objective epistemological perspectives such as the cognitive-behavioral approach.

The Individual Psychology of Alfred Adler and his followers (Adler, 1958; Ansbacher & Ansbacher, 1956; Dinkmeyer & Carlson, 1988) represents this position most clearly in contemporary psychology. It is from this position that most of the systemic approaches draw their roots (Sherman & Dinkmeyer, 1987). Nevertheless, formal acknowledgement of this theoretical position has seldom been noted.

Systems theory provides the chief contextual explanation for the conduct of marital therapy. Although the family is the primary contextual system in which individuals are formed and function, other systems are also important. Marriage itself is a system or, more appropriately, a subsystem of family therapy (Nichols, 1988, p. 43).

Strategic, structural, and systemic approaches to therapy are concerned with how couples organize and communicate. All three approaches are effective. Although there are some fundamental differences among these approaches, we are grouping them together because their similarities outshine their differences.

## STRATEGIC THERAPY

Strategic therapy has its roots in the Palo Alto Research Group, which was founded in the early 1950s and was led by Gregory Bateson. Jay Haley, John

Weakland, Don D. Jackson, and Virginia Satir were among those involved with early research on family communication and schizophrenia. Many articles and books were published by this group describing communication strategies for changing marital and family relationships. Strategic therapy evolved from this work at the Mental Research Institute (MRI) in Palo Alto and was further influenced by the work of Milton Erickson and his use of hypnosis and paradoxical strategies.

Strategic therapy has been generally known for its use of specific strategies for addressing relational problems (Madanes & Haley, 1977). Treatment is directed toward changing presenting complaints and is usually accomplished by the therapist assessing the cycle of interaction and breaking it with either straightforward behavioral procedures or paradoxical directives. The therapeutic process is not growth-oriented; it is solution-focused or change-oriented. The therapist focuses on the interaction between the couple, not on the interpretation of behavior or the exploration of past intrapsychic events. The therapeutic process is terminated once the defined problem has ceased.

Although which therapeutic approaches fit in the strategic, structural, and systemic approaches is unclear, most theorists feel that two approaches are most commonly associated with strategic therapy: Haley/Madanes and MRI. Nevertheless, there are many proponents of these various approaches, and the distinction of who fits where is by no means hard and fast. Our goal in this chapter is to present the diversities and the differences, as well as the similarities, of these three intervention therapies.

## Haley/Madanes

Jay Haley and Cloe Madanes are husband and wife and believe that problems are maintained by a faulty hierarchy within the marital relationship (Haley, 1976, 1980, 1984; Madanes, 1981, 1984). The goal of therapy is to alter the interactions and change the structure of the relationship. Haley and Madanes believe that the presenting problem is actually a metaphor for the real problem or issue the couple is experiencing. Haley and Madanes often work with couples while focusing on problems of the children. By realigning problematic hierarchies and triangulated relationships (Haley, 1976, 1980), Haley and Madanes are able to make changes and strengthen the couple's relationship. Intervention strategies used are paradox, reframing, ordeals, "pretending," and unbalancing through the creation of alternative coalitions.

## MRI

The MRI approach focuses on the process rather than on the organization of the relationship. Interventions are made that change the interaction between the spouses. Issues of hierarchy and power are not viewed as important. How a couple resolves a conflict or attempts to solve a life cycle challenge is assumed to be maintaining the presenting problem (Watzlawick, Weakland, & Fisch, 1974). The therapist identifies a pattern of spousal behavior by asking questions and observing. The therapist then prescribes a specific homework assignment for the couple. The homework assignment may be done directly or in a paradoxical fashion with the end goal to disrupt the existing sequence of couple behavior. Traditional therapists often exhibit a less direct, more one-down position in dealing with the couple than does Haley or Madanes (Fisch, Weakland, & Segal, 1983).

## STRUCTURAL THERAPY

In structural therapy the focus is less on theory of change than on theory of family (Stanton, 1981). The primary concept is that of proximity and distance, which are defined through the boundaries or rules that specify who participates and in what way (Minuchin, 1974). Proximity/distance may be determined by examining the spouses' respective turfs, such as where one member has primary influence concerning budgets and children compared to the other member. Boundaries can also connote coalitions, such as when one or all children are united with one parent against the other or when one or more of a spouse's parents are involved in a coalition against the other spouse.

A central concept in the structural therapy is the continuum of enmeshment-disengagement. These are the extremes of proximity/distance or boundary functioning. An enmeshed subsystem is overly tight, and members are allowed little or no autonomy. If the integrity or closeness of the system is threatened, the enmeshed couple often responds rapidly and defensively. Furthermore, behavior change or reaction to stress in one spouse greatly affects the other and may reverberate throughout the system. The heightened sense of belonging in enmeshed systems or subsystems comes at the expense of individual independence (Minuchin, 1974). In disengaged couples, members may function autonomously, but there is little loyalty and a distorted sense of independence. They cannot request support when needed and lack a capacity for interdependence. In such marriages, individuals tend to operate within their own separate little domains relative to their partners. Stresses in one member do not readily affect the other (Minuchin, 1974). In general, then, the thrust of structural therapy is toward differentiating enmeshed members and increasing the involvement of disengaged couples.

## Salvador Minuchin

Structural therapy was born out of Salvador Minuchin's work with low socio-economic status families (Minuchin, Montalvo, Guerney, Rosman, & Shumer, 1967). Minuchin uses an active problem-solving approach. He has extended his work to include psychosomatic families (Minuchin, Rosman, & Baker, 1978), as well as patients of varying socioeconomic classes (Minuchin & Fishman, 1981). His approach to therapy is characterized by an emphasis on hierarchical issues. Therapy usually involves changing the structure by modifying the way people relate to each other. The focus is on the present, and the therapist uses direct, indirect, and paradoxical procedures. Therapy is terminated once the structure is positively altered and able to maintain itself without the use of the presenting problem (Minuchin, 1974).

# SYSTEMIC THERAPY

Systemic therapy has its roots in the work of Gregory Bateson and contends that problems are maintained by behavioral sequences (Selvini-Palazzoli, Boscolo, Cecchin, & Prata, 1978). The therapist takes responsibility for observing the patterns of behavior and changing the interaction through either direct or indirect interventions. The couple is viewed as a constantly changing and evolving system. Problems arise when the old procedures for handling issues do not fit current situations. The therapist's role is to help the couple develop a new way for handling the problem by creating an environment in which new information is introduced and change occurs spontaneously.

## Milan Associates

Mara Selvini-Palazzoli, Luigi Boscolo, Gianfranco Cecchin, and Guiliana Prata worked collaboratively in Milan, Italy, and developed an innovative method for helping families with severe emotional problems (Boscolo, Cecchin, Hoffman, & Penn, 1987). Milan Associates explain their in-session behavior in terms of three themes: hypothesizing, circularity, and neutrality (Selvini-Palazzoli et al., 1980). The therapist is constantly generating hypotheses about why the couple acts as it does. These hypotheses create a map by which questions can be asked of the couple and interventions can be made. All hypotheses, including those developed by the couple, are seen as equally valid. Circularity exists in the ways in which the therapist conducts the session. Partners are often asked to comment on what is going on between them. The therapist is also involved in the same process. In this way new information is introduced that allows partners to experience themselves in new contexts. According to Selvini-Palazzoli et al. (1980), simply conducting a session in this way may introduce enough new information to produce change. The therapist remains neutral throughout the session. He or she avoids issues of hierarchy, power, and side-taking and is therefore free to experience the system in its entirety. Within this sense of neutrality, the couple is free to decide whether it wishes to change.

One of the interesting features of this Italian intervention team is the scheduling of appointments. Often sessions are spread a month or two apart, and each session may last several hours. Interventions are given implicitly through the use of a ritual or explicitly through the use of paradoxical prescriptions that may ask the couple not to change. The interventions are different from those that are used in strategic approaches in that their aim is to put new information into the system, not necessarily to alter patterns of interactions. Whether the couple does a task or accepts the hypothesis is not important. The important aspect is that the partners are exposed to a different way of viewing their problems.

## SIMILARITIES IN THE APPROACHES

All three approaches believe that individuals can best be understood within the context in which they live and that the marital relation is a rule-governing system. All see the presenting problem in terms of what function it serves within the marriage, and all believe the problem can best be understood by examining the marital interactions. All employ general systems concepts such as homeostasis and positive feedback in understanding how a dyad functions. All are similar in practice. They observe the results of the therapeutic interventions in order to assess and plan future interventions. Adherents of all three therapies maintain that they use whatever techniques work. There are many techniques common to these schools, including joining, reframing, and therapeutic paradox. All emphasize process over content and present behavior over past behavior. All use both in-session as well as homework assignments to produce change. The therapist takes a directive role, and all approaches are basically brief (between 10 and 20 sessions).

## KEY CONCEPTS

These approaches are concerned with how people organize and communicate. The focus of the intervention is on current behaviors, communication, and roles. The fundamental belief of these approaches is that whatever affects one part of a system affects all parts.

## Organization

According to Gurman and Kniskern (1981), key concepts for organization are wholeness, boundaries, and hierarchies. *Wholeness* refers to the understanding of patterns, rather than to an analysis of elements. Rather than looking at a marital interaction and seeing only that Bob is a bore or that Sally is wild, the therapist sees the larger pattern of interaction: withdrawal-> nagging-> passive-aggressive behavioral outburst-> withdrawal-> attacking-> passive-aggressive behavioral outburst, and so on. The concept of *boundaries* refers to who is included within a system and to the quality and process that occur (Nichols & Everett, 1986). Boundaries are invisible lines of demarcation in a marriage that may be defined, strengthened, loosened, or changed as a result of therapy. Boundaries range from "rigid" (extreme separateness) to "diffuse" (extreme togetherness). Ideally, boundaries are "clear" and help the marital relationship to function effectively. The term *hierarchies* refers to the fact that systems have several different levels. The marriage, which is composed of two individual subsystems (units within a family based upon characteristics such as gender or age), is itself a subsystem of the nuclear family, which consists of man, woman, and child(ren). The nuclear family in turn is a subsystem of an extended family system (Nichols, 1988).

## Homeostasis

Homeostasis is the tendency within a system to seek equilibrium or balance through maintenance of the status quo and resistance to change. Couples can use various mechanisms to maintain balance and stability.

## Communication

Within a systems perspective, all behavior is considered to be communication. Verbal communication and nonverbal communication are both viewed as very important. It is impossible, according to systems theorists, for an individual *not* to communicate. Patterns of communication not only help to shape the behavior and functioning of family members; they also provide clues to the relative openness/closeness of the system and its interaction with other parts of the environment (Nichols, 1988). Systems cannot be either too closed or too open and still function in a healthy manner.

Communication and feedback processes can help to maintain a steady state condition in which the disequilibrium that produces growth and development and the continuity of the system are adequately balanced. Negative feedback is a communication process used to correct system deviations by reestablishing a previous state of equilibrium. For example, this process is at work in families in which a child acts out in order to bring quarreling parents back together again. Positive feedback is a change-activating process within systems. Any tactic, whether from a therapist or a family, that challenges the family homeostasis and changes the family's way of behaving is an example of positive feedback.

Systems theorists are also concerned with a process known as metacommunication, which is communication about communication. This term usually refers to the covert, nonverbal message (tone of voice, inflection, body language) that gives additional meaning to an overt, verbal message.

A double bind, another systems concept, is a form of communication that leaves a responder "damned if you do and damned if you don't." A double bind includes (1) a double message, such as saying, "I'm glad to see you" while looking away, (2) within an emotionally important relationship, (3) where the receiver of the message is unable to comment on the message.

### Equifinality

This concept indicates that there are many different paths or procedures that will yield the same results. It is not necessary to begin at the same place or in the same way. Systemic theory indicates that a therapist can work with couples individually or conjointly and on any of their problems and make a significant intervention.

### Circular Causality

This concept purports that both parties are involved in any problem. Partner A influences Partner B and vice versa. Does Jim leave and go out drinking with the boys because Jane nags him, or does Jane nag him because Jim goes out drinking with the boys? The answer is, of course, both. The clinical implication associated with the concept of circular causality is that the therapist does not need to search for a cause but can intervene from any one of several starting points and be successful. Any change in one aspect in one partner will affect the other.

## Nonsummativity

The marriage as a whole is different from the sum of its parts. Marriage is not understandable merely through a summarizing of the attributes or characteristics of the individual marital partners. To describe Judy as an individual and Tom as an individual is not the same as describing the pair in relationship. Summing up of the parts does not provide the whole picture. That can be done only by looking at the picture as a whole.

It is also fair to say that the whole is different than the sum of the parts. According to Bateson (1980, p. 3), to use an analogy, a house is made of nails, lumber, electrical wiring, and other materials, but to say that a house is composed of so many nails, so much lumber, and so on does not describe the house. Rather it is necessary to look at the parts and sum them up *and* to pay attention to the pattern that connects them in order to appreciate the structure. The clinician must similarly look for the pattern that connects, not merely the bits and pieces of behavior that form a marital relationship.

## Change

According to Watzlawick, Weakland, and Fisch (1974), change can be either first-order or second-order. First-order change pertains to those alterations in a system that leave the fundamental organization of that system unchanged.

> A symptomatic marriage could thus be said to undergo first order change whenever it adapts in response to a therapeutic intervention but does not cease its symptomatic functioning. Daniel, for example, may no longer "blow up" at Estelle, but substitute a "cold war" for the "hot war" by treating her with cool irony. Estelle no longer nags, but "gets under the skin" of Daniel as strongly as ever by ignoring him. Formerly the marriage was symptomatic in one way, but now it is symptomatic in another way. (Nichols, 1988, p. 47)

Second-order change refers to alterations in a system that change the fundamental organization of the system. Second-order change is generally considered better than first-order change because it is more structural and more permanent.

## TREATMENT PROCESS

Working with couples from a systems perspective allows the therapist to operate in myriad ways. Therapists can make changes anywhere within the marital system and expect changes to occur within the marital relationship. Interventions can be made directly with the couple, with the partners individually, or with the larger family. Boundaries can be strengthened and clarified, communication improved, and the marital relationship enriched. This flexibility affords many available techniques to change the system. The therapist can operate as a systems consultant (Wynne, McDaniel, & Weber, 1986) and design/tailor an appropriate change. The following are some of the clinical skills utilized by systemic therapies.

### Boundary Marking

This is a strategy in which the therapist reinforces appropriate boundaries and defuses inappropriate boundaries by modifying transactional patterns. For example, the therapist may sit next to one partner to strengthen that person's position and weaken the other's.

### Circular Questioning

Introduced by Selvini-Palazzoli and her associates (Selvini-Palazzoli, Bocolo, Cecchin, & Prata, 1978), circular questions are interview questions used to learn more about changes and differences in relationships that might provide clues to recursive family patterns. Circular questions are useful in generating systemic hypotheses and interventions and in allowing a couple to begin viewing itself systemically. The questions force people to stop and think rather than react in a stereotypical way. The person who is not talking also listens attentively. These questions cut into escalations and fights and address a difference or define a relationship. Examples are questions that ask a client to comment on his parents' marriage, to rank family members on the basis of "who has suffered the most from someone's death," or "to rate on a scale from 1 to 10 his mother's and then his father's anger when the client came home late at night." Even hypothetical questions are used: "If you'd not been born, what do you think your parents' marriage would be like now?" "If you would not have married each other, how would your life be today?"

### Family Ritual

Used extensively by Selvini-Palazzoli and her associates (1978), this is an individualized prescription of an action or a series of actions designed to change family members' roles.

## Joining

Joining is an accommodating maneuver in which the therapist establishes rapport with family members and temporarily becomes a part of the family system. As a result, the family accepts the therapist more openly, thus enhancing the therapist's ability to bring about change.

## Therapeutic Paradox

This is a strategic intervention that has been defined and implemented in many ways (Weeks & L'Abate, 1979). Generally it entails maneuvers that are in apparent contradiction to the goals of therapy yet are actually designed to achieve them (Haley, 1976). Major classes of therapeutic paradox are 1—prescribing, 2—restraining, and 3—positioning.

### Prescribing

This is a strategy in which the therapist encourages or instructs the client to engage in or practice his or her symptom. For example, a depressed spouse may be asked to stay depressed on a particular day and keep notes on his or her depression, ostensibly so that the therapist can learn more about the depression. The client either rebels against the directive and gives up the symptom or obeys the therapist and continues the symptom, thus putting the maintenance of the symptom under his or her conscious, voluntary control.

### Restraining

Restraining is a strategy in which the therapist discourages change, usually by outlining the dangers implicit in improving. For example, the therapist might say, "If your son got better, you and your husband might not have anything to talk about."

### Positioning

Positioning is a strategy in which the therapist accepts and exaggerates what the client is saying. This often has the effect of underlining the absurdity in the situation and forces the client to take a different position. For example, when the couple complains about how awful their marriage is, the therapist could say, "Why not get a divorce?" and thereby move the couple to take a position defending rather than attacking the relationship.

**Restructuring**

Any therapeutic intervention that confronts and challenges the family and facilitates structural changes is a restructuring. Examples of restructuring maneuvers include assigning tasks, shifting power systems, escalating stress, and marking boundaries.

**Relabeling/Reframing**

This is the use of language to give new meaning to a situation, which invites the possibility of change. For example, relabeling a wife's depression as caring in order to keep her husband home and from working so much may change the partner's response to that behavior.

# CONCLUDING NOTE

Systems theory is at the basis of all marital interventions. This chapter discussed structural, strategic, and systemic approaches, their major proponents, and their similarities. The key concepts were highlighted and the various treatment strategies indicated. The more serious student will want to read each of these approaches in their original sources and understand the differences among them.

# REFERENCES

Adler, A. (1958). *The practice and theory of individual psychology.* Paterson, NJ: Littlefield, Adams.

Ansbacher, H. L.,& Ansbacher, R. R. (1956). *The individual psychology of Alfred Adler.* New York: Harper & Row.

Bateson, G. (1980). *Mind and nature.* New York: Bantam Books.

Boscolo, L., Cecchin, G., Hoffman, L., & Penn, P. (1987). *Milan systemic family therapy.* New York: Basic Books.

Dinkmeyer, D., & Carlson, J. (1988, Winter). Adlerian marriage therapy. *American Journal of Family Therapy.*

*Family Process* (1982), *21*(1), 1–127; *21* (4), 383–434 .

Fisch, R., Weakland, J. H., & Segal, L. (1982). *The tactics of change: Doing therapy briefly.* San Francisco: Jossey-Bass.

Gurman, A. S., & Kniskern, D. P. (Eds.). (1981). *Handbook of family therapy.* New York: Brunner/Mazel.

Haley, J. (1976). *Problem-solving therapy.* San Francisco: Jossey-Bass.

Haley, J. (1980). *Leaving home: The therapy of disturbed young people.* New York: McGraw-Hill.

Haley, J. (1984). *Ordeal therapy: Unusual ways to change behavior.* San Francisco: Jossey-Bass.

Madanes, C. (1981). *Strategic family therapy.* San Francisco: Jossey-Bass.

Madanes, C. (1984). *Behind the one-way mirror: Advances in the practice of strategic therapy.* San Francisco: Jossey-Bass.

Madanes, C. & Haley, J. (1977). Dimensions of family therapy. *The Journal of Nervous and Mental Disease, 165,* 88–98.

Minuchin, S. (1974). *Families and family therapy.* Cambridge, MA: Harvard University Press.

Minuchin, S., & Fishman, H. C. (1981). *Family therapy techniques.* Cambridge, MA: Harvard University Press.

Minuchin, S., Montalvo, B., Guerney, B. G., Jr., Rosman, B. L., & Schumer, F. (1967). *Families of the slums: An exploration of their structure and treatment.* New York: Basic Books.

Minuchin, S., Rosman, B. L., & Baker, L. (1978). *Psychosomatic families: Anorexia nervosa in context.* Cambridge, MA: Harvard University Press.

Nichols, W. C. (1988). *Marital therapy: An integrative approach.* New York: Guilford Press.

Nichols, W. C., & Everett, C. A. (1986). *Systemic family therapy: An integrative approach.* New York: Guilford Press.

Selvini-Palazzoli, M., Boscolo, L., Cecchin, G., & Prata, G. (1978). *Paradox and counter-paradox: A new model in the therapy of the family in schizophrenic transaction.* New York: Jason Aronson.

Selvini-Palazzoli, M., Boscolo, L., Cecchin, G., & Prata, G. (1980). Hypothesizing-circularity-neutrality: Three guidelines for the conductor of the session. *Family Process, 19,* 3–12.

Sherman, R., & Dinkmeyer, D. (1987). *Systems of family therapy: An Adlerian integration.* New York: Brunner/Mazel.

Stanton, M. D. (1981). Strategic approaches to family therapy. In A. S. Gurman and D. P. Kniskern (Eds.), *Handbook of family therapy.* New York: Brunner/Mazel.

Watzlawick, P., Weakland, J. H., & Fisch, R. (1974). *Change: Principles of problem formation and problem resolution.* New York: Norton.

Weeks, G., & L'Abate, L. (1979). A compilation of paradoxical methods. *American Journal of Family Therapy, 7,* 61–76.

Wynne, L. C., McDaniel, S. H., & Weber, T. T. (1986). *Systems consultation: A new perspective for family therapy.* New York: Guilford Press.

# 7

# *Integrative Approaches to Marital Therapy*

T he key conceptual and therapeutic techniques of the traditional models of marital therapy were described in some detail in the preceding chapters. At times, the competing and often conflicting claims of the pioneers and loyal proponents of these approaches have taken on an evangelical fervor. In fact, the development of all individual therapy approaches seems to have gone through an initial, evangelical phase in which the new approach is viewed as transcending the mistakes of previous therapy systems and seems to possess unlimited therapeutic potential. Proselytizing of converts to the new approach actually begins with workshops, publications, and independent training institutes and then advances to university training programs. Psychoanalysis went through such an era between 1900 and 1930; the mid-1950s to the early 1970s were the evangelical years of behavior therapy.

The 1970s and 1980s witnessed the same fervor in the field of marital and family therapy. Too often the proponents of the psychoanalytic, systems, and behavioral marriage therapy models espoused purism and denounced attempts at eclecticism or integration. This evangelical era in marital therapy is passing, however, and the general expectation that marital therapists must adhere to a particular model of marital therapy has lessened. The past few years have been replete with published accounts of ingenious and successful efforts at integrating the concepts and techniques of the traditional models of marital therapy.

An integrative model affords the therapist a more comprehensive map to follow in explaining and potentially changing the marital relationship. Like purist models, integrative models can be therapist-centered, but they can likewise be couple-centered. A couple-centered perspective is usually referred to as an "integrative-tailored" approach. Basically, this orientation is a modification of Paul's (1967) famous dictum: What treatment, by what therapist, is most appropriate and effective for this couple, with this particular set of problems and expectations for change, and under what set of circumstances?

If this chapter were to have a subtitle, it would likely be "From Theory to Tailoring." This chapter surveys a number of integrative efforts to blend key concepts and constructs as well as attempts to integrate various models of marital therapy. It also reviews three significant clinical research models of marital therapy and three approaches for tailoring treatments. Finally, the chapter concludes on a more personal note with a description of the stages of professional development in the career of the marital therapist.

## INTEGRATIVE CONCEPTS FROM VARIOUS MARITAL THERAPY MODELS

Fish and Fish (1986) have proposed that the basis of marriage is the "quid pro quo" agreement, which they believe is the structural base of all systemic marital theories and therapies. Quid pro quo, which literally means "something for something," is a term used to describe the overarching pattern of roles and interactional sequences that defines a marital relationship. Fish and Fish contend that symmetry and complementarity are divergent ways in which couples work out the quid pro quo inherent in their marriages. Problems arise only when the couple becomes locked into a particular complementary or symmetrical style and is not able to break out of these time-bound patterns or styles for managing issues. Symmetry and complementarity are two ways in which the three basic marital issues of power, intimacy, and boundaries are worked out in any marital relationship.

Using categories similar to those Fish and Fish used, Doherty, Colangelo, Green, and Hoffman (1985) analyzed 13 models of marital and family therapy according to the dimensions of inclusion, control, and intimacy. This analysis yielded the classification of therapy models listed in Table 7.1.

Doherty and associates also rated the secondary and tertiary emphases of each of the 13 models. They believed that their conceptual analysis provided a guide for therapists wishing to become more eclectic or integrative in their clinical practices. They felt the analysis suggested a way to match therapy techniques from different family and marital therapy models to the presenting couple or family issue that each model emphasizes most strongly.

**TABLE 7.1** Marital Therapy Models Classified According to Inclusion, Control, and Intimacy

| *Inclusion (Boundary)* | *Control (Power)* | *Intimacy* |
| --- | --- | --- |
| Contextual | Strategic | Couples contract (Sager) |
| Bowen | Behavioral | Family of origin (Framo) |
| Structural | Problem-centered | Symbolic-experiential (Whittaker) |
| Functional | (McMasters) | Integrative (Duhl & Duhl) |
| | Interactional | Communications (Satir) |

*Source:* Doherty Colangelo, Green, and Hoffman. (1985).

# CLINICAL RESEARCH MODELS

The traditional approaches to marital therapy described in preceding chapters were developed from clinical work with couples. Usually, the clinician who pioneered a particular approach was dissatisfied with the methods he or she had previously been employing and gradually developed a unique approach. Often such an approach followed a pragmatic and an experiential rather than an experimental line of inquiry. For the most part, research was not a consideration or priority in the early stages of theory development. It was later, after the theory and approach were sufficiently developed, that researching the effectiveness of the approach, usually in comparison with other approaches, became a consideration.

The three—the McMaster's model, Olson's circumplex model, and the Beavers system model—have a different history. All were developed in a clinical research format, which means that theory, methods of assessment, and treatment strategies and techniques stemmed from a more inductive and experimental rather than an experiential approach to science. These three approaches are excellent examples of clinical research approaches to marital theory and therapy.

## The McMaster's Model

The McMaster's model of marital functioning was developed in the early 1960s by Epstein, Bishop, and Levin (1978) at McMaster's University. The model is a useful tool for evaluating marriages and families and is based on the systems approach. As such, it describes the structure, organization, and transactional patterns of the family and marital unit. It allows an examination of marriage or family relations along the total spectrum ranging from healthy to severely pathological. Unlike other models that conceptualize marital behavior in terms of a single dimension such as communication, power, boundaries, or intimacy, the McMaster's model considers six aspects of family functioning: problem solving, communication, roles, affective responsiveness, affective involvement, and behavioral control.

## Problem Solving

This dimension is defined as a couple's ability to resolve problems at a level that maintains effective family functioning. Thus, in this framework a marital problem is an issue that threatens the integrity and functional capacity of the family. Problems are divided into instrumental and affective types. Instrumental problems involve everyday issues such as finance and housing, whereas affective problems are those related to feelings. Seven stages are operationally defined as components of the problem-solving process: identification of the problem, communication of the problem to the appropriate person or resource, development of alternative action, decision on one alternative action, action, monitoring of the action, and evaluation of success of the action. The most effective couple or family carries out all seven stages, whereas the least effective couple or family usually cannot even identify the problem.

## Communication

Communication is defined as how the couple and family exchange information. The focus is solely on verbal exchange. Verbal communication is subdivided into types: instrumental and affective. According to Epstein, couples and families can have marked difficulties with affective communication and still function adequately with instrumental communication, but the reverse is rarely seen. Communication is assessed on two other vectors: clear versus masked and direct versus indirect. These dimensions yield four patterns of communication: clear and direct, clear and indirect, masked and direct, and masked and indirect. The McMaster's group proposes that the most effective communication is clear and direct, whereas the most ineffective is masked and indirect.

## Roles

Roles are defined as the repetitive pattern of behavior by which individuals fulfill marital and family functions. Functioning is divided into the instrumental and affective areas, with all the implications previously mentioned. The functions are then subdivided into necessary family functions and other family functions. Necessary functions, which can comprise instrumental, affective, and mixed types, are those that the couple and family must address repeatedly if they are to function well. Necessary functions include provision of resources, life skills development, nurturance and support, sexual gratification of marital partners, and systems management and maintenance. Other functions are those that are unique to a family and arise in the course of daily living but are not necessary for effective couple functioning. Effective couple and family functioning results when all necessary functions have both clear allocation to appropriate individuals and built-in accountability. Functioning in the least effective couples and families is not addressed or allocated, and no accountability is maintained.

## Affective Responsiveness

Affective responsiveness is defined as the ability to respond to a range of stimuli with the appropriate quality and quantity of feelings. Two classes of responses are welfare feelings and emergency feelings. Love, tenderness, happiness, and joy are examples of welfare emotions; fear, anger, sadness, disappointment, and depression are examples of emergency emotions. The most effective family has the broadest repertoire of affective responsiveness, whereas the least effective has the narrowest repertoire.

## Affective Involvement

The degree to which the couple and family show interest in and value the activities and interests of individual members is called affective involvement. The focus here is on how much and in what way individuals express and invest themselves in each other. This range of involvement has six styles: lack of involvement, involvement void of feelings, narcissistic involvement, empathic involvement, overinvolvement, and symbiotic involvement. Empathic involvement is the most effective form, with designations moving to either end of the spectrum implying increasingly ineffective forms of functioning.

## Behavioral Control

This dimension is defined as the pattern the couple adopts for handling behavior in three types of situations: those involving physical danger; those involving psychobiological needs, such as eating, sleeping, sex, and aggression; and those involving socializing behaviors both within and outside the family. The standard for acceptable behavior determines the style of behavioral control of the particular couple or family. Styles of control can be classified as rigid, flexible, laissez faire, and chaotic. Obviously, flexible behavior control is the most effective form and chaotic the least effective. To maintain its style of behavior control, the couple tends to develop a number of functions to enforce what it considers acceptable behavior, and this becomes part of the system maintenance and management function mentioned earlier.

## The Treatment Model

In addition to the conceptual model of couple and family functioning, Epstein and colleagues have proposed a corresponding treatment model— problem-centered family systems therapy (PCFST). This model provides the therapist with a detailed and systematic approach to marital and family therapy that stresses directness and collaboration between the couple and the therapist in accessing and resolving specific problems of the marital or family system.

In this model, therapy has two phases: macrostages and micromoves. Macrostages are the large sequential blocks of the treatment process, such as assessment or closure. Micromoves are the numerous interventions made by the therapist while carrying out the macrostages and include, for example, techniques for labeling, focusing, and clarification. PCFST focuses primarily on the macrostages of treatment. PCFST stresses the need for the couple's collaboration with the therapist at each stage to ensure that spouses understand, accept, and are prepared for each step of treatment. This process tends to foster a positive response to the treatment.

Usually the treatment is short-term, consisting of approximately 6 to 12 sessions. The model provides the couple with an implicit approach to problem solving that it can generalize and use in resolving future difficulties. There are four macrostages to treatment: assessment, contracting, treatment, and closure. Each stage contains a sequence of substages, the first of which is always orientation. After a general orientation, each substage is approached systematically with the therapist guiding the process. Upon completion, the therapist and couple review and reach agreement before moving onto the next stage. Epstein and his colleagues indicate that this model has proved useful in a variety of clinical settings, printing programs, and research projects.

The McMaster group has developed the Family Assessment Device, a questionnaire designed to evaluate families according to the McMaster model of family functioning. It is made up of seven scales: the six areas of functioning and an area designated as "general functioning." (This assessment device will be further discussed in the chapter on assessment.)

## Olson's Circumplex Model

Olson and colleagues (1979, 1983) and Sprenkle and Olson (1978) have described a "circumplex" model for understanding and assessing couples and families. This model builds on the "interpersonal circumplex"—a circular classificatory system of personality characteristics generated from factor analytic study and analysis. Olson's research began at the National Institute of Mental Health, where he studied normal families. Because the Olson group has not articulated a treatment approach, this section describes the circumplex model and assessment system.

After an intensive review of the literature, Olson and his colleagues identified two aspects of family and marital behavior—cohesion and adaptability—that they considered basic to an understanding of marital and family processes. *Cohesion* is a measure of the emotional bonding that family members have toward one another. Cohesion is represented on a continuum from high to low functioning. At the high end, the family is overidentified intellectually, emotionally, and/or physically. In other words, the family is an enmeshed system. At the other end of the continuum, there is a low cohesion, and the members are disengaged. Olson and his colleagues assume that a moderate degree of couple or family cohesion is most conducive to effective functioning. This concept is very similar to the "enmeshment-disengagement" continuum described by Minuchin (1974).

*Family adaptability* is the ability of the marital and family system to change its power structure or role relationship and relationship rules in response to situational or developmental stresses. Family adaptability is a measure of the degree to which the family tolerates change and the extent to which the family requires stability. Adequate functioning of marital and other family relationships requires both an element of stability and the capacity for change.

### Assessment Methods

A couple or family can be assessed with either a structured interview or an inventory. (Inventory instruments will be described in some detail in the chapter on assessment.) After assessment the couple or family can be rated on two axes as noted in Figure 7.1.

Figure 7.1 illustrates how couples or families can be grouped into 16 possible types. The central area of the figure is the one in which the most-well-functioning families or couples are expected to be situated. These four types—flexibly separated, flexibly connected, structurally separated, and structurally connected—represent various combinations of adaptability and

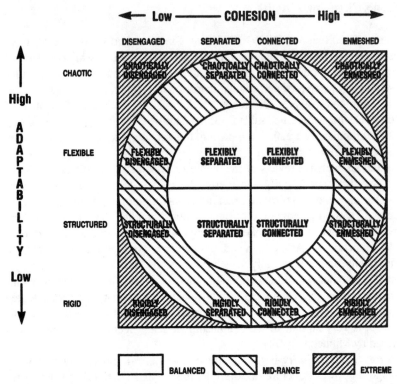

**Figure 7.1   Circumplex Model: Sixteen Types of Marital and Family Systems**

*Source:* Olson, Russell, and Sprenkle (1983).

cohesion. Within the limits of this inner circle, couples or families are free to move in any direction as the situation or life cycle demands. The four extreme types, in the corners of the figure, are those most likely to be associated with marital problems or problems in an individual spouse or family member. These are the chaotically disengaged, chaotically enmeshed, rigidly disengaged, and rigidly enmeshed. Olson and his colleagues believe that the relationship between the dimensions of cohesion and adaptability is curvilinear—that is, too little or too much cohesion or adaptability is not optimal. This is a controversial issue (Beavers & Voeller, 1983; Green, Kolevzon, & Vosler, 1985).

In a study of 25 couples receiving marital counseling and 25 not receiving counseling, Sprenkle and Olson (1978) reported some major differences with regard to adaptability. The dimensions of creativity and support were also examined. Sprenkle and Olson found that under stressful circumstances the better adjusted couples had a more egalitarian leadership pattern. A combination of high support and egalitarian leadership was especially characteristic of those couples who were not in counseling. These couples were significantly more creative, more supportive, and more responsive to each other than were the couples receiving counseling. Sprenkle and Olson also noted that negative supports and verbal putdowns, rather than the absence of positive support, typified the distressed couples.

### The Beavers System Model

This model was described by W. Robert Beavers, (1981), and grew out of research on normal family functioning conducted by the Timberlawn group. This model was developed to provide a classification system for therapists based on integration of systems research on healthy and disturbed couples and families and on clinical data. The goal was to provide a process-oriented family assessment method based on couple and family style and competence. The model thus has two axes. One involves "stylistic quality family interaction," which is classified as either centripetal, mixed, or centrifugal. This classification represents a curvilinear continuum where optimal couple and family functioning involves a mix of centripetal and centrifugal rather than extremes of centrifugal or the centripetal. The other axis is called the "health competence dimension," a continuum ranging from the extremes of severely dysfunctional to healthy. Five types of competence are derived: severely disturbed, borderline, midrange, adequate, and optimal. See Figure 7.2.

In his book, *Successful Marriage* (1985), Beavers described couples that came from severely dysfunctional, borderline, or midrange families. He noted that in all of these families the partners came from families with about the same degree of distance, trust, and toleration of intimacy. Furthermore, he noted that individuals tended to marry partners who had similar family rules regarding distance and intimacy. These three levels of couple functioning are briefly described.

### Severely Disturbed

Beavers stated that this group represented about 20% of the couples that he treated in his private practice but that many more were seen in public agencies. Among these couples, coherence and hope were the primary deficiencies. Enmeshment, lack of gratification, nonexistent choice, and unresolved ambivalence characterized these couples. The severely disturbed centrifugal

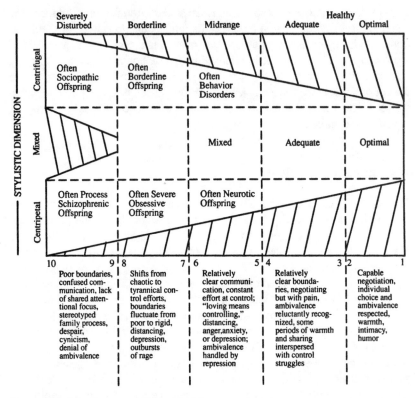

**Figure 7.2 The Beavers System Model**

*Source:* Beaver and Voeller, 1983.

couples were described as denying the need for warmth and closeness, where-as the severely dysfunctional centripetal couples tended to deny anger and a desire for separateness. For the centripetal couple being loving meant both partners believed they had to think and feel the same way.

Psychosis was occasionally an issue in the severely disturbed marriages. With both the bipolar disorder—manic-depressive illness—and schizophre-nia, Beavers treated patients in couple and/or family context. In addition to medication, Beavers found that his focus on relationships, communication, boundaries, and choice was effective and relatively safe with these couples. Finally he noted that triangles, particularly involving the couple, a parent, or a child, were ordinarily tenacious and persistent in the severely dysfunctional family.

*Borderline*

These couples comprised about 40% of his practice, and he noted that they were the most difficult of the groups to treat, many of them having had several previous treatment experiences. These couples were identified with an extreme concern with control, often of a bizarre nature. Beavers found that relatively few centrifugal borderline couples remained in treatment, particularly after a crisis was settled. He noted that this group tended to be treated in public clinics and usually in an individual rather than a marital treatment mode. The centripetal couple was usually involved in more intensive treatment, and a central issue in therapy was the power struggle. Because of this, Beavers was likely to use indirect methods such as paradox and storytelling.

*Midrange*

Beavers noted that this group comprised about 40% of his patient load. He noted that these couples were the easiest and most gratifying to treat. As with other types of couples, the midrange centrifugal couples seldom stayed in treatment. The midrange centripetal couples were less demoralized and had more successful experiences with intimacy than had the other two groups of couples. With these couples, Beavers tied the control issue to the intimacy issue and helped the individuals to see that intimidation was a method that ultimately reduced and eliminated any possibility of intimacy.

*Assessment Methods*

Two assessment methods have been developed with the Beavers approach. The Beavers/Timberlawn Family Evaluation Scale is a therapist-rated scale. The Self-Report Family Instrument is a couple-rated instrument (Beavers, Hampson, & Hulgus, 1985). (Both of these instruments will be described in more detail in the assessment chapter.)

# EVALUATION OF THE CLINICAL RESEARCH MODELS

Both Olson's circumplex model and the Beavers systems model are cross-sectional, process-oriented, and capable of providing the structure for both marital theory research and marital therapy. Both have been evaluated by a number of other research teams. Beavers and Voeller (1983) and Green, Kolevzon, and Vosler (1985) leveled a number of criticisms at the circumplex model.

These authors indicated that the Beavers model appears to conform better to clinical reality than does the circumplex model. They also believe the Beavers model can easily interface systems theory with developmental theory, whereas the circumplex model cannot. Finally, they noted that the adaptability scale is curvilinear rather than unilinear. In short, they believe that the Beavers model is designed to take into account increased couple functioning potential, whereas Olson's curvilinear model allows only for "adjustment."

The McMasters, circumplex, and Beavers systems models represent major advances in the field of marital dynamics, therapy, and research. There have been numerous published commentaries on these models that have led to further refinements in each. For example, Lee (1988) reported an integrated model synthesizing features of both Beavers's and Olson's models. Lee focused on the concept of "adaptability" as measured by the Beavers and Olson models and concluded that several levels of adaptability are implicit in the circumplex model.

The search for a conceptually mature and research-based model of marital functioning continues. The goal is to develop an assessment method that best fits the reality of marital functioning and dysfunction. Beavers and Olson both acknowledge that the evolution of a workable marital model will follow a progression similar to the American Psychiatric Association's evolution of a diagnostic scheme for classifying individual diagnoses from DSM-I, published in 1952, to DSM-IV, scheduled for publication in 1992. Evolutions in the McMasters model (Will & Wrate, 1985) further attest to this progression.

It has been only a few years (Sprenkle & Olson, 1978; Beavers, 1981; Epstein, Bishop, & Levin, 1978) since the first versions of the McMaster's, Olson, and Beavers models were first widely disseminated. The 1980s were easily the most exciting years in the history of marital theory and therapy. It is anticipated that the 1990s will witness the evolution of even more mature and clinically useful theory and treatment approaches for clinicians working with couples.

# INTEGRATIVE CLINICAL MODELS

The two approaches described in this section are examples of attempts to integrate several of the traditional approaches to marital therapy. By far, the most common integrative efforts involve attempts to combine two systems, such as the psychoanalytic and the behavioral (Sager, 1976; Pinsoff, 1983; Feldman, 1982; Segraves, 1982) or the psychoanalytic and the systems (Framo, 1982; Kirschner & Kirschner, 1986). Historically such efforts have been necessary but not sufficient to develop a truly integrative approach. Presently, a number of clinician-writers have been describing efforts to combine three or more models. Two of the more promising efforts to integrate three different models are presented in this section.

### Nichols's Integrative Approach

Nichols (1988) has proposed a form of marital therapy that not only integrates the systems approach with the behavioral and the psychoanalytic orientation but also integrates the understanding of the individual spouse with the subsystem of the marriage and the family system. This is by far the most ambitious of the integrative approaches to marital therapy. Nichols believes that the theoretical foundation for a truly integrative marital therapy approach has to deal with (a) the contexts in which personality and marriage evolve and function, (b) intimate attachment processes, and (c) the processes of motivation, change, and learning.

Nichols says his efforts to develop a workable theoretical perspective of marital interactions evolved from his clinical work with couples and was supported by theoretical and empirical research on marriage and marriage interactions. Nichols indicates it was quite difficult to synthesize concepts from three very different orientations to explain marital interaction. He used the metaphor "lumps in the oatmeal" to indicate that the various concepts do not necessarily combine without some disjunctive and disconcerting lumps and bumps. A smooth blend can be obtained only at the expense of admitting distortions.

Nichols has synthesized concepts from systems theory, object relations, and social learning theory. Systems theory provides Nichols with the chief contextual explanation for the conduct of marital therapy. He describes eight concepts that he has utilized from systems theory: wholeness, boundaries, hierarchy, communications, equifinality, circular causality, nonsummativity, and change. In deriving therapeutic interventions from the systems orientation, Nichols indicates that any of the structural and strategic techniques for clarification, strengthening, or reworking boundaries and power alliances can be utilized with most couples. He focuses on total systems or their parts, their structure, their processes, or all of these, depending on what the marital system requires. Specific techniques such as sculpting, genograms, family rituals, reframing, and paradoxical maneuvers are all possible interventions.

For Nichols, the objects relations approach is a useful bridge between individual systems and the marital system. Nichols noted that five concepts are particularly useful for the marital therapist: splitting, projective identification, collusion, ambivalence, and model of relationship. These are models of how a parent should act, models of what effective interaction between spouses should be, and models of how parents should act as a system. Such models are learned through the direct experience of observing the behaviors of others and identifying with them.

Nichols utilizes three therapeutic interventions derived from the object relations/psychoanalytic approach: interpretation of the unconscious fear, confrontation of the spouse's mispreconceptions, and use of family-of-origin sessions in which both spouses are seen with their parents and other family members for the purpose of altering internalized perceptions from the past.

For Nichols, social learning theory emphasizes the environment and the importance of learning in therapy. The goal is to define the problem clearly in work behavior terms and to develop problem-solving solutions. Nichols utilizes four concepts from social learning theory: behavior exchange and reciprocity, contingencies, modeling, and positive reinforcement. Behavior exchange is basically a quasieconomic theory applied to marital relationships in which spousal behavior is seen to have specific costs and benefits. The cost/benefit ratio determines the amount of marital satisfaction experienced by each spouse. The concept of reciprocity requires involvement by both spouses to secure change and develop cooperation. Nichols indicates that there are two therapeutic interventions that the integrative marital therapist can derive from the social learning approach: contingency contracting and communication and problem-solving training. Nichols also indicates that the therapist's ability to tailor interventions to the particular needs of the couple is greatly enhanced by the tenets of social learning theory.

## Problem-Centered Psychodynamic Marital and Family Therapy

Problem-centered psychodynamic family and marital therapy (PCPFT) is a blending of the object relations model and two systems models. Will and Wrate (1985) have blended the structural model of Minuchin (1974) with the problem-centered systems model of the McMaster's group. Their purpose is to establish an approach in which the therapist can work collaboratively with the couple or family so that the homeostasis of the marital or family system can be openly explored, understood, and worked with. They describe this focus on collaboration as open, directive marital and family therapy in contradistinction to strategic therapy, in which there is often no attempt to establish a negotiated collaborative relationship with the family or couple.

Blending object relations concepts and techniques allows the therapist to make the bridge between the couple as a system and spouses as individual persons. This blending of three models provides a depth of understanding that cannot be derived from the systems approaches alone.

The range of therapeutic techniques available in PCPFT makes it possible to "tailor" therapy to suit the needs of different couples and families. Variation in the emphasis on specific therapeutic techniques depends both on the general characteristics of the couple and on the nature, meaning, and causes of the couple's difficulty. Therefore, treatment of multiproblem couples whose disorganization affects basic problem-solving skills often entails extensive use of clear setting of tasks between sessions. Relatively stable couples with basically affective issues, such as unresolved grief, are better treated with the use of interpretation.

During the course of therapy, however, both types of techniques—systems and object relations—prove necessary for most couples. Some couples may respond more readily to action-oriented techniques such as task-setting, whereas others may respond more readily to interpretation. In PCPFT, the therapist can move along a technical continuum that extends from the most basic action-oriented techniques to interpretation that links the present with the remote past.

Will and Wrate, like the McMaster's group, have provided a useful treatment manual for marital and family therapists. Although primarily taught and practiced in Canada, the PCPFT approach deserves widespread dissemination. Of particular benefit is Will and Wrate's 1985 discussion of the common difficulties they encountered in attempting to teach and practice an integrative psychoanalytic/systems approach to marital therapy. They noted four common problems facing trainees who have some experience in psychoanalytic theory. The first is the tendency to conduct individual interviews with one spouse while ignoring the other. The second is the tendency to avoid being appropriately active throughout the course of therapy. Although this is rarely a problem for the systems-trained therapist, it is for the psychodynamically trained therapist, whose education has been based on a passive interviewing style designed to encourage the individual patient's free-flowing associations. The third is the tendency to devalue the power of reality-oriented techniques. Dynamically trained therapists are schooled to intervene at the "deep" levels of psychological functioning. Therefore, they experience a certain degree of dissatisfaction when intervening at the level of "surface behavior." The authors did note, however, that this attitude is usually modified after the therapist experiences the results of systems interventions. The fourth occupational hazard of the psychoanalytically trained therapist is the tendency to focus on the couple's pathology rather than on the couple's strength. The authors noted that these difficulties in integration of analytic and systems thinking can be overcome and that previous experience in psychoanalytic treatments is often very helpful for the therapist learning PCPFT.

## INTEGRATIVE-TAILORING APPROACHES

Previous sections have described integrated approaches to marital therapy. At the beginning of this chapter we noted that the integrative models were midway on the continuum between therapist-centered (traditional) and couple-centered (tailoring) models. It might be helpful at this point to define and differentiate the terms *eclectic, integrative,* and *tailoring.* Eclectic basically refers to a philosophy of treatment in which the therapist selects concepts and treatment methods from a variety of theoretical sources. Eclectic therapists practice the way they do because they have found that such an approach works. Integrative refers to the treatment philosophy in which the therapist incorporates and combines discrete parts of theories and treatment methods into a more total and fuller understanding of the treatment process. Although integraters are eclectics, not all eclectics are integraters. Both eclectic and integrative positions are basically therapist-centered, which is to say that the therapist personalizes therapeutic concepts and techniques to meet his or her own needs for therapeutic effectiveness, intellectual synthesis, or whatever. Tailoring refers to the philosophy of basing treatment decisions on what is best for the client or couple system. Tailoring is basically a client- or couple-centered orientation.

Norcross (1986) estimated that approximately 40% of psychotherapists classified themselves as the eclectic or integrative. He cited survey data of the eclectic orientation among professional disciplines: 40% of counseling psychologists, 35% of clinical psychologists in independent practice, 42% of behavioral therapists, and 54% of clinical social workers. No data seem to be available to indicate the percentage of marital therapists who primarily identify themselves as operating from an eclectic, integrative, or tailoring perspective.

Norcross found no differences between those espousing an eclectic and noneclectic perspective except for clinical experience. Clinicians espousing eclecticism tended to be older and more experienced than were their noneclectic counterparts. Robertson (1979) identified six factors that appear to facilitate the adoption of the eclectic viewpoint. The first is a lack of pressure in training and professional environments to bend to a doctrinal position; this includes the absence of charismatic figures to emulate. The second factor is length of clinical experience. As therapists gain experience with a heterogeneous client population and a wide variety of problems, they tend to reject a single theory or model approach. The third factor is the extent to which they consider the practice of psychotherapy a career or a vocation/personal philosophy of life. According to Robertson, eclecticism is more likely to follow the former. Fourth is an obsessive/compulsive desire to synthesize all of the interventions in the therapeutic universe. Fifth is a maverick temperament allowing the individual to move beyond his or her therapeutic model of origin. Sixth is a skeptical attitude toward the status quo.

Although integration and tailoring may be only theoretical considerations for the marital-therapist-in-training, they often become specific and practical considerations in the consulting room. If tailoring is not an issue at the outset of treatment, it often becomes one in the later stages of marital therapy, particularly when noncompliance is an issue. Noncompliance may involve missed appointments and failure to do intersession tasks, or it may present as resistance. Noncompliance is one of many indicators that the couple's needs and expectations are not being recognized and met in the therapy process. Wood and Jacobson (1985) found that noncompliance is the most perplexing issue facing marital therapists.

Only recently has the process of tailoring been described in the marital therapy literature (Sperry, 1986). There are several bases for tailoring. The most common involves tailoring treatment according to levels of marital conflict, levels of systems functioning, and areas of individual functioning.

## Tailoring by Levels of Marital Conflict

According to Guerin, Fay, Burden, and Kautto (1987), marital conflict differs significantly from one couple to another, not only with respect to specific issues but, more importantly, with respect to the duration and intensity of the conflict. Accordingly, Guerin tailors treatment to the level of severity (intensity and duration) of marital discord. He describes couples in terms of four stages of marital discord.

### Stage One

Stage one involves couples who demonstrate a preclinical or minimal degree of marital conflict. Often the conflict has lasted for less than 6 months, and most often the couples are newlyweds. These couples readily respond to formal group sessions focusing on how marriages do and do not work. These couples are able to apply this information to change their relationships for the better. Thus, marital therapy for this type of couple is primarily group psychoeducational intervention. Occasionally, a few couples sessions are necessary as an adjunct to the group sessions. This psychoeducation treatment involves six weekly sessions of 90 minutes each. Developed in the Bowenian tradition, the sessions focus on concepts such as multigenerational transmission, triangles, behavioral styles, and differentiation as well as on common problems that couples are likely to present in the beginning stages of a marriage.

### Stage Two

Stage two consists of couples who are experiencing significant marital conflicts lasting more than 6 months. Although communication patterns remain open and adequate, criticism and projection have increased. When the therapist dissects the conflictual marital process, however, both spouses can generally move to a self-focus within six to eight sessions. Then the intensity of the conflict can be substantially reduced. Therapy in stage two provides a structure for the couple that lowers emotional arousal and anxiety and helps the spouses reestablish self-focus.

### Stage Three

Stage three couples present with severe marital conflict. Often this conflict has lasted longer than 6 months, and projection is intense. Levels of anxiety and emotional arousal are high, as are the intensity and polarization of surrounding triangles. Communication is closed with marked conflict. The level of criticism is high, and blaming is common. Therapy at this stage is primarily focused on trying to control the couples' reactivity (the tendency to react emotionally without thinking). Even when a positive result is obtained through therapy, a recycling of conflicts inevitably occurs within the ensuing 6 to 8 months. Guerin notes that such recycling is a common phenomenon at all levels of marital conflict, but particularly at this stage. When this recycling continues to occur, both spouses have probably lost much of their resilience and tend to be unresponsive to further treatment.

### Stage Four

Couples at stage four are characterized by extremes in all the criteria that Guerin uses for a marital evaluation of conflict. That is, communication is closed, information exchange is poor, criticism and blaming are very high, and self-disclosure is basically absent in the relationship. Relationship time and activity together are either minimal or nonexistent. The definitive marker for this stage is the engagement of an attorney by one or both spouses. Such a situation is likely to be more adversarial than conciliatory. In the vast majority of cases, attempts to keep the marriage from dissolution appear doomed. Therefore, therapy is aimed at diminishing emotional damage to the spouses, their children, and their extended family. The goal becomes the successful disengagement from the relationship. In short, mediation is the treatment of choice.

## Treatment Protocols

Guerin and his associates detail treatment protocols in which specific dynamic, behavioral, and systems interventions are utilized with couples at different levels of functioning. Assessment of each of the four stages of couple functioning is aided by specific behavioral indices.

## Tailoring by Levels of Systems Functioning

Weltner (1985) believes in tailoring treatment to a couple's or family's level of systems functioning. He describes four levels of functioning in terms of treatment issues and then proposes a corresponding intervention strategy and set of techniques for each level. The first two levels describe two kinds of underorganized couples or families, the third describes the overorganized couple, and the fourth describes the adequately functioning couple.

According to Weltner, intervention must first address the level of a couple's most basic problem before moving on to higher-level intervention. He believes that the effective therapist must be sufficiently conversant with the major therapeutic approaches to marital therapy in order to mix and match techniques appropriately to a specific level, rather than unilaterally applying one approach to all couples or families.

## Level One

For level one, the main issue involves parental capacity to provide basic nurturance and protection. Therefore, the basic treatment strategy is to mobilize available outside support to assist the single parent or the strongest member of the family in facing the severe stress of illness, including alcoholism. The therapist's role is that of advocate, convener, teacher, and role model. Structural interventions and support are key interventions.

## Level Two

In level two, issues of authority and limits are prominent for the couple and family. Expectations may be unclear or unmet. The basic strategy is to clarify expectations and power issues by means of techniques such as written contracts, formation of coalitions, and behavioral reinforcers.

## Level Three

Level three families and couples are more complicated. They have a structure and a style that appear to be functional, yet issues regarding boundaries are prominent. Resistance to change is another hallmark of this type of family or couple. The basic strategy is to create sufficient inner space for a spouse or specific family member and to protect that spouse, family member, or subsystem from overinvolvement. Therapeutic techniques at this level include rebuilding of alliances, paradox, and development of generational boundaries.

## Level Four

Issues for level four couples and families are usually focused on intimacy and inner conflict. Whereas families and couples at levels one to three are immersed in day-to-day survival issues, level four couples are able to consider self-actualizing concerns. Insight is a basic therapeutic strategy, and techniques include marital and family enrichment, gestalt and experiential marital therapies, and individual psychodynamically oriented psychotherapy.

## Other Models

Schultz (1984) has proposed a similar model of family and couple functioning based more specifically on DSM-III psychopathology. Schultz likewise describes four levels. He labels the first level of family functioning as "psychotic" and matches this with the family transactional approach developed by Wynne (1983). The second level is labeled as "immature" and is matched with a structural-system approach such as that of Minuchin. The third level is called "neurotic" and is matched with various strategic methods. The fourth level is labeled "mature" and is matched with growth-focused approaches such as Satir's (1983) communication approach, the symbolic-experiential approach of Whitaker and Keith (1981), or the psychodynamic approaches.

## Tailoring by Areas of Individual Functioning

Lazarus (1976, 1981) advocates the matching or tailoring of therapeutic techniques to seven specific areas of spousal functioning: behavior, affect, sensation, imagery, cognition, interpersonal (functioning), and drugs/biology (BASIC-ID—biology is identified as D and refers to drugs in particular and physical health in general). The therapist's role is to assess these areas of functioning, to develop a problem list, to prioritize their importance to the spouses' functioning, and to direct a focused intervention for each.

Lazarus's orientation is an eclectic form of cognitive-behavior therapy. Research studies attest to the effectiveness of focused multimodal intervention as compared to unimodal intervention (Lazarus, 1981). Lazarus notes that couples constitute the overwhelming majority of referrals to his clinical practice. The BASIC-ID profile provides both couples and therapists with a blueprint for assessing the spouses' as well as the couple's current level of functioning and for setting clear objectives for change. This unique methodology helps therapists establish a one-to-one correspondence between diagnosis and treatment. Each item on the problem list is matched or tailored with a specific treatment intervention.

The spouses are seen together in the initial interview to discuss the main presenting problems. They are then helped to prepare a list of undesirable behaviors that they note in themselves and in each other. Each spouse independently fills out a life history questionnaire, which is discussed with the therapist in a subsequent individual session. During this session the modality profile is constructed. A conjoint session follows to compare the two profiles and to tailor the treatment process to each individual and to the couple. Table 7.2 illustrates the modality profile for one couple in therapy.

**TABLE 7.2**   Modality Profile for One Couple

| Area of Functioning | Wife | Husband |
|---|---|---|
| Behavior | Shy in social settings<br>Overeats<br>Uses sex as weapon | Hard driving, Type A<br>Occasionally impotent<br>Loses temper often |
| Affect | Anxiety, panic attacks<br>(2–3/month)<br>Guilt feelings | Hostility<br>Dysphoria |
| Sensations | Minimal sexual awareness<br>Palpitations, tremors,<br>and hyperventilation | Tension headaches<br>Nervous stomach |
| Imagery | Romantic fantasies<br>Image of herself as obese<br>and unattractive | Images of rejection and<br>ridicule by others |
| Cognitions | Strong desire for social<br>approval<br>Belief that she may die or<br>go crazy during panic attacks | Perfection<br>Belief that a man must be<br>strong, head of<br>household |
| Interpersonal<br>(functioning) | Difficulty making requests<br>Difficulty expressing<br>negative feelings | Few close friends; depends<br>on wife for support<br>Subtly manipulative |
| Drugs/Biology | High caffeine intake | Inderal for hypertension |

We have now completed our overview of integrative and tailored approaches to treating marital discord. The final section of this chapter shifts from the marital therapist as a provider of services to the therapist as a developing person and professional.

# BECOMING AN INTEGRATIVE THERAPIST

Moultrup (1986) has offered a model for understanding the personal process involved in the journey toward integration. He has articulated five progressive stages in the process of becoming an integrative therapist. Each stage reflects both the breadth and depth of theoretical material integrated and the breadth of application of that material. He makes the assumption that the more mature stages of integration are characterized by greater complexity in the theoretical material that has been integrated and greater complexity in the application of that material.

### Stage One

In stage one, a small amount of material is integrated in such a way that the range of application is relatively narrow. At this stage a therapist is able to offer only a limited style of therapy. Moultrup notes that trainees usually begin at stage one. Typically, they adopt the psychoanalytic, systems, behavioral, or structural approach and then apply this to all cases. This seems to be true even when students are exposed to an "integrative" training program. More experienced therapists who claim that it is impossible to integrate models may take on such "true believer" qualities, maintaining that there is only one "right" approach to therapy.

### Stage Two

In stage two, the therapist has integrated a broader range of material and can use it more flexibly. The therapist starts becoming aware of the expansive possibilities of multiple theoretical models. A vague sense of an "eclectic" style begins emerging. But material has not been organized so that it is consistently available to the therapist. This, of course, limits the breadth and depth of application of the material.

## Stage Three

In stage three, the therapist integrates and incorporates a somewhat broader range of material. The limiting characteristic in stage three is application, however. Material has not been sufficiently integrated so that it can be creatively and flexibly utilized. Instead, it tends to be used in a rigid and mechanical fashion.

## Stage Four

At this stage of integration, the therapist has incorporated a fairly broad range of material that can be flexibly, creatively, and sensitively applied in the treatment setting. Moultrup notes that a pattern of practice emerges that matches the therapist's own personal style and that stylistic differences among therapists are the result of a synthesis of clinical experience, professional training, and personal history. Some therapists at stage four disavow allegiance to any particular orientation. Moultrup notes that others who claim to identify with a particular orientation have actually transcended the limits of that approach because they have integrated personal life experiences into their therapies.

## Stage Five

Therapists functioning at this stage of integration have expanding boundaries. A mature, solid, stage four foundation is supplemented by the creative integration of new material and the development of innovative applications and conceptualization. These accomplishments are the hallmark of the master therapist. Moultrup notes that relatively few therapists function at this level of integration all the time. He notes that even the pioneers in the field, who at one time displayed the openness and creativity characteristic of this stage, do slip into a more predictable, circumscribed level of functioning similar to that of stage four.

This stage-oriented process provides a sense of direction in the therapist's journey to become not only an integrative professional but a more integrative person. This journey is not without difficulties. It is not particularly easy to teach beginning therapists to think in terms of dynamic, systems, behavioral, and other models and to blend these into an integrative approach. It may be necessary for some beginning therapists to maintain a stronger attachment to a particular orientation or set of techniques that are less than integrative and focused because of these learners' personal needs for security and certainty at that point in their careers. As Nichols and Everett (1986) pointed out, however, it is still important to keep learners abreast of findings in clinical and empirical research.

# REFERENCES

Beavers, W. (1981). A systems model of family for family therapists. *Journal of Marital and Family Therapy, 7,* 299–307.
Beavers, W. (1985). *Successful marriage: A family systems approach to couples therapy.* New York: Norton.
Beavers, W., Hampson, R., & Hulgus, Y. (1985). Commentary: The Beavers systems approach to family assessment, *Family Process, 24,* 398–405.
Beavers, W., & Voeller (1983). Family models: Comparing and contrasting the Olson circumplex model with the Beavers systems model. *Family Process, 22,* 85–98.
Doherty, W., Colangelo, N., Green, A., & Hoffman, G. (1985). Emphasis of the major family therapy models: A family FIRO analysis. *Journal of Marital and Family Therapy, 11,* 299–303.
Epstein, N., Bishop, D., & Levin, S. (1978). The McMaster model of family functioning. *Journal of Marriage and Family Counseling, 4,* 19–31.
Feldman, L. (1982). Dysfunctional marital conflict: An integrative interpersonal-intrapsychic model. *Journal of marital and family therapy, 8,* 417–428.
Fish, R., & Fish, L. (1986). Quid pro quo revisited: The basis of marital therapy. *American Journal of Orthopsychiatry, 56,* 317–384.
Framo, J. (1982). *Explorations in marital and family therapy.* New York: Springer.
Green, R., Kolevzon, M., & Vosler, N. (1985). The Beavers Timberlawn model of family competence and the circumplex model of family adaptability and cohesion: Separate but equal? *Family Process, 27,* 73–85.
Guerin, P., Fay, L., Burden, & Kautto, J. (1987). *The evaluation and treatment of marital conflict: A four stage approach.* New York: Basic Books.
Kirschner, D., and Kirschner, S. (1986). *Comprehensive family therapy: An integration of systematic and psychodynamic treatment models.* New York: Brunner/Mazel.
Lazarus, A. (1976). *Multimodal behavior therapy.* New York: Springer.
Lazarus, A. (1981). *The practice of multimodal therapy.* New York: McGraw-Hill.
Lee, C. (1988). Theories of family adaptability: Toward a synthesis of Olson's circumplex and the Beavers systems model. *Family Process, 27,* 73–85.
Minuchin, S. (1974). *Families and family therapy.* Cambridge, MA: Harvard University Press.
Moultrup, D. (1986). Integration: A coming of age. *Contemporary Family Therapy, 8,* 157–167.
Nichols, W. C. (1988). *Marital therapy: An integrated approach.* New York: Guilford Press.

Nichols, W., and Everett, C. (1986). *Systematic family therapy: An integrative approach.* New York: Guilford Press.

Norcross, J. (1986). Eclectic psychotherapy: An introduction and overview. In J. Norcross (Ed.), *Handbook of eclectic psychotherapy.* New York: Brunner/Mazel.

Olson, D., Russell, C., & Sprenkle, D. (1983). Circumplex model of marital and family systems: VI. Theoretical update. *Family Process, 22,* 69–83.

Olson, D., Sprenkle, D., & Russell, C. (1979). Circumplex model of marital and family systems: I. Cohesion and adaptability dimensions, family types and clinical applications. *Family Process, 18,* 3–28.

Paul, G. (1967). Strategy of outcome research on psychotherapy. *Journal of Consulting Psychology, 31,* 109–118.

Pinsoff, W. (1983). Integrative problem-centered therapy: Toward a synthesis of family and individual psychodynamics. *Journal of Marital and Family Therapy, 9,* 19–35.

Robertson, M. (1979). Some observations from an eclectic psychotherapist. *Psychotherapy: Theory, Research and Practice, 16,* 18–21.

Sager, C. (1976). *Marriage contracts and couples therapy: Hidden forces in intimate relationships.* New York: Brunner/Mazel.

Satir, V. (1983). *Conjoint family therapy* (3d ed.). Palo Alto, CA: Science and Behavior Books.

Schultz, S. (1984). *Family systems therapy: An integration.* New York: Jason Aronson.

Segraves, R. (1982). *Marital therapy: A combined psychodynamic-behavioral approach.* New York: Plenum Press.

Sperry, L. (1986). Contemporary approaches to family therapy: A comparative and meta-analysis. *Individual Psychology, 42,* 591–601.

Sprenkle, D., & Olson, D. (1978): Circumplex model of marital systems: An empirical study of clinic and non-clinic couples. *Journal of Marriage and Family Counseling, 4,* 59–74.

Weltner, J. (1985). Matchmaking: Choosing the appropriate therapy for families at various levels of pathology. In M. Mirkin & S. Koman (Eds.), *Handbook of adolescents and family therapy.* New York: Gardner Press.

Whitaker, C., & Keith, D. (1981). Symbolic-experiential family therapy. In A. Gurman & D. Kniskern (Eds.), *Handbook of family therapy.* New York: Brunner/Mazel.

Will, D., & Wrate, R. (1985). *Integrated family therapy: A problem-centered psychodynamic approach.* London: Tavistock.

Wood, L., & Jacobson, N. (1985). Marital distress. In D. Barlow (Ed.), *Clinical handbook of psychological problems.* New York: Guilford Press.

Wynne, L. C. (1983). A phase-oriented approach to treatment with schizophrenics and their families. In W. MacFarlane (Ed.), *Family therapy in schizophrenia.* New York: Guilford Press.

# 8

# *The Treatment Process*

N ow that we have examined the biological and psychosocial dynamics and stages of marriage and have introduced the major theoretical orientations to marital therapy, we turn our attention to the actual practice of marital therapy. This chapter surveys the processes and stages of marital therapy. Because psychotherapy is as much an art as a science, different clinicians approach couples in different fashions, depending on the clinician's orientation, training, experience, and personality style. In this chapter, we discuss the stages of therapy for a few representative integrated approaches and then indicate their commonalities. Then we provide a "map" of how a therapist might think and function during the course of a particular session. Thus, the purpose of this chapter is to provide the reader with an overview of the treatment process and a perspective for understanding subsequent chapters on assessment and treatment methods.

## STAGES OF MARITAL THERAPY: INTEGRATIVE PERSPECTIVES

### L'Abate

L'Abate (1986) offers an integrative approach to marital and family therapy that combines the systems approach with the psychoeducational, which for L'Abate, blends behavioral and communication methods. He offers a very systematic approach to the therapy process. He believes that the process of

133

marital and family therapy takes place sequentially for most couples and families who seek professional help. He lists four stages: engagement and stress reduction, skill training and education, termination, and follow-up.

### Engagement and Stress Reduction

The first stage is to make contact, establish a relationship of trust and confidence with the couple, and reduce symptomatic behavior to controllable or bearable proportions. This stage may last from 1 to 10 or more sessions. L'Abate emphasizes the need for both couple and therapist to be active at this stage. Interventions include contextual and "change" activities and are based on assessment of both systems dimensions and the couple's level of interpersonal relationship skills.

### Skill Training and Education

The therapeutic emphasis at this stage is to teach deficient interpersonal skills. Usually this involves conflict resolution and negotiation skills. L'Abate reports that systematic homework assignments have been successful when other treatment interventions have failed. He notes that these assignments are particularly useful in getting a couple beyond impasses. Rebalancing of the relationship occurs once these power issues have been addressed.

### Termination

This stage deals with unfinished business, particularly issues of intimacy. After developing better skills in communication and negotiation, the couple is usually ready to confront intimacy issues, which are often terrifying and frightening. Intimacy homework assignments are given at this stage. L'Abate indicates that issues of separation, loss, dependency, individuation, and loneliness are likewise dealt with during this stage with both direct and indirect treatment methods. He describes this third stage as the semifinal stage, meaning that dealing with termination issues does not signal the end of therapy.

### Follow-up

Once most marital problems have been successfully dealt with (stages one and two) and a certain degree of intimacy has been obtained (stage three), the issue of termination needs to be considered by both therapist and couple.

L'Abate believes that therapy should not be terminated abruptly; it should contain the message that the couple is still not out of the woods and is still "on trial" to the extent that it needs to demonstrate that it has profited by therapy. L'Abate tells couples, "I'm not sure I have done any good for you as a couple until you've been on your own for at least 6 months." He communicates to the partners that they have the responsibility to apply whatever training they have received. He offers a contract of follow-up to the couples to help them consolidate their gains. He believes that this follow-up contract reduces relapse.

## Nichols

Nichols (1988) describes a three-stage process model for marital therapy: early, middle, and termination.

### Early Stage

The early stage involves three main tasks for the clinician: to assess the spouses' needs, problems, strengths, motivation, and expectations; to establish a collaborative relationship between the spouses and the therapist; and to provide immediate help to the couple. Nichols indicates that it is critical for the therapist to secure a reasonable degree of congruence between his or her goals for therapy and those of the couple. He notes that clarification and establishing of goals may go on continually throughout the course of treatment because what happens at one point determines subsequent therapeutic work. The therapist's level of activity is usually high during this first stage.

### Middle Stage

The mainstay of therapeutic interventions occurs during this stage as basic treatment issues are addressed. These include relational issues, individual issues, and family-of-origin issues. The therapist's activity level during this stage depends on particular issues and the couple's style and needs. The choice of treatment method depends on the issue and developmental stage of the couple. The basic goal is to rebalance the relationship and help the couple develop the skills, awareness, and experiences necessary to function effectively and independently. Deficits in communication, negotiation, problem-solving, and time management skills are assessed and remediated. The couple's use of projective identification and collusion, as well as family-of-origin issues, is addressed.

*Termination Stage*

Nichols reports that there are at least four ways in which couples terminate. The least desirable pattern is for one or both partners to drop out of treatment without examining with the therapist the reasons for doing so. Termination can occur during the course of one or two sessions if and when the couple is ready to terminate. A second pattern comprises gradual termination in which sessions may be scheduled at widely spaced intervals. A third pattern involves termination with a "checkup" session scheduled for a period of 1 to 3 months later. A fourth pattern involves termination with the understanding that the couple can call back to arrange an appointment at any time it elects to do so. Just as Nichols believes that treatment goals should be collaboratively negotiated, he believes that termination should be a cooperative decision between couple and therapist. Two criteria for termination are that the presenting symptom and problem have been resolved and that additional problems that arose during the course of the therapy have been adequately resolved.

**Glick, Clarkin, and Kessler**

Glick, Clarkin, and Kessler (1987) offer another integrative approach to marital therapy. These authors work from a generic, biopsychosocial orientation that combines biological, psychodynamic, and system approaches. According to these authors, the typical course of marital therapy has three stages, or phases: early, middle, and termination.

*Early Stage*

The primary goals for this stage are detailing the primary problems and nonproductive couple patterns, clarifying the goals for treatment, solidifying the therapeutic contract, strengthening the therapeutic relationship, shifting the focus from the identified spouse to the marital system, decreasing guilt and blame, and increasing the couple's capacity for empathy. Glick notes that the early stage is probably the most difficult for the trainee to master.

*Middle Stage*

This is the stage in which the major work of change takes place. What the therapist does during this stage varies, depending on which negotiated treatment goal becomes the focus. Glick notes that transference distortions between husband and wife and negative transference distortions toward the therapist must be addressed quickly and decisively. Whereas some realignment of boundary structures may have occurred during the early stage, boundary issues involving collusive processes and projective identification need to be dealt with directly in the middle stage.

The therapist also must link individual experience, including past experience and inner thoughts, to the marital relationship. This is accomplished in several ways. The therapist may prescribe tasks that encourage the spouse to differentiate between the impact of the other's behavior and the other's intent; the therapist may focus awareness on the concrete behavior of the spouse that contradicts past perceptions of that partner; or the therapist can encourage each spouse to acknowledge behavior changes that are incompatible with the maladaptive ways each has seen himself or herself and has been seen by the partner. So whereas changes in the first stage focus on the relationship, the focus in the second stage is more on changes in the individual spouses. Behavioral techniques including communication and problem-solving training are utilized to help the spouses reintegrate denied aspects of themselves and of each other.

### Termination Stage

In the termination phase the therapist reviews with the couple the course of treatment beginning with the original problems and goals and the degree to which they have or have not been achieved. The authors offer four criteria suggestive of successful treatment outcomes. First, the couple shows new coping patterns and enhanced empathy. Second, nonproductive quarreling and conflict are reduced and replaced by more productive conflict and management skills. Third, the couple is more flexible in its marital rules and organization and appears more able to grow and develop. Fourth, individual spouses are symptomatically improved, and positive channels of interaction and increased agreement about each spouse's role and function exist. The authors note that during the termination phase there may be an exacerbation of presenting symptoms that often represents a temporary response to the anxiety of termination rather than a sign of treatment failure. This indicates that separation is a key issue to be addressed in the termination phase.

### Other Stage Approaches

A few other stage approaches merit brief mention. Epstein and Bishop (1981) describe four stages of marital or family therapy based on the McMaster's model: assessment, which involves development of therapeutic alliance, data gathering, problem description, clarification, and agreement on a problem list; contracting, which involves orientation, outlining of options, negotiation of expectations, and contract signing; treatment, which involves orientation, clarification, setting of tasks, and task evaluation; and closure, which involves orientation, summary of treatment, long-term goals, and follow-up. Will and Wrate (1985) describe the same four stages in their modification of the McMaster's model. Gurman (1981) offers another integrative approach based on objects relations theory in which he blends treatment techniques from the systems model and the behavioral model. He delineates four phases or stages of treatment: treatment goals and assessment; early intervention and therapeutic alliance; midphase issues, including transference, countertransference, resistance, and the use of specific techniques; and termination. Gurman's overriding goal in this therapy approach is to achieve change in each spouse as well as in the marital interaction. This is the same goal as that of Glick, Clarkin, and Kessler (1987), Nichols (1988), and Will and Wrate (1985).

### Composite Stages

There is a great degree of concordance among these integrative approaches regarding the stages, or phases, of the treatment process. It may be useful to delineate a four-stage model of treatment which recognizes these similarities: engagement, assessment, negotiated treatment plan; early intervention for symptom reduction; continued intervention; and termination and follow-up.

## THE IMPORTANCE OF
## THE INITIAL STAGE OF THERAPY

Glick, Clarkin, and Kessler (1987) have indicated that the first stage of treatment is usually the most difficult for the trainee to master. There are several reasons for this. First, the initial face-to-face meeting of the couple and therapist is crucial in determining whether therapy will continue. The attrition rate for couples is high. Of the couples, 30% to 40% do not return for a second appointment (Nichols, 1988). Second, in the first stage the trainee must contend with a rather large number of treatment tasks and goals that must often be addressed in the first interview. Not only must the therapist complete an adequate assessment; he or she must formulate the case so as to understand the individual and systems dynamics and develop some treatment goals and strategies in order to negotiate a treatment plan with the couple. Finally, the therapist must make a series of decisions about treatment format and treatment interventions. Should the couple be seen in a conjoint format, in individual marital therapy, in concurrent therapy, or in couples groups? It is for these reasons that we would like to focus in some detail on the importance of the initial interview or interviews.

## Engagement

All approaches that we have surveyed emphasize the importance of engagement, which involves the development of a rapport or an alliance between the couple and the therapist. Engagement connotes a sufficient degree of commitment and cooperation for the couple and the therapist to work productively together. Engagement is a necessary condition for effective therapeutic outcomes.

Feldman (1976) has noted that the writings of marital and family therapists commonly emphasize the empathy, respect, concern, and genuineness in the therapist's manner of relating to a couple or family members. These are the same qualities that Rogers (1957) and Carkhuff (1976) considered essential for individual and group therapists. Therapists who can effectively engage a couple in treatment are those who are able to manifest a wide range of feelings and serve as both a model and a catalyst for change. To the extent that therapists represent themselves as genuine and clearly identifiable persons, they reduce the chances for the formation of transferences to themselves. As a result transference reactions remain primarily between the spouses.

Engagement is not merely a function of a therapist's being and skills. Olson (1987) has noted that engagement of the "reluctant spouse"—usually the husband—can often be facilitated through the use of formal assessment inventories. Olson has found that the reluctant spouse may return to the second session because he or she is curious about the results of the formal assessment, particularly when a computer-generated report is expected.

## Assessment

Assessment of the various levels of functioning of the marriage relationship as well as of each spouse begins on the phone. It continues more formally through clinical interview, formal inventories, enactment, observation, and so on. Most writers agree that the answer to the "why now" question provides important information. That spouses choose to seek professional help now rather than 2 months previously, or 6 months in the future, is often suggestive of their levels of coping abilities in the face of particular stressors.

Just as a therapist adopts a particular course of treatment based on his or her orientation, training and experience, and personality style, so does he or she adopt a particular assessment mode. The more integrative and the more couple-centered the approach to marital therapy, the more the approach advocates a comprehensive assessment. A comprehensive assessment includes at least four dimensions: *situation*—symptoms, stressors, problems, circumstances; *system*—system factors, stage of the marriage, relating skills; *spouse*—personality style, health status; and *suitability for treatment*—expectations and readiness for therapy, previous therapeutic efforts.

Traditional, nonintegrative approaches emphasize formal assessment of the situation and system dimension but minimize or deny the value of assessing the spouse and suitability dimensions. This results in a reductionistic, noncomprehensive assessment. The integrative approaches that incorporate a psychodynamic or psychoanalytic model compensate for this omission by emphasizing how the individuality of each spouse impacts the marital system. Comprehensive assessment protocols that involve all four dimensions are noted in the works of Will and Wrate (1985), Nichols (1988), and Glick, Clarkin, and Kessler (1987).

## Psychiatric Disorders in One Spouse

A spouse with a serious DSM-III-R Axis I disorder such as depression, panic disorder with agoraphobia, substance dependence, manic type bipolar disorder (manic-depression), or schizophrenia puts considerable strain on a marriage. The marital relationship prior to, during, and following the onset of such symptoms in the spouse is influenced by many factors and is quite variable across couples. To assume that the interaction between spouses brought on or caused the mental disorder and symptoms in the other spouse is an unwarranted assumption. In some cases the marital interaction neither caused nor precipitated the disorder in a spouse who was biologically predisposed to such symptoms. In other cases the marital interaction was a stressor that contributed to the onset of symptoms in a vulnerable spouse. Occasionally, the marital interaction does not initially stress the vulnerable spouse, but as symptoms emerge the marital interaction begins to become dysfunctional, which results in further distress and more symptoms. Finally, in some marriages, psychiatric symptoms can be fully explained as a function of an interactional pattern between the spouses. Whatever the case, the diagnostic and symptom picture of the psychiatrically disordered spouse and characteristics of the other spouse are related to the symptoms in the marital interaction and should influence treatment planning. Such is the case when one spouse has a major depression with no clear, precipitating stressful life event. The marital interaction can be a chronic stressor and contributor to the condition. Here marital therapy is probably the treatment of choice. For the spouse suffering from a bipolar illness where the marital interaction prior to the episode was good, psychoeducational interventions may be the treatment of choice, with little or no therapeutic attention focused on the marital interaction itself.

### Case Formulation

After the informal and formal assessment data are elicited and reviewed, the therapist's task is to make some sense of them and come to some conclusions about treatment goals and direction. This is called a case formulation. Basically, a case formulation is a written statement that conveys the therapist's understanding and logical explanation of the case. It forms the basis of the treatment plan if treatment is indicated. But a case formulation is more than a summary statement of the couple's problems and the story of their relationship, more than a diagnostic label. Rather, a case formulation is an explanation of the pattern of individual and relationship dysfunction. Through the formulation, the therapist describes his or her understanding of this dysfunctional pattern in terms of precipitating and predisposing factors. Finally, a formulation suggests what factors perpetuate the level and degree of dysfunction. Not surprisingly, the formulation is based on and reflects the therapist's theoretical model of marital functioning.

There are two versions of the formulation. The first is the formal written statement, which forms the basis of the treatment plan when treatment is indicated. The treatment plan indicates the intermediate and outcome goals for therapy, the format, general treatment strategies, and the duration of treatment. If a psychiatric or medication evaluation is indicated, the treatment plan includes this. The formulation, treatment plan, specific background information, and summary of the findings of the assessment constitute a report that is commonly referred to as the Initial Evaluation and Treatment Plan. This report becomes part of the couple's record. As such, it is a legal document and may be requested by other health care providers, insurance companies, or the courts.

The second type of formulation is the verbal report and recommendation that the therapist shares with the couple. This verbal feedback is not a simplified explanation of the written formulation. Generally, a therapist providing insight into the couple's dynamics is not particularly helpful to the couple at this point (Barker, 1986). Knowing how the therapist understands their problem does not necessarily lead the spouses to change. In fact, when a strategic approach to treatment is planned, it might actually impede the treatment. Rather, the therapist can make a concise, explicit statement about the marriage in language a couple can understand. For instance, the therapist might say, "I think your bulimia has to do with some of the feelings you and your husband have about each other. Maybe it has to do with your feeling that eating is one of the few areas of your life in which you can have some control. From his point of view, he feels that you don't understand the demands of his job and how hard he has to work. I think we should meet together to see how things could be better in your marriage and explore what has happened." Such a statement could be used as a springboard for discussion of the treatment plan.

## Treatment Goals

The formulation of therapeutic goals has at least two levels. The first involves the couple's immediate or mediating goals regarding the present complaint and the therapist's goals regarding symptoms. The second set of goals involves the couple's longer-range goals and the therapist's overall outcome goals for treatment.

The mediating goals of marital therapy include establishment of a therapeutic alliance, specification of interactional problems, recognition of the spouses' mutual contribution to the problem, clarification of marital boundaries, clarification and specification of each spouse's needs and expectations in the relationship, increased communication skills, decreased coercion and blame, increased differentiation, and resolution of marital transference distortions (Glick, Clarkin, & Kessler, 1987). The most common outcome goals of marital therapy involve resolution of presenting problems, reduction of symptoms, increased intimacy, increased role flexibility and adaptability, tolerance of individual differences, improved psychosexual functioning, balance of power, appropriate boundaries, resolution of conflictual interactions, player communication, and improved relationships with children and families of origin (Glick, Clarkin, & Kessler, 1987).

## Negotiation

Research suggests that a cooperative, negotiated approach to treatment planning results in positive therapeutic outcomes and increased adherence and satisfaction with treatment (Francis, Clarkin, & Perry, 1984; Beutler, 1983).

The negotiation process begins as the therapist acknowledges the couple's explanation of its marital difficulties as well as its treatment expectations. The therapist then relates the formulation and suggests some general treatment goals and strategies. Differences can be discussed, and the therapist can educate and correct any misconceptions the couple may have about the treatment process, treatment goals, strategies, or involvement in the therapy process. Agreement about general outcome goals must be articulated. Obvious differences of opinion about the general outcome goal of treatment can seriously jeopardize the course of treatment.

It is particularly helpful for the therapist to frame the treatment plan as a means of giving the couple more choices and more effective alternatives for responding to one another, rather than allowing the couple to frame treatment as a condemnation or life constriction. This is one of many opportunities in the course of therapy to encourage the couple and in so doing begin to reverse both spouses' sense of demoralization.

In this context, a mutually agreed upon treatment contract should be the outcome of the negotiation phase. A clearly defined contract regarding goals, treatment roles, and responsibilities should be established. The contract should include who is to be present at the sessions; the location, times, estimated length, and frequency of sessions; and the fee, contingency plans in individual sessions with a spouse, and missed appointments. The contract should also specify both therapist and couple responsibilities in sessions and between sessions regarding matters such as focus, homework, telephone contact with the therapist, and the like.

### Individualizing Treatment

Throughout this chapter the reader has been encouraged to think not only of the marital interaction as a whole but of the two individuals who make up the marital system. Each spouse has a history, personality style, and unique coping abilities. A knowledge of individual personality theory and psychopathology is essential for anticipating what to expect from each spouse as well as from the marital system. At times it may be necessary to direct specific attention toward or provide specific treatment to one spouse—for example, when one spouse is acutely psychotic—with individual sessions and sometimes with hospitalization. But even under ordinary circumstances, a thorough understanding of each spouse's strengths and weaknesses can help individualize treatment.

As mentioned earlier, negotiated treatment goals and realistic expectations for the outcome of treatment are basic to individualized or tailored treatment.

After that, the therapist's skill and creativity play a role in matching particular treatment techniques to individual spouse's cognitive style and need. It has been said that matching goals with the most efficient therapeutic strategies and techniques at the right time and in the right sequence is, by definition, the art of psychotherapy. Marital therapists who can tailor treatment to the styles of the spouses and the couple are no mere technicians. Rather, they are caring and committed professionals and artists.

## Mode of Treatment: Individual, Concurrent, Conjoint, or Group

During the 1980s it became axiomatic to associate conjoint marital therapy with effective therapeutic outcomes. Conjoint therapy refers to two spouses working therapeutically with a marital therapist. In an influential review of the marital therapy outcome research, Gurman and Kniskern (1978) summarized data indicating that conjoint marital therapy was superior to concurrent therapy, conjoint plus individual therapy, and individual therapy. Gurman and Kniskern reported that the rate of deterioration—that is, the "worsening" of positive effects over time— for conjoint, group, and concurrent/collaborative marital therapies was one half that of individual marital therapy. In a critical reappraisal of the same outcome studies Gurman and Kniskern reviewed, Wells and Giannetti (1986) reported that Gurman and Kniskern's conclusions about individual marital therapy were suspect because these outcome studies had serious flaws in their design and implementation. Thus, Wells and Giannetti believed that statements claiming that IMT was a harmful treatment were not justified. Gurman and Kniskern (1986), in a commentary on Wells and Giannetti, partially capitulated on their contention about the deterioration effect of individual and marital therapy.

Often only one spouse is willing to come for treatment, or one spouse drops out after therapy has begun. Were marital therapy dependent on a conjoint mode of treatment, the less motivated spouse could consistently sabotage progress by simply refusing to work on the relationship. It is possible, however, to effect significant change in the relationship through work with the motivated spouse alone. Friedman (1985) has developed a systems approach based on Bowen's work for "coaching" one spouse with the focus on the marital relationship. Friedman coaches the motivated spouse alone on how to extricate himself or herself from dysfunctional marital patterns and achieve more self-differentiation. Friedman finds that the more motivated and coachable spouse is generally the one who sets the appointment, who articulates the problem, and who is capable of defining his or her position in a nonblaming way. This spouse tends to be the overfunctioner or the pursuer in the relationship. Conversely, it is the underfunctioner or the distancer who is reluctant to be involved in treatment.

The coaching approach is an effort to stimulate a relationship's strengths rather than shore up its weaknesses. The goal of coaching is to rebalance the marital system. After some initial focus on the nonattending spouse, the emphasis shifts to empowering the coached spouse to change his or her behavior in the relationship. Detriangulation is the major treatment intervention. Ultimately, the coached partner is helped to focus on unresolved issues in his or her own family of origin rather than on issues in the marital relationship. As the coached partner becomes more involved in his or her own goals and destiny, he or she is able to reduce dependence to a minimum and can decrease feedback to the spouse's systemic responses. At this point the coached spouse makes changes that could not have been brought about by a continuing focus on a specific problem. As a result the whole system shifts. Friedman maintains that the differentiating spouse becomes the more attractive one, and the unmotivated one becomes the pursuer.

The coaching approach described elegantly by Friedman allows marital therapy to be effectively practiced in an individual therapy mode. Friedman does caution that the therapist runs the risk of being triangulated or of being seen by either spouse as having joined in an alliance against or with him or her. Nevertheless, to the extent that therapists focus on differentiation through the relationship, they should be able to remain objective about the underlying process even when coached spouses are not totally truthful.

# A CROSS SECTIONAL VIEW OF A THERAPY SESSION

Previous sections have provided a longitudinal map of the treatment process in marital therapy. This section provides the reader with a cross-sectional map for a single session in the middle phase of treatment. This map has been useful in training therapists to recognize and establish a rhythm and pattern to the treatment process during the middle stages of therapy.

### Sperry's ERIC Model

The acronym ERIC is useful as a label for the phases present in any clinician/client or couple interaction (Sperry, 1987). We believe that to the extent that the therapist is aware of these processes and their relationship to one another and has developed some of the skills associated with each phase, he or she can maximize the outcome of a single treatment session. ERIC is articulated as:

E—engagement, exploration or evaluation, empathy, and enactment
R—renegotiation, reformulation and reframing, reversal of demoralization
I —immediate interventions, information, instruction, interference, and intervening strategies
C—continuing intervention, collaboration, consultation, compliance enhancement

## The "E" Phase

The engagement process begins with the development of a therapeutic alliance in the initial stage of therapy. Typically, the process solidifies and deepens in the middle stages of treatment even though transference, counter-transference, and resistance issues may temporarily intervene. As each session begins, the therapist and couple must engage anew—that is, "warm up" to each other. It is important for the therapist to note delays or difficulties with this warming up process in the middle stages of therapy. Long silences at the beginning of a session or inordinately superficial talk may indicate some sort of disengagement. The therapist does well to explore the reasons for this.

Evaluation (and reevaluation) is likewise considered in the middle stages of therapy. There may be a specific intersession task that the couple has been given at the previous session, and the therapist may structure treatment such that these intersession tasks are reviewed in the beginning of the session. During the course of the session the therapist may also be evaluating the progress of this couple to this point. The therapist may use indices such as level of skills, level of awareness, or changes in commitment. Based on this brief review of homework and/or general progress in individual and marital functioning, the therapist may decide to focus the conversation on a particular conflict, circumstance, or skill.

As a way of evaluating the couple's progress and as a way of developing more couple awareness and skills, the therapist can use enactment. For example, the therapist may use enactment in the formal role playing of a past situation to stimulate more positive and prosocial interactions or to have the couple practice a particular communication skill.

## The "R" Phase

As mentioned earlier, the immediate goals of treatment are subject to change during the course of treatment, usually because of a change of circumstances for the couple. Specific aspects of treatment may also be renegotiated, such as homework or the consequences of noncompliance with appointments. Reframing is a basic and essential treatment method in all forms of individual, marital, and group therapy. Even within the first 10 minutes of the therapy session, the therapist is likely to have opportunities to reframe specific conflicts, incidents, thoughts, or feelings.

### The "I" Phase

During the course of a particular session the therapist may find that an immediate or very specific intervention is called into play, usually related to a specific concern of the couple. So a couple may have experienced significant loss or conflict or a stressor that demands immediate attention. The immediate intervention may be grief work, information or advice giving, teaching of specific relaxation techniques or thought stopping techniques, or cognitive reversal.

### The "C" Phase

Continuing intervention refers to the ongoing agenda for therapy that includes both the outcome goals of treatment and increases in dimensions such as communication skills, conflict resolution, self-efficacy, and the like. Long-term interventions may extend from the very beginning of treatment through the time of termination. They may be a continuing focus of therapy in every session and may occupy a significant amount of time in any given session. These continual interventions are the "background music," or motif, for the course of treatment; the immediate interventions are particular "movements" superimposed on the background music.

An example of a continuing intervention is the use of "I statements" and "absolutizing." In an early session, the therapist might have pointed out the absolutizing statements of one or both spouses: "You never . . ."; "I always . . ."; "We never . . . ." The therapist would have taught as well as modeled relativizing statements such as, "I sometimes. . . ." From session to session the therapist would have monitored the couple's communication for "I statements" and relativizing statements, pointing out failures of usage when appropriate and reinforcing positive usage.

There are also times when the therapist considers the necessity for a medical or psychiatric consultation on one spouse or for a specific consultation for one spouse with a mental health professional who performs particular treatments such as smoking cessation or alcohol or drug counseling. The therapist may also collaborate with another family member, an employer, or any other individual who can provide additional information, support, or stability for a spouse or the couple.

Often there are problems with relapse or noncompliance with medications, medical treatments, job attendance, or even therapy sessions. Probably the most common noncompliance issue in marital therapy involves intersession tasks or homework. A basic therapeutic rule of thumb is that nonadherence with any aspect of treatment should be an immediate treatment consideration. This means that therapy cannot continue on a specific personal or couple issue until the underlying compliance issue is resolved. The underlying issue may be as simple as a lack of information or a failure to understand instructions, or the issue may be a basic power struggle between an individual spouse, or both spouses, and the therapist.

In short, we encourage beginning therapists to use a schema such as ERIC as a plan for conducting individual sessions. If they do, they are likely to have a focus and direction for a specific conjoint session. We have found this strategy particularly valuable in dealing with nontraditional couples who tend not to be as goal-directed and focused as more traditional couples. In whatever setting and with whatever kind of couple, the ERIC schema has proved useful.

## CONCLUDING NOTE

We have reviewed several integrative approaches to the practice of marital therapy and have proposed a composite four-stage model of the treatment process. We then emphasized the importance of the initial stage of treatment. A cross-sectional map—ERIC—was described to aid the therapist in planning and structuring individual sessions.

## REFERENCES

Barker, P. (1986). *Basic family therapy* (2d ed.). New York: Oxford University Press.

Beutler, L. (1983). *Eclectic psychotherapy: A systematic approach.* New York: Pergamon Press.

Carkhuff, R. (1976). *The art of helping* (3d ed.). Amherst, MA: Human Resources Development Press.

Epstein, N., & Bishop, D. (1981). Problem centered systems therapy of the family. *Journal of Marital and Family Therapy, 7,* 21–23.

Francis, A., Clarkin, J., & Perry, S. (1984). *Differential therapeutics in psychiatry.* New York: Brunner/Mazel.

Feldman, L. (1976). Goals of family therapy. *Journal of Marriage and Family Counseling, 2*, 103–113.

Friedman, E. (1985). *Generation to generation: Family process in church and synagogue.* New York: Guilford Press.

Glick, I., Clarkin, J., & Kessler, D. (1987). *Marital and family therapy* (3d ed.). Orlando, FL: Grune and Stratton.

Gurman, A. (1981). Integrative marital therapy: Toward the development of an interpersonal approach. In S. Budman (Ed.), *Forms of brief therapy.* New York: Guilford Press.

Gurman, A., & Kniskern, D. (1986). Commentary: Individual marital therapy—have reports of your death been somewhat exaggerated? *Family Process, 25*, 51–62.

L'Abate, L. (1986). *Systematic family therapy.* New York: Brunner/Mazel.

Nichols, W. (1988). *Marital therapy: An integrative approach.* New York: Brunner/Mazel.

Olson, D. (1987, October). *Assessment in brief marriage therapy.* Paper presented at the American Association of Marriage and Family Therapy Convention, Chicago, IL.

Rogers, C. (1957). The necessary and sufficient conditions of therapeutic personality change. *Journal of Consulting Psychology, 21*, 95–103.

Sperry, L. (1987). ERIC: A cognitive map for guiding brief therapy and health care counseling. *Individual Psychology, 43*, 237–241.

Wells, R., & Giannetti, V. (1986). Individual marital therapy: A critical reappraisal. *Family Process, 25*, 43–51.

Will, D., and Wrate, R. (1985). *Integrated family therapy: A problem-centered psychodynamic approach.* London: Tavistock.

# 9

# *Assessment*

T he way in which a therapist thinks about and carries out a marital assessment is based upon his or her theoretical model of how marital relationships become functional and dysfunctional. This model is an extremely useful guide in helping the therapist make sense out of the complex, sometimes confusing mixture of information, behavior, and communication elicited and observed during the marital assessment. Of necessity, this model is reductionistic in that the therapist ignores some input and focuses on data that fit his or her tentative formulation and treatment plan. Many such models exist. Chapters 4 through 7 surveyed the most common and current ones. During the course of their careers, many marital therapists develop their own personal theory or model of marital functioning and dysfunction, and so it is not too surprising that the way in which therapists conduct assessment interviews changes.

This diversity in assessment approaches can be briefly illustrated. Framo (1981) utilizes only one method of assessment, the clinical interview, while forsaking any use of formal questionnaires, guided interview schedules, or enactment. In fact, he strongly objects to the use of questionnaires or inventories. In his initial interviews with the couple, he considers three areas of inquiry: the husband, the wife, and their relationship. Because of his object relations/systems orientation, Framo is interested in the spouses' intrapsychic intermesh. Specifically, he focuses on referral source, brief statement of the problem from each spouse, age, occupation, length of marriage, age and gender of children, previous therapies, prior marriages, basis of mate selection, families' reaction to choice of partner, each partner's fight style, whether the spouses basically love each other, whether they each had a good relationship, commitment to the marriage, the quality and quantity of their sexual relationship, a brief history of each family of origin, current relationship with parents and siblings, how the partners relate to each other in the interview, and motivation for therapy.

Nichols (1988), who also operates from an object relations/systems approach, utilizes standardized inventories, enactment, observation of the spouses' interaction between themselves and with the therapist, and the clinical interview in completing his assessment. In addition to collecting similar information to that of Framo, Nichols assesses relationship skills such as commitment, caring, communication, and conflict/compromise abilities.

Both Framo and Nichols place considerable emphasis on object relations and systems factors in their assessments. Fisher (1976) reviewed several clinical assessment schemas and integrated a summary list of the most frequently used assessment criteria common to many theoretical orientations. He listed five main categories:

I.  Structural Descriptors
    1. Role: complementarity, acceptance, confusion, adequacy
    2. Splits: alliances, scapegoating
    3. Boundaries: internal and external
    4. Patterns of interaction and communication: rules and norms of relating
    5. Conflicts and patterns of resolution
    6. Family views of life, people, and the external world
II.  Controls and Sanctions
    1. Power and leadership
    2. Flexibility
    3. Exercise and control
    4. Dependency/independency
    5. Differentiation/fusion
III.  Emotions and Needs
    1. Methods and rules for affective expression
    2. Need satisfaction: giving and taking
    3. Relative importance of needs versus instrumental tasks
    4. Dominant affect themes
IV.  Cultural Aspects
    1. Social position
    2. Environmental stresses
    3. Cultural heritage
    4. Social and cultural views

V. Developmental Aspects:
  Appropriateness of structural, affective, and cultural aspects to developmental stage

# GOALS AND PURPOSES OF ASSESSMENT

A common perception among trainees as well as couples is that a marital assessment is a formal, verbal evaluation performed face to face with the couple by the therapist in the first interview(s). A corollary is that the same therapist who completes the assessment will undertake therapeutic interventions. In our experience this is a rather limited view of assessment. We view the assessment phase as a process beginning with the couple's first contact with the therapist or clinic, usually by phone, extending throughout the course of treatment, and including follow-up after treatment is formally terminated. As we shall point out later, initial telephone contact prior to the first appointment offers important assessment information. Also important are the assessment nonverbal behaviors, data from forms and inventories that the couple completes before or after the first sessions, and medical and psychological reports from other professionals.

The purpose of this chapter is to advance an approach to assessment that is relatively comprehensive and integrative. This approach is based on a biopsychosocial perspective and has been found to be useful for assessing all couples, particularly the nontraditional couple who is referred for marital therapy.

Before formal therapeutic interventions are initiated, the therapist must make at least three decisions. The first regards the relative indications for a marital assessment and therapy. Are the presenting symptoms predominantly related to the marital system in terms of etiology or affect? Even though the marital system is relevant in considering the spouses' concern or symptoms, there are instances in which other factors may be more important. Physical overlays and symptoms such as medication side effects, medical conditions such as hypothyroidism, and a number of neurological and psychiatric disorders are conditions that can greatly impact marital functioning. Usually, when these physical conditions are appropriately treated, the marital relationship improves, probably without formal marital intervention. But marital therapy may also be needed for predisposed couples in which medical conditions are extraordinarily stressful. With a few exceptions, the marital literature has avoided a discussion of the indications and contraindications for marital therapy. The assumption is made that marital therapy is a treatment of choice whenever a spouse seeks help. Besides being somewhat cavalier, this attitude can be harmful to the couple or spouse. It has and may continue to be the basis of malpractice suits brought against marital therapists.

The second decision is based on the results of the marital evaluation. Which of the modes of marital therapy (conjoint, collaborative, couples groups, family or marital therapy alone or in conjunction with couples sessions) is the optimal treatment for a particular couple?

If conjoint marital therapy is the treatment of choice, the third set of decisions involves the type, duration, focus, and particular strategies utilized in the treatment of a particular couple. This effort to match treatment to a couple's needs and styles, strengths, and previous positions is called differential therapeutics. These differential therapeutic considerations were discussed in the previous chapter.

## INDICATIONS AND CONTRAINDICATIONS FOR MARITAL THERAPY

Based on their clinical experience, a number of clinicians have attempted to establish indications and contraindications for the use of marital therapy. Haley (1963) suggested five indications: when individual therapy has failed, when individual therapy cannot be used, when sudden onset of symptoms in a patient coincides with marital discord, when therapy is requested by partners who are unable to resolve their distressful conflict, or when there are indications that a patient's individual improvement will result in divorce or the appearance of symptoms in the spouse. These indications are rather inclusive, whereas those described by Beavers (1981, 1985) are more restrictive.

Beavers offered five indications and three contraindications for the use of marital therapy. The first involves a request from a spouse or a couple, neither of whom is psychotic or severely depressed, for such help. Although both spouses wish for the relationship to continue, the request usually comes from one of the spouses, with the other reluctantly agreeing. Beavers noted that this is the most common indication of marital therapy. The second indication is the existence of a stalemate in individual psychotherapy because of the projection of power, control, and responsibility onto the absent spouse. The third indication involves an individual seeking help from a therapist who describes his or her problem primarily in terms of marital therapy. The fourth indication stems from a family evaluation that ostensibly involves child dysfunction but in which the central issues are basically marital issues. The fifth indication is acute psychosis, severe depression, or acute drug or alcohol abuse in a spouse assigned to outpatient treatment. When medication and individual psychotherapy are not sufficient and a supportive environment can be mobilized, marital therapy may be a potent therapeutic strategy.

Beavers listed three contraindications. The first is a lack of a stated desire on the part of both spouses to secure a satisfying relationship. Beavers noted that successful therapy requires a minimum investment of effort and a conscious desire for change. Beavers distinguished the joint commitment of a couple to therapy with the commitment to stay together in a relationship and not change. The second contraindication is the presence of a highly invested, ongoing, extramarital romantic and/or sexual relationship on the part of one spouse that is revealed to the therapist but is kept a secret from the other spouse. The third contraindication consists of overt, pervasive, and disruptive paranoid ideation on the part of one spouse toward the other.

## COMPREHENSIVE APPROACH TO MARITAL ASSESSMENT

A clinician who has any question about the value of a comprehensive assessment would do well to seriously consider the statistics on treatment failure in marital and family therapy. In *Failures in Family Therapy*, Coleman (1985) noted that 83% of treatment failures were primarily due to inadequate initial assessments. These data confirm our own clinical and supervisory experience. For this reason we have advocated comprehensive and competent assessments.

We have looked briefly at a few examples of assessment schemes as well as some of the decisions the marital therapist faces during the process of a marital assessment or evaluation. This section describes a simple but comprehensive model for planning a marital assessment (Sperry, 1989). Briefly stated, the model is:

Comprehensive          =   Situation + System + Spouse + Suitability
Marital Assessment                                         for Treatment

We believe that a comprehensive and integrative marital assessment involves eliciting information in each of these four components: situation, system, spouse, and suitability for treatment.

*Situation* refers to the symptoms, stressors, and the situation, circumstances, and demographics that form the context for the couple's presenting concerns, complaints, or problems.

*System* refers to the spousal subsystem—that is, the relationship between the spouses. Assessment here is concerned with the history of the relationship in its present stage of functioning. The assessment focuses on important system factors such as boundaries, power, and intimacy and includes the level of the couple's relational skills, object relations—particularly projective identification and collusion—and level of social interest and cooperation. A final system consideration involves family-of-origin and multigenerational issues that impact on the marriage relationship.

*Spouse* refers to the individual system dimension, including the physical and psychological health of each spouse as well as cognitive and constitutional style.

*Suitability for treatment* refers to the couple's qualification for marital therapy. It is common for marital and family therapists to assume that marital therapy is the treatment of choice for most conditions and circumstances and that most couples are suitable for marital treatment. Research by Beutler (1983; Beutler & Crago, 1987) has indicated, however, that suitability for treatment is a function of motivational readiness for change and realistic expectations for the outcome of therapy. Included in this dimension is an assessment of the couple's expectation and previous efforts to make changes in the relationship.

We have found this comprehensive model particularly useful for the nontraditional and "difficult" couple for whom age, cultural, health, medical, or psychiatric factors complicate the treatment picture. Until recently, the systems approach to marriage and family therapy has tended to focus on the marital subsystem at the expense of the individual subsystem. Because this view is reductionistic, we suggest a more comprehensive view. Table 9.1 lists 20 types of information helpful in leading a comprehensive couple evaluation or assessment. Each of these factors is briefly described in the following pages.

## Age of Spouses/Years Married

Researchers have noted an inverse association between age at the time of marriage and the probability of divorce. Those who marry at a very young age have the highest divorce rates, probably because they had not yet developed the necessary relationship skills at the time of marriage or because during the marriage they were too preoccupied with other personal and professional issues and responsibilities to commit the time and energy necessary to make the relationship work (Stuart, 1980).

Length of marriage is another factor. There is a curvilinear or U-shaped relationship between years married and marital stability and satisfaction. The majority of couples report more satisfaction with their spouses in their relationship before and after the childrearing years. As the spouses experience the untoward effects of increased age, illness, and a gradual loss of control of the forces that shape their lives, they may be more likely to remain together because of the shrinking range of options. The price of this stability, however, tends to be a diminished satisfaction with the relationship. A knowledge, then, of the ages of each partner can sensitize the therapist to a time factor that may strain even the most well-intentioned spouses.

**TABLE 9.1**  Assessment Factors in a Comprehensive Couple Evaluation

| *Component* | *Factor* |
|---|---|
| Situation | 1. Age of spouse/years married |
|  | 2. Family size |
|  | 3. Finances and employment |
|  | 4. Cultural values and social class |
| System | 5. Presenting complaint and problems |
|  | 6. History of the relationship |
|  | 7. Stage of relationship and degree of synchronicity |
|  | 8. Boundaries, power, intimacy |
|  | 9. Cooperation and social interest |
|  | 10. Relational skills |
|  | 11. Family-of-origin issues and genogram |
|  | 12. Commitment to the relationship |
|  | 13. Expectations for the marriage |
| Spouse | 14. Individual evaluation/psychological functioning |
|  | 15. Individual style—cognitive and constitutional |
|  | 16. Individual evaluation of health status |
| ·Suitability for Treatment | 17. Motivation for treatment |
|  | 18. Expectations for marital therapy |
|  | 19. Level of marital functioning and discord |
|  | 20. Prognostic factors |

*Source:* (Sperry, 1989.)

### Family Size

Generally speaking, researchers have found divorce-proneness to be positively correlated with family size. But, most specifically, researchers have found a U-shaped distribution in which childless couples and those with large families were more likely to divorce than were those with families of moderate size (Thornton, 1977). Other researchers have suggested that having children may be a barrier to divorce, which may explain the greater divorce-proneness of childless couples. Economic hardships experienced by the parents of large families could explain the upsurge in divorces at the upper end of the continuum. For families of moderate size, children may be an alternative source of love and satisfaction for spouses whose relationship with each other is less than they desire.

## Finances and Employment

Often a couple's problems are exacerbated by financial pressures. Family income is more strongly and negatively associated with divorce than is any other available census variable (Levinger, 1976). Generally it has been assumed that the husband's income is positively related to marital stability—that is, the more he earns, the more stable the marriage. Similarly, income earned by the wife is thought to be positively related to divorce—that is, the more she earns, the greater the instability of the marriage. But recent statistics suggest the wife's educational level is a modulating factor, such that college educated wives who work are more likely to have more stable marriages than do wives with lesser education (Gibbs, 1977).

## Cultural Values and Social Class

Cultural values and socioeconomic status combine to shape the character of marriage, particularly role expectations and the nuances of daily experience. These cultural values stem from the early socialization experiences of each spouse and are reinforced almost daily with members of the subculture in which the spouses spend their time (Laner, 1978; Grunebaum & Christ, 1976). Certain aspects of the couple's interaction may be viewed as dysfunctional by the therapist and yet be "off limits" to intervention because they are values the couple is unwilling to challenge. Social class differences greatly affect the depth and range of spousal contacts with other members of the community. Upper-class spouses tend to have superficial contacts with more outsiders than do middle-class spouses, who have deeper contacts with fewer individuals outside their family. Thus, sociocultural norm can have a predictable impact upon a couple's willingness to discuss its interactions with outsiders, particularly about extramarital affairs. What may appear to the middle-class therapist as "poor communication" may actually be normative behavior for the lower-class couple (Stuart, 1980).

## Presenting Complaint and Problems

Couples who seek marital therapy or are referred for marital evaluation and treatment usually present with a list of relatively similar concerns. In a national survey, problems reported by couples seeking professional help were communications (86.6%), children (45.7%), sex (43.7%), money (37%), leisure (32.6%), relatives (28.4%), infidelity (25.6%), housekeeping (16.7%), physical abuse (15.6%), and other problems (8%) (Beck & Jones, 1973).

Nichols (1988) noted that couples contact therapists with complaints that are not always identical to the problems that disturb the couples. More often the vagueness of their difficulty, as well as their inability to alleviate their discomfort by themselves, may be part of their presenting complaint. Exploration of such complaints may lead to a discovery of other facets or more basic problems. In evaluating the current functioning of a marriage, the therapist must determine the severity of the basic problems and the extent of dysfunction for each partner as well as the overall relationship in comparison with the developmental tasks for the particular stage of the marriage.

Often, the common denominator of these problems involves boundaries, power, and/or intimacy. Assessment of these factors helps determine the level of system functioning. The answer to the "why now?" question provides valuable clues about the couple's coping abilities and tolerance for stress (Beavers, 1985; Nichols, 1988).

### History of the Relationship

Eliciting the history of the marital relationship begins with questions such as, "How did you meet? As best you know, what attracted you to your spouse? How did your dating go? How did you decide on getting married? How did things go when you were first married? How have things changed since then?" Research shows that spouses tend to be similar with respect to age, race, social class origin, educational level, religious preference, ethnic background, intellectual abilities, and physical characteristics such as height, weight, and attractiveness (Sternberg, 1988; Murstein & Christy, 1976). Persons with similar characteristics and backgrounds tend to meet one another in common places such as their neighborhoods, their churches, or their jobs and tend to be more comfortable with one another than they would be with others whose resources and interests are widely different from their own.

Continuation of this initial relationship can be explained by the bonding that occurs at a deeper and more unconscious level. In this view, persons are attracted to one another and remain in a relationship because the spouses each represent one half of a total personality, and staying in the relationship is the way the spouses seek to grow and attain personal integration. Projective identification and collusion often emerge as important clinical indicators of a couple's presenting problems.

### Stage of the Relationship and Degree of Synchronicity

Nichols (1988) described a four-stage marital life cycle model. This model is a helpful framework for the therapist in determining the developmental level of a couple and ascertaining the degree to which it has or has not met the particular developmental tasks at each stage. Very briefly, stage one, which is called formation, comprises the development of an initial commitment and a workable pattern of communication and conflict resolution such that the spouses can establish a mutually satisfying affectional/sexual relationship and separate from their respective families of origin while developing their identity as a couple.

Stage two, which is called expansion, begins with pregnancy. The main tasks for the couple are to adjust to the realities of being a nuclear family, to fulfill parental roles as a couple, and to take a new place in the extended family network as a couple.

Stage three, called contraction, requires that the couple maintain solid couple boundaries while coping with the difficulties of rearing adolescents. This involves reconciling personal and marital needs and desires while at the same time reworking the expectations of the marital relationship. More specifically, both spouses must learn to let go of their children and deal with the "empty nest" phenomenon.

Stage four, called postparental, requires the spouses to support each other and attempt to find new meaning, satisfaction, and productivity as they deal with issues such as retirement, declining physiological functioning, and eventual loss of a spouse by death.

To date there has been relatively little research on the developmental stages of a marriage. Davitz and Davitz (1986) have addressed the perplexing issue of the different levels of growth between spouses during the course of a marriage. They call this process "living in sync." They believe that the key to spouses' growth is a mutual awareness and satisfaction of each other's needs. According to the authors, three skills are particularly helpful: compromise; selective insensitivity—learning to tune out things about the spouse that cannot be easily changed; and ability to deal with one's own anger.

### Boundaries, Power, Intimacy

Berman and Leif (1975) and Fish and Fish (1986) have suggested a series of questions therapists can ask themselves during the evaluation to determine the systems formations of the marital relationship. For boundaries: Who else is considered to be part of the marital system? What is being excluded from the marital relationship and assigned to children or others? Who and what events or things are intruding into the marital relationship? For power: Who is in charge? How do the spouses deal with power in their relationship? For intimacy: How near, how far, and how do the spouses tolerate or respond to each other's needs and desires for intimate contact and closeness? How do spouses use emotional and geographical distance when struggling with their need for closeness? Answers to such questions provide significant data for the therapist in assessing the marital system.

### Cooperation and Social Interest

A global measure of a couple's level of functioning is the ability to cooperate and collaborate. Dreikurs (1946) indicated that there are four attitudes, or qualities, of cooperative, collaborative relationships: social interest (the expression of a sense of belonging together), confidence in the other spouse, self-confidence, and courage. These qualities are the polar opposites of hostility, distrust and suspicion, inferiority feelings, and fear.

### Relational Skills

In addition to systems factors, stages of the relationship, and the spouses' attitudes toward each other, the therapist should assess the level of relational skills that the spouses possess and utilize in relating to one another. Nichols (1988) listed five skills that he assesses at the beginning and at the end of therapy: communication, caring, conflict/compromise, commitment, and volunteering. Volunteering consists of behaviors offered by one spouse on behalf of the other without the expectation of immediate reward or benefit. Dinkmeyer and Carlson (1986) described 10 important skills for a functional, growing relationship: acceptance of responsibility, encouragement, setting of priorities and values, congruent communication, response to whole messages, capacity for listening, capacity for making choices, conflict resolution, application of conflict resolution abilities, and commitment to the maintenance of the quality in the marriage relationship. These skills can be rated by formal inventories, or the spouses may rate each other's level of skill on a Likert-type scale.

### Family-of-Origin Issues and Genogram

Exploration of the couple's marital history in relationship to their families of origin often proves useful. Such exploration is frequently helpful in explicating issues and bringing them into the therapeutic arena. This can be accomplished in several ways. A common method is the use of the genogram (McGoldrick & Gerson, 1985), which is a visual depiction of the family tree covering at least three generations for both spouses. Important information is reported on the genogram such as names, ages, marital status, divorces, separations, and years of deaths. Typically, the therapist constructs a genogram of one spouse and has the other spouse fill in information and make comments following the initial disclosures. Then the process is reversed. Some therapists who operate from an object relations perspective may collect additional information by asking one spouse, "What do you imagine it would have been like to be married to your spouse's mother?" "What do you imagine it would have been like for your father to be married to your spouse's mother?"

## Commitment to the Relationship

Perhaps one of the most pressing concerns for the therapist during the evaluation is determining the commitment of the spouses to each other. Nichols (1988) found it helpful to describe couples as being preambivalent, ambivalent, or postambivalent in their commitment. Nichols described the preambivalent person as one who does not seriously consider ending the marriage and the ambivalent person as one who regards the spouse and the marriage with mixed feelings. There are two types of postambivalent spouses. The postambivalent/ positive spouse has seriously struggled with the issue of remaining in the marriage and has decided to stay, whereas the postambivalent/negative spouse has decided to leave the marriage, although he or she may not have conveyed that decision to the other. Nichols noted that the four most common patterns are: both spouses are preambivalent, both are ambivalent, one is ambivalent and the other is preambivalent, or one is ambivalent and the other is postambivalent. Each of these patterns has significant implications for the spouses and their individual and joint commitment to therapy.

## Expectations for the Marriage

Marital satisfaction is at its highest when the marital experiences of each spouse match his or her expectations. But when hope conflicts with reality, conflict and dissatisfaction usually follow. Thus, it is particularly helpful for the therapist to list the expectations each spouse had of the marriage and of the other spouse at the time of the marriage and has at the present time. Some formal inventories can be used to elicit these data, or the therapist can directly question the couple about expectations about divisions of responsibility, decision-making, sharing, recreation, and so on.

### Individual Evaluation/Psychological Functioning

Stuart (1980) contended that determining the level of potential depression in both spouses is probably the most critical assessment the therapist can make. The diagnosis of major depression can blunt the spouse's willingness to engage in or follow through on the therapeutic plan and can also be a harbinger of therapeutic failure. Stuart noted that depressive symptoms not only lower the level of marital satisfaction but also blunt treatment effectiveness.

Beavers (1985) has described his experience working with psychotic spouses. He indicates that he treats the spouse with a manic-depressive disorder only in a conjoint marital setting. He found that both spouses typically had similar behavioral patterns, particularly involving control issues and shared magical thinking. He also found that the manic spouse was usually on a medication such as Lithium and that issues of medication compliance and noncompliance involved boundary issues. Similarly, in treating schizophrenic spouses, Beavers requires the other spouse and other family members to be involved in the treatment.

Treatment will be hindered if a diagnosable psychiatric disorder is not properly evaluated and considered in the treatment plan. If the therapist does not have the training and experience in conducting a DSM-III-R evaluation, a consultation should be arranged with another professional who can perform such an evaluation.

### Individual Style—Cognitive and Constitutional

Rarely are stylistic differences of individual spouses a formal part of the assessment. Nevertheless, such an assessment is extraordinarily useful in helping spouses improve mutual communication, respect, and problem-solving. For instance, each spouse processes information through one of many sensory modalities. This preferred style is usually visual, auditory, or kinesthetic. Cameron-Bandler (1985) suggested that communication between spouses can be facilitated when each is taught to match the other's dominant style or modality.

While a couple is courting and deeply in love, each partner responds to the other by actually "overmatching" modalities. That is, even though the male may be primarily visual and the female primarily kinesthetic, the male typically responds to the female in all three modalities and vice versa. But after the honeymoon is over, each spouse shifts back to the preferred modality. Thus, the visual male may attempt to show his love (a visual modality) by taking his wife out to dinner or buying her something (both visual activities). But the kinesthetic wife may not feel as loved with these visual activities as she would be with more kinesthetic activities, such as being held or caressed by her spouse.

Differences in constitutional styles may also contribute to marital dissatisfaction. Constitutional styles are cycles of energy and activation. For instance, when one spouse is a morning person (a lark) and the other spouse is a night person (an owl), there are bound to be misunderstandings and disagreements about things such as lovemaking, entertainment and recreation, and sleeping arrangements. Sperry (1984) discussed a number of other constitutional styles including high energy versus low energy spouses and type A versus type B styles.

## Individual Evaluation of Health Status

The importance of assessing health factors cannot be overstressed. In fact, omission of this aspect can be the basis for malpractice action, particularly in work with older couples. That certain medications and illnesses are the primary cause of impotency in males is an established fact. That injudicious lifestyle habits can affect marital functioning is more than speculation. Beavers (1985) listed a series of questions regarded as essential in the assessment of an individual's physical functioning. What are the sleep patterns for both spouses? What drugs are being used, both prescription and nonprescription? When was the last physical examination for each spouse? A medication evaluation is indicated especially for couples whose complaints are primarily sexual. A competent medical evaluation can diagnose physical problems, such as congestive heart failure, hyperthyroidism, drug-induced toxic states, malignancies, and hypertension, that mimic psychiatric disorders.

We have found it helpful to elicit data in eight different areas: the physical health status of each spouse, including any current illnesses, and family history of chronic medical and psychiatric illnesses; prescription and nonprescription medications as well as the history of compulsivity, including use of recreational drugs and alcohol; exercise fitness; diet and nutritional fitness; adequacy of sexual functioning; stress management skills; adequacy of sleep and relaxation; and occupation data. With regard to job or occupation, we ask specifically about shift work, commuting time, and job and occupational hazards. The value of this last information is inestimable.

Research on shift workers suggests that altered work schedules result not only in an increase in physical illness and sleep disorders but also in an increase in marital discord. It behooves the marital therapist to know about the couple's work demands in terms of hours and travel. Individuals who fly regularly often suffer the effects of jet lag for days. Fatigue, irritability, and temper outbursts clearly impact on marital functioning (Folkard, 1983).

## Motivation for Treatment

Clarification of the motivation of each spouse in collaborating with the therapist and in a course of marital therapy is crucial. As was indicated earlier, commitment to a marriage is not synonymous with motivation to change or commitment to engage in marital therapy. Therefore, it is necessary for the therapist to observe the spouses' behaviors and verbalizations concerning their relationship, themselves, and therapy, noting the degree of congruence between their behavior and their statements. The therapist may also ask questions such as, "What do you want to be different in this relationship? What role do you see yourself having to change? How willing are you to see this change through?"

## Expectations for Marital Therapy

By the end of the initial assessment, the therapist should have elicited the spouses' individual and collective expectations regarding their own role in treatment, his or her role as therapist, the length and duration of treatment, and the therapeutic mode. Couples should also be queried on their treatment objective: Do they want rebalancing or symptom relief, divorce mediation, relationship enrichment, and so on? It is also helpful to elicit each spouse's explanation for what went wrong with the relationship. Although blame is the common first response, the therapist who probes beyond that level uncovers miscommunications and deep-rooted fears as well as information useful for treatment formulation. Finally, a reasonable degree of concurrence between the couple's goals for therapy and the therapist's goals is necessary. Any discrepancies between goals and expectations should be discussed and negotiated before treatment continues.

## Level of Marital Functioning and Discord

Organization of all the information received to this point into a classificatory system can prove quite useful. Presently there are no agreed-upon marital classification systems correlated with individual psychopathology. Nevertheless, several attempts at classifications of marital relationship have been made. Fisher (1979) has reviewed several classification systems. The one we have found particularly useful was developed by Guerin, Fay, Burden, and Kautto (1987), who classified marital conflict in terms of four types: preclinical or minimal degree, active, severe and chronic, and at the point of termination of the relationship. As a way of organizing data and as a basis for treatment planning, we find such a classification schema particularly valuable.

### Prognostic Factors

Clinicians and researchers have yet to derive the factors needed to predict the outcome of successful marital therapy. It has been much easier to determine which variables are prognostic of poor treatment outcomes. These include a long history of problems and a persistent major symptom; previous treatment based on the individual rather than on the family system; a relatively severe diagnosis; and an external, rather than self-generated, motivation for treatment (Coleman, 1985).

Nevertheless, future success can often be predicted on the basis of past successes (and failures). Therefore, it is useful to know about a couple's and spouses' previous utilization of psychotherapy (individual, family, group, or marital), self-help groups (AA, Alanon, ACOA), and marriage encounter or other enrichment programs. It is also helpful to make an early determination of the spouses' response to external control and correction as well as their level of resistance. For instance, the therapist can assess the spouses' receptivity to interpretations as compared to directives. All of these factors can be useful in making the three major decisions involved in the assessment phase of marital therapy.

## METHODS OF ASSESSMENT

As we have indicated earlier, different marital therapists utilize different approaches to assessment. Some, such as Framo (1981, 1982), rely entirely on clinical interview, whereas others, such as Nichols (1988), rely on clinical interview, observation, enactment, inventories, and questionnaires. Enactment refers to the therapist's directive to the spouses to "show" rather than "talk about" a previous problem or conflict or to a task that a therapist presents to the spouses so as to observe their current interpersonal functioning. In this final section of the chapter we focus on several commonly used assessment instruments.

Marital assessment instruments have been used to enhance the effects of marital therapy. Olson (1987) indicated that he found assessment instruments particularly useful in engaging the "less interested" spouse in marital therapy. He noted that the male is likely to be more skeptical and hesitant about seeking professional marital consultation. Filling out a formal questionnaire or inventory often serves as a convenient "icebreaker" and entree into the therapeutic process. Olson further indicated that men respond very favorably to the computer-generated report following from a particular instrument.

Boen (1987) described a three-step process to integrate marital instruments into the assessment process. First, he meets with the spouses to determine the type of problems they have been experiencing, what they have done to resolve the problems, and what brings them for treatment at this particular time. Next, he selects a marital instrument that he believes will more adequately clarify the couple's problems, illustrate the couple's needs, and give additional insight into the current relationship. He selects an instrument based on several factors: socioeconomic status, the couple's ability to comprehend the results, the spouses' awareness and understanding of each other, and how well they understand the problems they are dealing with. The couple is then asked to complete this instrument after the first session. In the next session Boen discusses with the couple the results of the testing information and provides a personal copy for each spouse. Finally, he, like other therapists who utilize marital assessment instruments, rechecks the couple at a further point in the therapy process to gauge their progress or explore other issues. Following are brief descriptions of 15 commonly-used marital assessment instruments; 14 are self-report scales, and the last is an observation scale rated by the therapist.

### Dyadic Adjustment Scale (DAS)

This 32-item instrument is designed to assess the quality of the relationship as perceived by married or cohabiting couples. It is one of the most widely used self-report questionnaires in both clinical practice and research. The instrument was designed to serve a number of needs, including use as a general measure of overall satisfaction in an intimate relationship. In addition, there are four subscales: dyadic satisfaction, dyadic cohesion, dyadic consensus, and affectional expression. The DAS may be adapted for use in the clinical interview. It can be hand-scored or computer-scored. The computer form generates a brief computer report.

*PRIMARY REFERENCES:* Spanier, G. (1976). Measuring dyadic adjustment: New scales for assessing the quality of marriage and similar dyads. *Journal of Marriage and the Family, 38,* 15–28.

Spanier, G. (1984). *Dyadic adjustment scale: Users manual.* Willowdale, Ontario: Multi-Health Systems.

## Couples Precounseling Inventory (CPI)

The CPI can be used as a discussion tool with the couple regarding finances, childrearing practices, sexual practices, communication, conflict resolution styles, and other areas. The CPI can be computer-scored.

*PRIMARY REFERENCES:* Stuart, R. (1980). *Helping couples change.* New York: Guilford Press.

Stuart, R. (1983, 1987). *Couples' pre-counseling inventory, counselor's guide.* Champaign, IL: Research Press.

## Primary Communication Inventory (PCI)

The PCI is a 25-item instrument designed to assess marital communication. There are two main subscales for this instrument. The first is the individual's perception of his or her communication ability, and the second is the partner's perception of the individual's communication abilities. Specific items address issues such as talking about pleasant/unpleasant events, sulking, voice tone, and facial expressions.

*PRIMARY REFERENCE:* Navran, L. (1967). Communication and adjustment in marriage. *Family Process, 6,* 173–184.

## Waring Intimacy Questionnaire (WIQ)

The WIQ is a 90-item, true/false questionnaire specifically developed to measure the quality of marital intimacy. Because intimacy problems constitute the largest single cluster of problem behaviors for which individuals seek psychotherapy, this instrument is particularly useful. Items on the inventory involve eight subscales: conflict resolution, affection, cohesion, sexuality, identity, compatibility, expressiveness, and autonomy. There is also a scale to measure social desirability.

*PRIMARY REFERENCE:* Waring, E., and Reddon, J. (1983). The measurement of intimacy in marriage: The Waring inventory. *Journal of Clinical Psychology, 39,* 53–57.

## Marital Satisfaction Inventory (MSI)

The MSI is a comprehensive, psychometrically sound self-report and spouse-report instrument containing both global and specific measures of marital interaction. The MSI contains 280 true/false items divided into 11 scales. The scales are conventualization, global distress, affective communication, problem-solving communication, time together, disagreement about finances, sexual satisfaction, role orientation, family history of distress, dissatisfaction with children, and conflict about childrearing. A computerized scoring and test report is also available. The report focuses specifically on identification of areas in which a couple may be satisfied or dissatisfied. It prioritizes those areas and produces a narrative as well as a graphic report and summary of issues to consider in work with couples. This report has been quite helpful in work with couples who are at a loss about where to begin in dealing with their issues. The MSI has been helpful for therapists in formulating differential treatment interventions.

*PRIMARY REFERENCE:* Snyder, E. (1981). *Marital satisfaction inventory (MSI)*. Los Angeles: Western Psychological Services.

**Marital Comparison Level Index (MCLI)**

The MCLI is a 32-item instrument designed to measure an individual's perception of the degree to which his or her marital relationship is living up to his or her expectations. The MCLI is a global assessment of each spouse's complaints about the marriage and is based on the notion that a person complains about some aspect of the marriage only when that aspect fails to meet his or her expectations. Factor analysis found the MCLI to have only one dimension: expectations. Each of the 32 items is scored on a seven-point scale with the midpoint on the scale reflecting the respondent's expectation level. This allows the respondent to indicate the degree to which his or her relationship outcomes fall above or below expectations.

*PRIMARY REFERENCE:* Sabatelli, R. (1984). The marital comparison level index: A measure for assessing outcomes relative to expectations. *Journal of Marriage and the Family, 46,* 651–662.

**Caring Relationship Inventory (CRI)**

The CRI is a commercial 83-item inventory designed to measure seven dimensions of caring or love in the relationship. The inventory measures how each spouse sees the relationship and then compares this response to how each partner sees the ideal relationship. The seven subscales are affection, friendship, heroes, empathy, self-love, received love, and deficiency love. The instrument can be either hand-scored or computer-scored (which generates a computer report).

*PRIMARY REFERENCE:* Shostrom, E. (1975). *Manual, caring relations inventory.* San Diego, CA: Educational and Industrial Testing Service.


## Marital Alternatives Scale (MAS)

The MAS is an 11-item multiple-choice questionnaire that evaluates the likelihood that a couple will divorce or separate. In short, this scale measures the unspoken thought of many marital partners: "Could I do any better if I were not married or if I were married to somebody else?" This scale adds significant information that cannot be assessed in a marital satisfaction survey. The MAS is predictive of marital disruption and it also provides an objective perspective to the dissatisfied spouse on the situation and alternatives.

*PRIMARY REFERENCE:* Udry, J. (1981). Marital alternatives and marital disruption. *Journal of Marriage and the Family, 43,* 889–897.


## Marriage Counseling Report (MCR)

The MCR has been found helpful in assessment of the personality of each spouse within the relationship and in examination of the interaction effects of the spouse's personality. This test is based on the 16 Personality Factors Questionnaire (16 PF). The MCR, which is computer-scored, generates a seven- or eight-page report of each individual's personality with a graphic display and a narrative display. The MCR also contains a report of a couple's 16 PF that is essentially a combination of the two individual profiles.

The most helpful part of the report is called the "marital adjustment prediction," which predicts the couple's potential for adjustment, including anticipated problem areas. The unique aspect of the MCR is a printout on marital relationship issues *and* on the individual personality or psychological issues that may be contributing to the relationship's difficulties. This inventory suggests the converse: how relationship difficulties may be exacerbating the individual's psychological difficulties.

*PRIMARY REFERENCE:* Russell, T., and Madsen, P. (1985). *Marriage counseling report user's guide.* Champaign, IL: Institute for Personality and Ability Testing.


## Myers-Briggs Type Indicator

The Myers-Briggs Type Indicator is probably the most widely used personality and counseling instrument for "normal" populations. First published in 1943, a revised, shortened version in 1983 led to a resurgence of use of this instrument in business and organizational settings as well as among research groups, secondary school and colleges, and couples groups. Jung's theory of personality types underlies the Myers-Briggs Indicator. Jung stressed complementarity in marital relationships and suggested that a person marries another to provide what is lacking in his or her own personality. The Myers-Briggs identifies four separate orientations: extroversion/introversion; sensation/intuition; thought/feeling; and judgment/perception. Insight into the spouse's type is meant to enhance understanding and communications. The test has 126 items and can be either hand-scored or computer scored.

*PRIMARY REFERENCE:* Myers, I. (1977). *The Myers-Briggs type indicator.* Palo Alto, CA: Consulting Psychologists Press.

## PREPARE-ENRICH Inventory

The PREPARE-ENRICH Inventory is part of a comprehensive package of assessment devices designed to meet the needs of professionals engaged in marriage preparation, enrichment, or marital therapy. (PREPARE stands for Premarital, Personal, and Relationship Evaluation; PREPARE-MC stands for Premarital, Personal, and Relationship Evaluation—Marriage with Children; ENRICH stands for Evaluating and Nurturing Relationships Issues, Communication, and Happiness.) These inventories are all based on Olson's circumplex model discussed earlier in this book.

PREPARE and PREPARE-MC can be used preventively with premarital couples so they become aware of potential problem areas in their relationships. ENRICH is designed for couples seeking marital therapy or marriage enrichment. All three inventories contain the following categories or subscales: idealistic distortion, realistic expectations, and marital satisfaction. PREPARE and ENRICH also contain these categories or subscales: personality issues, communications, conflict resolution, financial management, leisure activities, sexual relationships, children and marriage, family and friends, egalitarian rules, and religious orientation.

The PREPARE-ENRICH inventories are 8-page booklets that contain 125 items pertaining to marital issues. The items relate to the individual, the spouse, and the relationship rather than to marriage in general. The inventories are computer-processed and include a 15–20 page computer printout that includes couple feedback forms to facilitate discussion of results with the couple. Also included is a therapist feedback form designed to help the therapist organize results and make choices about issues most in need of discussion.

*PRIMARY REFERENCE:* Olson, D., Fournier, D., and Druckman, J. (1982). *PREPARE-ENRICH: Counselor's manual.* Minneapolis: Prepare-Enrich.

## Family Adaptability and Cohesion Evaluation Scale (FACES-III)

FACES-III is a 20-item instrument designed to measure family cohesion and adaptability. FACES-III, like PREPARE-ENRICH, is based on Olson's circumplex model of marital and family functioning. FACES-III was originally intended for families, but it can also be used with couples simply by changing the wording of some of the items. This instrument is particularly valuable in that it takes only a few minutes for couples to complete, it can be hand-scored, and it has been the subject of a great deal of research.

*PRIMARY REFERENCE:* Olson, D., Portner, J., & Labee, Y. (1985). *FACES-III.* St. Paul: University of Minnesota.

## Family Assessment Device (FAD)

The FAD is a 60-item questionnaire designed to evaluate marital and family functions according to the McMaster's model. The FAD is made up of seven subscales. Six measure the dimensions of the McMaster's model: problem-solving, communications, roles, affective responsiveness, affective involvement, and behavioral control. The seventh subscale measures general functioning.

*PRIMARY REFERENCE:* Epstein, N., Baldwin, L., & Bishop, D. (1983). The McMaster's family assessment device. *Journal of Marital and Family Therapy, 9,* 171–180.

## Self-Report Family Instrument (SFI)

The SFI is a 36-item instrument based on the Beavers-Timberlawn model of family competence and is designed to distinguish levels of competence in marriages and families. The five dimensions of the SFI are family conflict, family communication, family cohesion, directive leadership, and family health.

*PRIMARY REFERENCE:* Beavers, W., Hampson, R., and Hulgus, Y. (1985). Commentary: The Beavers systems approach to family assessment. *Family Process, 24,* 398–405.

## Verbal Problem Checklist (VPC)

The VPC, a therapist-rated instrument, includes 49 categories of verbal behavior, which are rated on a four-point Likert scale. Examples of some of the 49 response categories are overtalk, undertalk, monotone speech, quibbling, dogmatic statements, illogical talks, too much information given, and topic content avoidance. An additional rating of the categories on a 1–3 scale is used to identify the degree to which each category represents a problem area for the couple. Although it is less rigorous and systematic than other observation coding systems used in marital therapy research, the VPC can be used during the session itself or afterward through rating of an audiotape of the session. The VPC can also be used as a serial rating of subsequent sessions.

*PRIMARY REFERENCE:* Thomas, E. (1977). *Marital communication and decision-making.* New York: Free Press.

## CONCLUDING NOTE

This chapter has put forward an approach to marital assessment that is both comprehensive and integrated. Based on the biopsychosocial perspective, this assessment model targets 20 key factors subsumed under four components of marital functioning/dysfunctioning. The chapter has also reviewed 15 commonly available marital assessment instruments useful in the assessment and evaluation process. Because this book proposes an integrative and comprehensive approach to marital therapy, and because assessment is a necessary ingredient in the planning and execution of effective therapeutic processes and outcomes, the contents of this chapter have been based on a careful review of the research literature as well as on clinical practice.

## REFERENCES

Beavers, W. (1981). Indications and contraindications for couples therapy. In M. Goldberg (Ed.), *Marital therapy, the psychiatric clinics of North America.* Philadelphia: Saunders.

Beavers, W. (1985). *Successful marriage: A family systems approach to couples therapy.* New York: Norton.

Beck, D., & Jones, M. (1973). *Progress on family problems.* New York: Service Association of America.

Berman, E., & Leif, H. (1975). Marital therapy from a psychiatric perspective: An overview. *American Journal of Psychiatry, 132,* 583–591.

Beutler, L. (1983). *Eclectic psychotherapy: A systematic approach.* New York: Pergamon Press.

Beutler, L., & Crago, M. (1987). Strategies and techniques of prescriptive psychotherapeutic intervention. In R. Hales & A. Frances (Eds.), *Psychiatric updates: APA annual review* (Vol. 6). Washington, DC: American Psychiatric Press.

Boen, D. (1987). A practitioner looks at assessment in marital counseling. *Journal of Counseling and Development, 65*, 484–486.

Cameron-Bandler, L. (1985). *Solutions: Practical and effective antidotes for sexual and relationship problems.* San Rafael, CA: Future Pace.

Coleman, B. (Ed.). (1985). *Failures in family therapy.* New York: Guilford Press.

Coleman, S. (1985). *Failures in family therapy.* New York: Guilford Press.

Davitz, L., & Davitz, J. (1986). *Living in sync.* New York: Bergh.

Dinkmeyer, D., & Carlson, J. (1986). TIME for a better marriage. *Journal of Psychotherapy and the Family, 2*, 19–28.

Dreikurs, R. (1946). *The challenge of marriage.* New York: Duell, Sloan, and Pearce.

Fish, R., & Fish, L. (1986). Quid pro quo revisited: The basis of marital ʾherapy. *American Journal of Orthopsychiatry, 56*, 371–384.

Fisher, L. (1976). Dimensions of family assessment: A critical review. *Journal of Marriage and Family Counseling, 2*, 367–376.

Fisher, L. (1979). On the classification of families. In J. Howells (Ed.), *Advances in Family Psychiatry* (Vol. 1). New York: International Universities Press.

Folkard, S. (1983). Diurnal variations. In R. Hockey (Ed.), *Stress and fatigue in human performance.* New York: Wiley.

Framo, J. (1981). The integration of marital therapy with family of origin sessions. In A. Gurman and D. Kniskern (Eds.), *Handbook of family therapy.* New York: Brunner/Mazel.

Framo, J. (1982). *Explorations in marital and family therapy.* New York: Springer.

Gibbs, A. (1977). Traditional and companionship variation within high and low satisfied black marriages. *Dissertation Abstracts, 37*, 5830.

Grunebaum, H., & Christ, J. (Eds). (1976). *Contemporary marriage: Structures, dynamics and therapy.* Boston: Little, Brown.

Guerin, P., Fay, L., Burden, S., & Kautto, J. (1987). *The evaluation and treatment of marital conflict: A four stage approach.* New York: Basic Books.

Haley, J. (1963). *Strategies of psychotherapy.* New York: Grune and Stratton.

Laner, M. (1978). Love's labors lost: A theory of marital dissolution. *Family Coordinator, 25*, 175–181.

Levinger, G. (1976). In conclusion: Threads in the fabric. *Journal of Social Issues, 32*, 193–207.

McGoldrick, M., & Gerson, R. (1985). *Genograms in family assessment.* New York: Norton.

Murstein, B., & Christy, P. (1976). Physical attractiveness and marriage adjustment in middle-aged couples. *Journal of Personality and Social Psychology, 34*, 537–542.

Nichols, W. (1988). *Marital therapy: An integrative approach.* New York: Guilford Press.

Olson, D. (1987, October). *Assessment in brief marriage therapy.* Paper presented at the meeting of the American Association of Marriage and Family Therapy, Chicago, IL.

Phillips, E. (1985). *Psychotherapy revisited: New frontiers in research and practice.* Hillsdale, NJ: Lawrence Erlbaum Associates.

Sperry, L. (1984). *The together experience: Getting, growing and staying together in marriage.* San Diego, CA: Beta Books.

Sperry, L. (1989). Assessment in marital therapy: A couples-centered biopsychosocial approach. *Individual Psychology, 45*, 446–451.

Sternberg, R. (1988). *The love triangle.* New York: Basic Books.

Stuart, R. (1980). *Helping couples change: A social learning approach to marital therapy.* New York: Guilford Press.

Thornton, A. (1977). Children and marital stability. *Journal of Marriage and the Family, 39*, 531–540.

# *10*

# *Intervention*

According to Simon, Stierlin, and Wynne (1985), "Strategy is a plan of action, a modus operandi in more or less predictable situations that allows one to make decisions likely to facilitate reaching a specific goal" (p. 338). A marital therapist uses strategy when intervening in a couple's relationship. The therapist needs to know how to make interventions in the here-and-now and in the future that will lead to the desired goal. Interventions are made within the therapy hour and take the form of suggestions for action to be taken before the next meeting. The types of strategies and interventions used by marital therapists are many. This chapter discusses some of the possibilities.

## TREATMENT MODALITIES

There are many different treatment modalities used in marital therapy. According to Nichols (1988), the most common approaches are as follows.

### Conjoint Marital Therapy

According to Berman and Lief (1975), conjoint marital therapy, in which one therapist meets with husband and wife together, is the most frequently used form of marital therapy. This is to be differentiated from co-therapy, in which there are two therapists.

## Couples Groups

Working with several couples at once in a group setting is a popular and, according to outcome research (Gurman & Kniskern, 1978), an effective approach for dealing with marital discord. Kaslow and Lieberman (1981) have presented the rationale, dynamics, and process of using couples group therapy. Many therapists prefer this approach and feel that it is a good use of time for all who are involved. We have found this to be a very effective intervention approach for the right couples at the right stage of treatment.

## Family-of-Origin Intervention

Framo (1983) and Napier (1988) are among the proponents of this technique. It often involves two therapists meeting with clients and the members of their families of origin. This is often an adjunct to marital therapy. Framo has described a pattern in which a therapist meets with the client and his or her nuclear family for 2 hours on a Friday night and then 2 hours on the next Saturday morning as a supplement to marital sessions. This can be a very powerful intervention technique. Skilled marital therapists use it whenever occasions develop in which family members are together, such as at holidays.

## Combining Techniques

All of the previous techniques can be done in conjunction with one another as well as in conjunction with individual therapy. Many therapists routinely use a combination of weekly individual sessions and conjoint sessions. It is often used by therapists with an intrapsychic point of view who are attempting to change characterological structure. The disadvantage of this type of an intervention is financial.

We routinely see couples conjointly and then meet with each individually before beginning marital therapy. The individual session(s) allows us to better understand each person. Sometimes this involves more than one session as histories are often complex.

During individual sessions the therapist is able to prepare the individual to participate effectively in marital therapy. Sometimes individual partners are so dysfunctional that they are unable to be with their partners without hurting and attacking. Sometimes they are confused about whether to continue the relationship and ambivalent about participation in therapy. Sometimes individuals need to work through grief from the ending of an extramarital relationship or loss of a parent. Sometimes there are concerns that do not directly involve the partner.

## ADJUNCTIVE MODALITIES

There are many useful adjunctive modalities. These include various types of skill-training such as relationship enhancement efforts (Dinkmeyer & Carlson, 1984a) and communication facilitation (Gottman, Notarius, & Markman, 1976). Bibliotherapy (Sperry & Carlson, 1990; Dinkmeyer & Carlson, 1989) is also a helpful procedure for learning skills and preventing future problems. Self-help groups such as Alcoholics Anonymous, Alanon, and Adult Children of Alcoholics are all helpful adjuncts, as are sexual therapy and financial counseling.

## GENERAL ELEMENTS OF MARITAL THERAPY

According to Marmor (1975), there are at least seven elements that most schools of psychotherapy share in common.

1. A good patient-therapist relationship
2. Release of emotional tension
3. Cognitive learning
4. Operant reconditioning of the patient toward more adaptive behavior patterns by explicit or implicit approval-disapproval cues and by a corrective emotional relationship with the therapist
5. Suggestion and persuasion
6. Identification with the therapist
7. Repeated reality testing or practicing of new adaptive techniques in the context of implicit or explicit emotional therapeutic support

Marital therapy involves these elements in the context of a dyadic relationship. The particular mix of these therapeutic elements varies with the specific needs of the couple. There is hardly any specific technique utilized in other therapy formats and orientations that could not be adapted in some way for use in marital therapy (Glick, Clarkin, & Kessler, 1988).

## TECHNIQUES

So far in this chapter we have discussed strategies, which can be composed of many techniques or systematic procedures by which a task is accomplished. Techniques are often thought of as moves, prescriptions, or suggestions made by the therapist that require the client to perform a series of actions that yield greater understanding or stimulate change. Techniques may be very complicated or very brief interactions or tactics such as changing the seating order, asking a simple question, or making an empathic or encouraging comment. Sherman and Fredman (1986) have identified eight common variables used in developing techniques.

1. Expansion or reduction of the number of members in the therapeutic system.
2. Variation of the time frame for meeting or tasks.
3. Change in the place in which therapy meeting or tasks occur.
4. Alteration of the activity or introduction of a new one.
5. Engaging of different levels of consciousness and thought processes.
6. Structuring of the patterns of communication.
7. Alteration or reversal of the place or roles of members of the system.
8. Variation of the therapist's mode of interacting with clients.

Many variables and tactics make up techniques, and many techniques are used in a strategy. Many of the decisions are arbitrary and depend upon the therapist, his or her skills, and the current situation. The therapist needs to feel comfortable with the medium and the style of the technique to be used as well as the theoretical rationale for using it. If the therapist is unassertive, for example, prescriptive behavior may be difficult. If the therapist is structured, the use of more ambiguous projective methods may present problems, whereas a passive type of therapist may have difficulty with more action-oriented methods. The techniques must fit the user, just like a shoe must fit the wearer. The personality of the therapist is a critical element (Combs, 1969).

## STRATEGIES

The number of techniques and combination of techniques is unlimited. Nevertheless, techniques and interventions can be grouped according to strategic intent. The following five categories of strategies, identified by Glick, Clarkin, and Kessler (1988) as basic to family therapy, are also basic to marital intervention.

1. Use of adaptive mechanisms to impart new information, advice, suggestions, and so on (the so-called psychoeducational approach).
2. Expansion of individual and couple emotional experience.
3. Explicit development of specific interpersonal skills.
4. Reorganization of the marital structure.
5. Increase in insight and fostering of conflict resolution.

According to Glick, Clarkin, and Kessler (1988), the five basic strategies, as listed, reflect an increasing depth of involvement. The earlier techniques are simpler and less involved and if they work should be used alone. As the marital problems become more complex and complicated and the couple shows resistance to change using simpler techniques, the more involved techniques are probably needed. In practice it is hard to separate these techniques in a clear, pure fashion. At any given session a therapist may be using all five strategies.

## TECHNIQUES FOR PSYCHOEDUCATION

Every couple has some health and some strengths. These should be recognized and actively encouraged. The therapist uses many skills and techniques to support these coping mechanisms. Active listening and concern, positive feedback about healthy behaviors, education about poor procedures, and advice are all helpful to couples in distress. The therapist is constantly modeling the role of teacher, either directly or indirectly. The therapist models the mood, tempo, and levels of interpersonal acceptance. Much of what the therapist teaches is done implicitly. The therapist shows respect by listening carefully to what each partner says. This in turn shows each member how to respect his or her partner. As the therapist listens and reflects what each partner is saying, the couple begins this important practice. The therapist also models an encouraging attitude that is contagious.

There has been a growing emphasis on prevention and skill-training. These approaches provide information that all couples need in order to cope and perform effectively in marriage (Sperry & Carlson, 1990). This approach is most obvious in the skill-training or marriage enrichment programs (Dinkmeyer & Carlson, 1984a; Guerney, 1977; L'Abate, 1981; Miller, Nunnally, & Wackman, 1975). Information can be communicated through written material, lectures, discussion in groups, and workshops. This approach also involves bibliotherapy and the use of directed study. Many therapists give couples homework assignments. In our practice we routinely provide spouses with the book *Time for a Better Marriage* (Dinkmeyer & Carlson, 1984a) or *Taking Time for Love* (Dinkmeyer & Carlson, 1989) and instruct them to read a chapter each week. When specific problems are identified, we give a directed reading assignment. We also use audiotapes in conjunction with the reading assignments. Audiotapes may involve learning relaxation strategies, mental imagery, self-encouragement, and other skills such as are available on the audiotape *Time to Relax and Imagine* (Dinkmeyer & Carlson, 1984b).

Many therapists find it helpful to involve couples in ongoing marriage enrichment groups along with therapy to help ensure that the couple has high-level skills. Marriage enrichment is a relatively new area. Many credit its beginnings to the early work of Dreikurs in the 1930s in Europe in which study groups were set up and focused on the book *The Challenge of Marriage* (Dreikurs, 1946). The modern marriage encounter movement began in 1961 in Italy with Father Gabriel Calbo. Currently the Association of Couples for Marriage Enrichment is coordinating and facilitating the various skill-training programs in this important area.

# TECHNIQUES TO EXPAND EMOTIONAL EXPERIENCE

Psychotherapy has many techniques to help individuals and couples expand their emotional experience. These techniques focus on here-and-now experience in the sessions themselves. The techniques are designed to help members become aware of their feelings and how to express them effectively. These procedures also help couples to slow down and to learn important relaxation skills. Furthermore, they help each person to live in the present. These techniques include the following.

## Gestalt Techniques

In these procedures the therapist stresses that the only time is the present; the past is not rehashed or considered. Each individual is responsible for his or her own behavior and symptoms, and conflicts are seen as here-and-now expressions of unfinished situations of childhood that can be finished in treatment. Gestalt therapists pay significant attention to nonverbal communication and behavior (Lawe & Smith, 1986).

## Role Playing

Much of marriage therapy involves role playing in which couples work through current problems and develop new patterns of response. In role playing or reverse role playing, each partner plays himself or his or her partner in a real or hypothetical situation. Often the roles are switched back and forth in a role reversal fashion, and the partners are asked to comment on observations, feelings, and behavior that has been elicited. Role reversal is useful in the development of empathy.

### Weekend Couples Retreats

Marriage encounter and other marriage enrichment groups are frequently scheduled. These intensive workshops often help couples to cathart and to become more aware of how they feel about their partners. These self-help groups are often led by clergy or paraprofessionals.

### Guided Fantasy

Through the use of guided fantasy, therapists can help couples become aware of many of their fantasies, thoughts, and goals regarding marriage, themselves, and their partners. It is through guided fantasy that couples can learn to develop and become aware of how to solve problems effectively. It is important to debrief or process guided fantasies. This helps individuals to become aware of their inner thoughts and for each partner to learn to be more empathic.

### Sculpting

The master therapist Virginia Satir (1982) frequently used sculpting with couples. In this procedure she created a physical representation of the relationship the couple was having by arranging the spouses' bodies in space. Both the content of the sculpture and the way the sculpture used mass and form were examined. This is an excellent procedure to use with nonverbal couples.

### Mourning and Grief

The procedures used in this process are often borrowed from gestalt therapy. The technique involves helping partners elicit long-hidden feelings, expectations, and emotion involving a loss. The loss can be of a parent, child, or even the loss of youth. Many partners in marriage feel confined and tend to lose their identities. This can evoke meaningful content for verbal therapeutic interventions.

## TECHNIQUES TO DEVELOP INTERPERSONAL SKILLS

Many couples do not utilize basic skills of communication, encouragement, choice making, and problem solving because they have never learned such skills. Furthermore, our society has very few good models of marriage. What models of effective marriage we do have are based upon traditional, rather than companionate, approaches.

As was mentioned previously, the therapist can help couples learn to express their thoughts and feelings more clearly to one another. The therapist promotes open and clear communication, emotional empathy, and positive rapport between partners. It is important to realize that these communication difficulties are at the heart of most dysfunctional relationships. Often couples will report, "We don't communicate." This is really a mistake, however. Communication occurs all the time in marriage. Every action or inaction communicates a message. Unfortunately, in troubled marriages what is communicated is generally negative feedback. Also, how a spouse spends his or her time every day communicates what he or she thinks is really important. It is important that the therapist interpret distorted or hidden messages so that the couple can learn to express them more congruently.

Often in marital relationships, one partner talks the majority of the time and the other lets him or her do so. It is important to balance communication time. The therapist does not allow either partner to monopolize a session or to speak for the other. The therapist works at teaching the more verbal partner to listen and the less verbal partner to speak.

Another important communication skill is specific, direct, and clear speaking. Vague, generalized speaking makes it impossible to resolve conflict and to achieve understanding. The therapist looks for any dysfunctional patterns in communication, points them out, and helps the couple see how these patterns and the resultant attitudes cause problems. This allows couples to open up blocked channels of communication and repressed feelings.

It is important to teach an effective problem-solving model. Very few couples who enter treatment have a clear model for handling their problems; yet problems occur throughout a marriage. We often stress a four-step method developed by Dreikurs (1946) that involves mutual respect, pinpointing of the real issue, identification of agreements, and mutual participation in a decision. This process works best when couples set aside time on a regular basis to resolve marital problems.

The skills of communication, encouragement, choice making, and conflict resolution are taught, as was indicated, in marriage enrichment/education programs. These programs also apply the skills to common areas of concern, such as finance, in-laws, alcohol and drugs, recreation, friends, religion, sex, and childrearing and parenting. It is often necessary to supplement therapy to help partners deal with overwhelming concerns in any of these areas.

# TECHNIQUES FOR REORGANIZING THE MARITAL STRUCTURE

In each marriage and family system, there is a balance that keeps relationships the same. This balance is maintained by structured behavioral sequences that contribute to the maintenance of symptomatic problems and behaviors. Glick, Clarkin, and Kessler (1988) have provided a graphic representation of some of the common family coalitions. (See Figure 10.1.)

In their representations, it becomes clear how relationships change as communication patterns change. This figure represents a typical four-member fam-

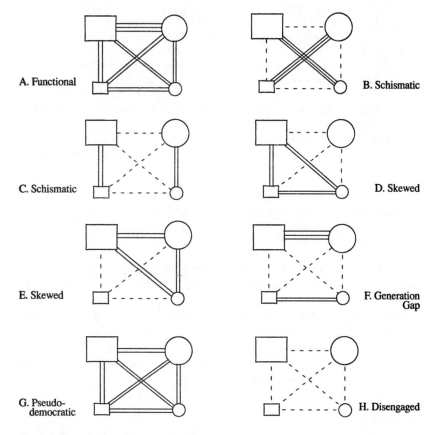

**Figure 10.1   Types of Family Coalitions**

*Source:* Glick, Clark, and Kessler (1988), p. 198.

ily unit. Rectangles represent the males and circles the females. The larger symbols stand for the spouse/parent, and the smaller symbols represent the offspring or siblings. The solid straight lines joining these symbols represent positive communication. Broken lines represent the relative absence or negative quality of interactions.

> In Example A, the *functional family*, the marital coalition is the strongest dyad in the family. The generation boundary is intact and all other channels are open and about equal to one another in importance. In contrast to this are the various types of dysfunctional families that follow.
> In Example B, the marital coalition is relatively weak or absent and instead there are strong alliances across the generations and sexes—between father and daughter, and mother and son—with a relative absence of other effective channels.
> In Example C, there are cross-generational alliances between same sex parent and child.
> Examples D and E depict *skewed* families in which one family member is relatively isolated from the other three who form a fairly cohesive unit.
> Example F represents the *generation gap family* in which the marital unit and the offspring each form a fairly cohesive duo with little or no interaction across the generational lines.
> Example G represents the *pseudo-democratic family* in which all channels seem to be of about equal importance with the marital coalition and the parental role not being particularly well-differentiated.
> Example H, the *disengaged family*, offers a representation of an extreme case in which each family member is pretty much cut off from every other member and in which one would expect very little sense of positive interaction, feeling, or belonging to a family unit. (Glick, Clarkin, & Kessler, 1988, pp. 199–200)

These representations are highly simplified and represent only a four-member family. Infinite variations could be added to include more children, step-families, and so forth. These representations enable a therapist to more clearly conceptualize just what is occurring in a particular family and how it affects the marital relationship. The goal is to move toward Example A, in which the marital coalition is the strongest.

The following are techniques that enable the marriage therapist to interrupt and change structured marital/family behaviors.

## Reframing

Everything can be something else. Each individual sees his or her reality from a unique perspective. When two people come together in a marital situation with both perceiving reality from their own frames of reference, difficulties often occur. Sometimes one partner has an unhealthy view; sometimes both have an unhealthy view. It is helpful when the therapist can counter with or enter into the relationship another competing view. This process is reframing. Reframing can be sudden, dramatic, and even humorous.

### Enactment

In this strategy, the couple is asked to enact or play out an actual interpersonal problem. Enactment allows the therapist to observe what is actually going on. A healthier solution can be interjected in a more meaningful fashion.

### Focusing

Many couples are overwhelmed with the question of just which problem is important. Recent developments in brief therapy have encouraged the therapist to help the couple find one focus to work on. The therapist selects the focus and then develops a theme for the conjoint marital session. It is important for the therapist to organize the session and have a clear idea of what needs to occur and just what is needed to reach that goal. Once the therapist understands this, he or she can use many techniques.

### Structural Techniques

According to Minuchin and Fishman (1981), boundary marking can be used to focus on and change the distance between partners. In this procedure, a therapist stops one partner from speaking for the other and requires each person to speak only for himself or herself. Boundaries can be made by verbal reconstructions, tasks, spatial rearrangements within the session, nonverbal gestures, and eye contact. Unbalancing is used in order to change the hierarchical relationship between the couple. The therapist can unbalance by affiliating closer with one partner than the other, ignoring one member, or taking sides. Another structural procedure is complementarity. This involves using mainly cognitive interventions to help each partner perceive and understand the workings of the marital relationship. Partners usually see themselves acting and reacting to one another, rather than seeing the larger picture of the marital system.

### Paradoxical Techniques

Paradoxical procedures are used with the couple to overtly strengthen or promote the homeostatic defenses while not arousing resistance. Paradoxical prescriptions are also called therapeutic double binds. In this procedure the therapist orders a partner to intensify the occurrence of a symptom. Then the symptom begins to lose its mystery and power. Whereas the symptom previously seemed out of control, it now seems to come under the therapist's control. For example, a marital couple that has engaged in nonproductive arguing now finds that the therapist has asked them to continue fighting and even to increase it. The couple is told to fight for one hour each evening. The injunction jars the continuing process, and both partners may rebel against the order. It is important for the therapist to follow through to make sure that the directions have been followed in the intended manner. This is done by asking the couple each week if it has completed homework (Mozdzierz, Macchitelli, & Lisiecki, 1976).

## TECHNIQUES FOR INSIGHT AND CONFLICT RESOLUTION

The goal of these techniques is to further the emotional-cognitive insights of the partner(s) in order to change behavior and/or character. The therapist uses techniques such as clarification, confrontation, and interpretation. This is done either with an individual partner or the marital dyad. *Clarification* involves asking the partner to clarify his or her understanding/emotional reaction to present and past events. *Confrontation* is the pointing out of contradictory aspects of the individual's behavior, often between verbal and nonverbal behavior. *Interpretation* occurs when the therapist links present contradictory behavior with past behavior. The therapist needs to clearly point out how current behavior is affected by past experiences. Interpretations can be made in the here-and-now interaction between partners or between therapist and each individual, or interpretations can link present behavior to past history. Dicks (1967), more than any other author, has spelled out the use of such dynamic techniques.

## DIFFERENTIAL USE OF THE FIVE BASIC STRATEGIES

Therapists are always interested in when to use various strategies and techniques. This is an unresolved area not only in the field of marital therapy, but in all psychotherapy. We are in the process of developing clear clinical research that will help practitioners to understand when certain techniques are indicated and when not.

Glick, Clarkin, and Kessler (1988) have maintained that the work of Beutler (1983) on individual therapy offers principles that can be applied to the marital/family treatment format.

> If the problem is a "neurotic-like" disturbance, therapy aimed at conflict-resolution is needed, whereas problems determined by habit formation and disorders can be approached by narrow-band behavioral approaches. Second, one must consider characteristic defensive style. Defenses that lead to impulsive, emotional activity need externally-focused treatment. On the other hand, those with ruminative anxiety magnifiers need treatment focused on cognitive control and refinement of internal cognitive structures. Finally, those with little emotional awareness need assistance with emotional arousal and awareness in the treatment. Third, one must consider the relative level of the patient; that is, the degree to which the patient is open to external influence or those who seek their own personal control and tend to reject assistance from others. The former will take a directive therapeutic approach, while the latter need a relatively non-directive therapist. (p. 208)

## CONCLUDING NOTE

This chapter has highlighted the various treatment modalities available to the marital therapist. The many techniques and strategies available to the therapist have been set forth. The differential use of these procedures has been discussed, and although marital therapy is in the process of becoming more scientific, much of it is an art. It is hoped that with continued exposure to the various strategies and couples, the marital therapist will develop the intuition necessary to know when strategies can be used effectively.

## REFERENCES

Berman, E. M., & Lief, H. I. (1975). Marital therapy from a psychiatric perspective. *American Journal of Psychiatry, 132*, 583–592.

Beutler, L. E. (1983). *Eclectic psychotherapy: A systematic approach.* New York: Pergamon Press.

Combs, A. W. (1969). *The Florida studies in the helping professions.* Gainesville: University of Florida Press.

Dicks, H. V. (1967). *Marital tensions.* London: Routledge and Kegan Paul.

Dinkmeyer, D., & Carlson, J. (1984a). *Time for a better marriage.* Circle Pines, MN: American Guidance Service.

Dinkmeyer, D., & Carlson, J. (1984b). *Time to relax and imagine.* Circle Pines, MN: American Guidance Service.

Dinkmeyer, D., & Carlson, J. (1989). *Taking time for love.* New York: Prentice-Hall.

Dreikurs, R. (1946). *The challenge of marriage.* New York: Hawthorn.

Framo, J. L. (1983). *Workshop on couples therapy.* Bay City: Michigan Psychological Association.

Glick, I. D., Clarkin, J. F., & Kessler, D. R. (1988). *Marital and family therapy* (3d ed.). Orlando, FL: Grune & Stratton.

Gottman, J., Notarius, C. I., and Markman, H. (1976). *A couple's guide to communication.* Champaign, IL: Research Press.

Guerney, B. G., Jr. (1977). *Relationship enhancement.* San Francisco: Jossey-Bass.

Gurman, A. S., & Kniskern, D. P. (1978). Research on marital and family therapy: Progress, perspective, and prospect. In S. L. Garfield & A. E. Bergin (Eds.), *Handbook of psychotherapy and behavior change: An empirical analysis.* New York: Wiley.

Kaslow, F. W., and Lieberman, E. J. (1981). Couples's group therapy: Rationale, dynamics, and process. In G. P. Sholevar (Ed.), *The handbook of marriage and marital therapy.* New York: Medical and Scientific Press.

L'Abate, L. (1981). Skill training programs for couples and families. In A. S. Gurman & D. P. Kniskern (Eds.), *Handbook of family therapy.* New York: Brunner/ Mazel.

Lawe, C. F., & Smith, E. W. L. (1986). Gestalt processes and family therapy. *Individual Psychology, 42*(4), 537–544.

Marmor, J. (1975, November 5). Marmor lecture. *Psychiatric News,* 1–15.

Miller, S., Nunnally, E. W., and Wackman, D. B. (1975). *Alive and aware: Improving communication in relationships.* Minneapolis: Interpersonal Communications Program.

Minuchin, S., & Fishman, H. C. (1981). *Family therapy techniques.* Cambridge, MA: Harvard University Press.

Mozdzierz, G., Macchitelli, F., & Lisiecki, J. (1976). The paradox in psychotherapy: An Adlerian perspective. *Journal of Individual Psychology, 32*(2), 169–184.

Napier, A. Y. (1988). *The fragile bond: In search of an equal, intimate, and enduring marriage.* New York: Harper & Row.

Nichols, W. C. (1988). *Marital therapy: An integrative approach.* New York: Guilford Press.

Satir, V. (1982). *Conjoint family therapy.* Palo Alto, CA: Science & Behavior Books.

Sherman, R., and Fredman, N. (1986). *Handbook of structured techniques in marriage and family therapy.* New York: Brunner/Mazel.

Simon, F. B., Stierlin, H., & Wynne, L. C. (1985). *The language of family therapy: A systemic vocabulary and source book.* New York: Family Process Press.

Sperry, L., & Carlson, J. (1990). Enhancing brief marital therapy with psychoeducational interventions. *Journal of Couples Therapy, 1,* 1, 57–69.

# 11

# *Common Problems and Issues in Marriage*

**M** arriage therapists are confronted with many common problems and issues. In this chapter, we present some of the common and perhaps most challenging areas: sexual problems; separation, divorce, and remarriage; nontraditional relationships; aging; alcohol and other substance abuse; and spouse abuse.

## SEXUAL PROBLEMS

Marital and sexual problems are interrelated. Researchers have estimated that as many as 75 to 80% of all couples seeking marital therapy have sexual difficulties (Greene, 1980; Sager, 1974) and that approximately 80% of the couples who are seen in sex therapy have significant marital problems (Heiman, LoPiccolo, & LoPiccolo, 1981). Most marriages will experience a sexual problem at some point. According to Masters and Johnson (1966), sexual dysfunction is usually the primary or core issue rather than a symptom of a deeper psychological or relational problem.

Due to the changes, however, in the purposes of sexual activity, many relational problems have occurred. Sex is often viewed as recreation rather than as marital obligation or as a procreative function. It has long been known that sexual activity is mixed with a variety of motives, such as power, hostility, dependence, and submission. This coupled with the changed attitude toward female sexuality has led to a change in the sexual relationship and demands between husband and wife. Historically, sexual functioning was largely done for the male's pleasure, whereas now women are increasingly expecting not only to receive pleasure but to achieve orgasm. Women participate in sexual activity in a more assertive way and have legitimatized sexual interest. This change in women to a more assertive sexual role has disturbed many men and has been a source of increased dysfunction. Men at times feel that they have failed if their partners have not reached orgasm (Glick, Clarkin, & Kessler, 1987).

Although sexual dysfunction and marital distress can operate independently of each other, they often do not. Therapists need to have good skills in assessment in order to determine which problems are primary and at what point to make an intervention. A thorough sexual history is often needed in order to determine which problems are primary. Exploration of a sexual complaint and the joint sexual history of the couple may or may not lead to the clinical decision that a complete sexual history for each spouse is necessary. The amount of information needed in order to determine the nature and extent of the dysfunction and the kind of treatment required is whatever information the clinician needs.

## Brief Sexual Therapy

Sexual problems can be divided into two categories: primary sexual problems, which are those that arise from sex-related stimuli and occur only in sexual situations; and secondary sexual problems, which are manifestations of a larger personal or relationship dissatisfaction. Classification of cases as secondary or primary helps to determine the appropriate counseling strategy. Primary problems usually respond well to brief therapy, whereas secondary problems require more in-depth, intensive therapy. The model that we endorse is the P-LI-SS-IT approach (Annon, 1974). It has four levels of approach with each letter or pair of letters designating a suggested method for handling the presenting sexual concern. The four levels are permission, limited information, specific suggestions, and intensive therapy.

### Permission

The first level, P, is the initial stage of treatment. Sometimes all that people want to know is whether they are normal, OK, not perverted, deviated, or abnormal. Once they find this out from someone with a professional background or someone who is in a position of authority, often the problems just disappear. One example of a presenting concern is the person who dreams of having sex with someone of the same sex. This can be dealt with very simply by saying, "Many, many, many people have sexual dreams with people of the same sex, opposite sex, groups, people of different races, and it's perfectly normal. The average person has an average of four or more sexual fantasies each day." Another concern may be when spouses worry about the fact that they are having sex only one time per month. Or another may be, "I can only come when he touches me with his tongue." Or another, "I get an erection when my baby daughter bounces on my lap; am I some kind of a pervert? Will I try anything with her?" These are all perfectly normal sexual concerns that normal people have. A number of popular books such as *The Joy of Sex* (Comfort, 1988) and *Super Marital Sex* (Pearsall, 1987) give people permission to operate in new ways.

## Limited Information

The second level of treatment involves giving the client specific factual information that is directly relevant to his or her sexual concern. This may result in the client's continuing to do what he or she was doing, or it may result in something different. Often the way to approach this is by providing books or videotapes. Questions can be as simple as, "Can germs be transmitted through oral-genital contact?" To this we suggest you respond with, "Yes, there are many, many germs in the mouth." Another concern may be, "I have small breasts, and I want to have plastic surgery so that I can have better orgasms." Another came from a gentleman we saw who wanted to have circumcision. He had an uncircumcised penis and was having trouble with premature ejaculation and thought that if he had his penis circumcised, this problem would be solved.

Further information can be very helpful in dispelling many of the sexual myths. Some of the common myths are as follows:

"It's coitus that counts. That's the normal or right way."
"The search for simultaneous orgasm is worthwhile; the couple that comes together stays together."
"Males need erections to make love."
"Sex must be spontaneous."
"Males are always ready. Females have to be made ready."
"All sexual problems are resolvable."
"Women don't get turned on by fantasies."

## Specific Suggestions

In order to practice the third level of treatment, specific suggestions, the therapist must first obtain specific information, which usually includes a thorough sexual problem history. Guidelines for taking a sexual problem history are as follows:

1. Description of current problem
2. Onset and course of problem

      a. Onset (gradual or sudden, precipitating events, consequences)
      b. Course (changes over time: increase, decrease, or fluctuation in severity, frequency, intensity; functional relationships with other variables)
  3. Client's concept of cause and continuation of the problem
  4. Past treatment and outcome
      a. Medical evaluation (specialty, date, form of treatment, results, current medication for any reason)
      b. Other professional help (specialty, date, form of treatment, results)
      c. Self-treatment (type and results)
  5. Current expectations and goals of treatment (concrete and general)

The main types of sexual problems that lend themselves to treatment fall into inhibited sexual desire, inhibited sexual excitement, inhibited female orgasm, inhibited male orgasm, premature ejaculation, functional dyspareunia, and functional vaginismus. Suggestions can be made to the male, the female, or the couple together.

*Intensive Therapy*

The fourth stage is used only when the others do not work. Often sexual problems, as we have indicated, have to do with ignorance of sexual anatomy and physiology, negative attitudes, self-defeating behaviors, or even the use of medication. Sometimes these problems are a symptom of a mental disorder. We will not describe or attempt to outline our approach to intensive therapy with sexual problems. Readers may want to read a detailed description of other approaches to intensive treatment and may find the following references helpful.

    Annon, J. S. (1975). *The behavioral treatment of sexual problems: Volume 2. Intensive therapy.* Honolulu, HI: Enabling Systems.

    Kaplan, H. S. (1974). *The new sex therapy: Active treatment of sexual dysfunction.* New York: Brunner/Mazel.

    Kaplan, H. S. (1979). *The new sex therapy: Volume II. Disorders of sexual desire.* New York: Brunner/Mazel.

    Weeks, G., and Hof, L. (1987). *Integrating sex and marital therapy: A clinical guide.* New York: Brunner/Mazel.

# SEPARATION, DIVORCE, AND REMARRIAGE

## Separation

Maintaining a lasting relationship is often more difficult than forming a new one. This is often a very insightful statement to pass on to couples. For this reason, therapists can often err in an attempt to hold the marriage together rather than breaking it up. It is important to understand just what your position is on marriage. Ours is very pro-marriage.

## Preseparation Agreements

It is important, however, to be realistic. Some people hold onto relationships that are not good for them in order to avoid change. Nevertheless, not every relationship can be improved, and some relationships are just not healthy for any of the participants. It is often important for husbands and wives to learn to change what can be changed and to accept what cannot be changed. Sometimes a separation can be helpful in allowing the spouses to learn more about themselves and what they really want in life. In order to make the transition time as smooth as possible, the therapist is wise to clarify and structure the separation beforehand. The following are areas that often need to be clarified and that require agreement between the spouses:

1. The purpose of the separation (Is it to get away in order to think clearly? Is it to see whether or not the spouses can live apart? Is it a time to work on individual issues?)
2. The time limit on the separation
3. Discretion in not injuring the reputation of the other by imprudent talk with relatives, friends, or others in the community; when necessary, discussion of personal matters away from the relationship
4. What to tell others about what is going on; confidentiality
5. No legal action before the separation is ended unless the action is mutually agreed upon
6. Convenient, regular, and arranged access by the noncustodial parent to the children; no negative use of the children
7. No one-sided action, such as withdrawal of savings, application for loans, sale of belongings, relocation, without consultation with the partner
8. Meetings with friends; dates
9. No changes, such as filing for divorce or taking or leaving a lover, without full discussion with a counselor
10. No sabotage of the other partner's care and discipline of the children
11. Nature of counseling sessions—individual or conjoint
12. How and when the spouses will see/date each other as well as participate (or not) in joint social functions
13. Other specific arrangements, such as money, visitation at home, laundering, meals, cars

*Talking to Children*

If children are involved, no matter what their ages, the reasons for separation and divorce should be openly and honestly discussed in a way that the children are able to understand given their age levels. Parents need to make clear that the separation and divorce are taking place because they cannot get along with each other, not because of any primary problems with the children. The children should be aware that both parents are still interested in them and love them, provided that this is true. The 11-item outline that follows indicates how to talk to children in these situations (Glick, Clarkin, & Kessler, 1987); marital therapists may want to have such an outline on hand, as separating and divorcing couples are often wondering what and how to tell the children.

(1) We are getting a divorce and explain.
(2) You did not cause it.
(3) You could not have prevented it.
(4) I am still your Mommy. I am still your Daddy.
(5) We both still love you. (This cannot be emphasized enough.)
(6) We always will.
(7) You do not have to choose between us. (Explain specifically what the living arrangements will be to the best of your ability.)
(8) People should be able to be fairly happy in marriage. If we had stayed together, you would have had to look at a bad marriage still longer and your view might have been set against marriage as having any possibility for happiness.
(9) We do not understand anything about the reasons for the divorce ourselves, but as we find out more, we will try to explain more to you. What do you think the reasons were?
(10) As time goes on, Mom and Dad may need to talk more about the divorce and you might need to talk about it too. Anytime you have any questions or feelings you want to talk about, we will always be ready to listen. Just do not make it the main topic of conversation when we have company.
(11) It is OK to tell your friends. It is not a secret. (p. 289)

Wallerstein and her associates (Wallerstein & Kelly, 1980; Wallerstein & Blakeslee, 1989) have done significant research on the effects of divorce on children. They found that the most important element seemed to be what happened after couples divorce and how the children were then treated. Effective parenting is important after divorce, as is a good relationship with the ex-spouse and an effective relationship with the next mate. If a healthier relationship is established in the next marriage, this can minimize the negative impact of the divorce on the children.

*The Postdivorce Crisis.* Family conflicts often escalate in the year following divorce, and the parenting skills of the ex-spouses decrease as parents become inconsistent, grow less affectionate, and exert less control over the children. Statistically, the risk of delinquency is much greater if the parents separated or divorced than if the parent died. Parental quarreling and mutual denigration can lead to the child's questioning of a previous positive evaluation of the parents. Criticism of the absent father by the mother can lead to disruption of sex-typing for boys and disruption of heterosexual relationships in adolescent girls. Custodial mothers are likely to develop a mutually coercive interaction with the children, especially the son. As the parents begin to date, the children, particularly preadolescents and adolescents, become aware of their parents as sex objects, and some develop precocious sexual behavior. The fact of divorce does not lead to any pathological consequences; what happens next may. Divorce can be a positive solution to a very destructive family situation.

It was often thought that boys suffered more as a result of divorce. According to Wallerstein and Blakeslee (1989), however, girls suffered, but there appeared to be a "sleeper" effect. Wallerstein and Blakeslee's studies strongly indicated that girls experienced the serious effects of divorce at the time they were entering young adulthood. The authors also found that other girls tended to become overburdened in taking on responsibility to make sure that their parents were OK.

## Divorce

### Divorce Therapy

Divorce therapy is a time-limited, usually 6–15 session intervention with the child and one or both parents in which the goal is to provide advice, information, and counseling about the common alternatives, problems, and emotional upsets involved in the divorce process. Sometimes it is not possible to bring together both parents and the children; in this case divorce therapy involves just one parent and the children. Divorce therapy attempts to aid families in mastering this crisis situation by investigating the normal phases of a separation process. Divorce therapy focuses particularly on the well-being of the children and attempts to find acceptable, fair, and functional solutions for all the family members to the problems posed by divorce. The problems in divorce are similar to those observed in the separation process in general and are analogous to the processes of individuation and mourning. The specific phases of divorce and separation are as follows.

*Disillusionment.* The initial phase is one of disillusionment and increasing feelings of dissatisfaction. In this phase the focus of attention is on the negative aspects of the relationship, and spouses tend to be overly critical of each other.

If the partners are able to express their disappointments and are willing to share the responsibility for changing the situation, an improvement of the relationship is possible. If this does not succeed, a specific type of family pathology—relational stagnation—is likely to develop, and the relationship increasingly erodes. This state of affairs can last for years because a vague, diffuse hope that "things might get better" maintains the status quo. Fear of separation and fear of being alone prove to be stronger than the realization that the present situation is unsatisfactory or even hopeless. The desire not to hurt anyone as well as consideration for the children's well-being can also lead to the denial of the status of the relationship.

*Distance.* This phase is usually followed by increased emotional distance, indifference, and finally the physical and spatial separation of the couple. At this point, the situation can no longer be denied, and the separation now has to be worked out emotionally. This process corresponds to a large extent to what Kübler-Ross (1969) has described as the stages of mourning: denial and anger, attempt to change the situation through action or compromise, depression, and final acceptance of loss. Once this process of mourning is complete, a second adolescence, an altered identity as it were, may develop.

At present there seems to be no consensus as to the best method for how to deal with problems in divorce. It is essential, however, that the therapist be familiar with the stages of separation and divorce and the specific emotional problems related to them (Kaslow & Schwartz, 1987).

In summary, divorce therapy is a process whereby the therapist helps those in the decision-making phase of divorce to assess their needs, strengths, and shortcomings and thus facilitates their arriving at a satisfactory decision to stay married or to divorce. The therapist further helps couples and families that are facing divorce in the process of restructuring their individual lives, present and future relationships, problems with their children, financial difficulties, and general adjustment to singlehood.

### Divorce Mediation

Divorce mediation is the process by which a couple meets together with a trained mental health professional or an attorney educated in mediation and the psychology of conflict resolution. The differences in issues for the couple are mediated in a task-oriented manner until a settlement is reached. In this process each person assumes responsibility for his or her actions. Respect for each other's concerns is expressed, and the integrity of the family unit is maintained. Although the husband and wife separate and obtain a divorce, the family continues and the agreement is discussed in terms of the relationships among mother, father, and children. An advisory attorney rewrites the mediated settlement in legal terms and relates impartially to the family as the client, "not to two parties in conflict." The settlement task for mediation includes division of marital property, possible spousal maintenance of rehabilitative alimony, required child support, shared parenting responsibilities, and custodial arrangements for the children (Folberg & Milne, 1988; Kaslow & Schwartz, 1987; Erickson & McKnight-Erickson, 1988).

In this type of intervention, the husband and wife come together with a mediator rather than an attorney to work out a solution to their marriage. In this situation there are no winners or losers. In divorce, once an attorney is hired, it becomes an adversarial system in which the participants need to do battle with one another. Lawyers are subject to malpractice if they do not get the best possible deals for their clients. Most mediators view divorce differently and really work toward a solution that is best for all parties. The mediator works hard to teach people how to cooperate. A communication process is used to resolve practical and emotional issues of divorce in a mutually cooperative manner. Given the two parties' different values, different abilities, and limited resources to face the future, mediation provides a participatory process for them to achieve a successful termination of a partnership that has created children, shared income, and accumulated assets. The goal is for each of them to receive the best settlement possible that will satisfy to the greatest extent possible their respective needs and interests now and in the future. The four areas that a mediator tries to influence in creating a cooperative settlement outcome are communication, attitudes, negotiating methods, and outcome goals (Erickson & McKnight-Erickson, 1988).

Coogler (1978) proposed that six conditions must be present for true conflict resolution to occur.

1. The physical well-being of each party involved is maintained during negotiations and in the resolution reached.
2. Each party maintains his or her feelings of self-worth during the negotiating process and in the resolution itself.
3. All involved parties are respected and tolerated as persons but with the understanding that this need not imply approval of others' morals or values.
4. All relevant facts, available options, and technical information are considered and used in reaching any solutions.
5. The consequences of each available option are considered by all parties before any resolution is agreed upon.
6. The resolution that is reached is agreed to by all parties even though other choices were available.

At the very least, the process consists of systematically isolating points of agreement and disagreement, developing options, and considering accommodations. Even if all the elements of the dispute cannot be resolved, the conflict may be reduced to a much more manageable level.

## Remarriage

A remarried family is a blended or reconstituted family or a stepfamily that is formed by the marriage or living together of two adults, one or both widowed or divorced, with their custodial or visiting children. Remarried, also called step- or reconstituted families, must be recognized as a viable form of a new commonplace American family. Acceptance of this reality is a necessary orientation for working with remarried families. These families have another set of problems, potentials, and options with which they may need professional help. There is very little history for how to live in these new family units, and without tradition there are many problems that occur. This type of living style, however new, is here to stay, and therapists must know how to deal with it. The special concerns of these families are the roles of stepparents vis-à-vis the children and vice versa. Relationships with the former spouse, financial arrangements, child custody, and visitation are issues that are often determined by the courts.

Psychoeducation is often a preferred method of intervention at this level. *Strengthening Stepfamilies* (Albert & Einstein, 1986) and *New Beginnings* (Dinkmeyer, McKay, & McKay, 1987) are complete educational programs that help people become aware of the special problems and skills needed to live in blended family units. Many therapists use these programs on an individual basis as well as offering them in the community as a preventive intervention. The major goals for work with this group are as follows:

1. Ensure that children have access and ongoing relationships rather than mere visitations with both their parents and their families in order to define their own identities and identifications.
2. Parents and children remain emotionally attached and responsible to each other.
3. Guilt and anger are reduced for children and parents.
4. A noncustodial parent's participation is increased.
5. Pains are taken by bioparents not to stimulate loyalty conflicts in the children.
6. Children can gain by experiencing two father and mother images and two different family cultures.

There are other goals as well. The primary problems, however, center on how to take people who have been wounded in a prior relationship into a new relationship in which the parents have very strong romantic feelings and are really overly involved in another adult. In this situation the children often feel neglected, that they are not getting their fair share. There is difficulty for the parent and children in mourning the old relationship as well as in learning how to deal with a new neighborhood, friends, and a new way of life. Another problem involves children from different families now being brothers and sisters. Still another involves establishing new boundaries within the family for what roles a new adult will take (Sager et al., 1983).

# NONTRADITIONAL RELATIONSHIPS

Nontraditional marital forms are more and more common today; in fact, many studies believe them to be the most common form. It is important for therapists to understand the various types of nontraditional unions because these are often the types that therapists see most. This section discusses cohabitating partners, gay couples, and ethnicity.

## Cohabitating Partners

Cohabitation is growing (or at least holding a status quo) in the United States. Couples may live together for years while not marrying for one reason or another. Often there are tax and other financial reasons for remaining unmarried. There may be doubts about the long-term viability of the relationship. As long as there is no desire for children, marriage may be seen as unnecessary. It is important to realize that just because people cohabit well together does not mean that they marry well together, and often couples will live in cohabitation for several years very well and then get married and have troubles begin. Strategies and techniques of intervention with cohabitating partners are synonymous with those of marital therapy.

## Gay Couples

Gay couples are in some ways different than nongay couples. There are no readily viable models and limited societal support for this type of relationship.

Gays really do not depend so much on the family unit as traditional marriages do. They depend a lot on friendships. There is less support from families and from society for the maintenance of these relationships, and there is no religious, legal, or tax consideration to stabilize the marriage. There is no offspring involved to keep the couple together and develop. In general, relationships do not seem to last as long as nongay relationships do. Often gays have a host of serial relationships. According to Mendola (1980), the average relationship lasts 2 to 3 years.

A gay couple is not composed of two homosexuals or two lesbians; it is composed of two men or two women. It is important to realize that when people come from a good, stable family, have a history of good psychosocial functioning, and have had successful relationships, these are the most crucial indicators of potential.

Stability in any couple's relationship requires both rapport and resistance. Rapport is a similarity of response and outlook and is important for closeness and affection. Resistance consists of attention, distance, and dissimilarity as the matrix for complementarity and sexual interest. According to this view, nongay couples would tend to be low on rapport or similarity and high on resistance or contrast. In male-female relationships there is greater social sex-role differentiation between partners, but this is not the case for gays. There is an excessive similarity between them, and this often produces fatigue or boredom. As a result these relationships tend to move on. Many people feel that gay couples tend to have stereotypical husband/wife role playing. This appears to be a false belief. There appears to be a considerable degree of variety and variability, and the situation is actually similar to gender role allocation. Many gays have open (nonmonogamous) relationships. Nevertheless, all of the same skills that are necessary in a nongay relationship—communication, problem solving, encouragement—are necessary for gay couples.


## Ethnicity

Everyone is a member of a family, and every family has an ethnic/cultural heritage. Cultural and ethnic values play a significant role in marital behaviors. Many of these values are not consciously held but just seem natural to the relationship. Many families do not come from just one background but are dual-culture families. Cultural dimensions are also involved in the relationships between the couple and the therapist. Therapists are influenced by their cultural values. Cultural issues are defined here as sets of common, adaptive behaviors and experiences derived from a membership in a variety of different contexts and include:

- Ecological setting—rural, urban, or suburban
- Philosophical or religious values
- Nationality and ethnicity

- Types of family organization
- Social class
- Occupation
- Migratory patterns and stage of acculturation
- Values derived from partaking of similar historic moments or particular ideologies

Cultural differences are tied to types of group membership or other forms of contextual inclusion or exclusion not necessarily subsumed under specific ethnic group memberships. Different cultures and subcultures organize different adaptive family arrangements and interactive styles. An understanding of the social/cultural context becomes crucial for assessing the meaning and function of marital behavior. Cultural issues are also present in the couple's interaction with other organizations and institutions. The manner in which problems and solutions are perceived, explained, and dealt with; pathways of seeking and obtaining help; what is expected; and how a person interacts with a professional are all affected by the cultural and social class factors. McGoldrick, Pearce, and Giordano (1982) have described how to work with a variety of different ethnic groups and to understand specific problems that are common to each. Kaslow and Ridenour (1984) did the same with military families.

## AGING

According to Maurice Chevalier, growing old is not so bad when you consider the alternative. Old age may actually hit in the 50s, but it may not appear until the 80s or even the 90s. It may be more attitudinal than physiological. Old age can be a way of life. It can have some similarities to depression. It can be giving up and awaiting death in the hope that death will come before disability, before the money runs out, before the children lose interest, before a nursing home is necessary, or before the partner dies.

Old people are not as likely to come to therapy as young people are. They are more likely to go to hospitals and less likely to seek outpatient solutions. There are some exceptions. The elderly still may be struggling with manic-depression, alcoholism, extramarital affairs, phobias, psychosomatic disorders, and even anorexia. It is no different at 80 than at 20. They can still struggle with the misinformation they got from their parents 70 or 80 years ago and with the disappointments of childhood.

They say the legs go first, then the mind. That is not quite true. It is the eyes, the teeth, and the spirit of adventure that go first. Physical strength lessens and stamina fades. It is not the muscles as much as it is the joints. You begin to creak and stiffen, and things that made you feel good begin to make you feel bad. You go past the point where you do things well for your age toward the point where doing them at all is cause for pride. A person was heard to say that if it does not hurt, it does not work anymore. Sex need not shrivel up and fall off, but it often does.

The onset of old age is quite different. It signals the loss of real powers and the first signs are frightening. At this stage, people begin to prefer the comfort of the familiar to the stimulation of the novel.

## Turning Points in the Aging Process

There are definite turning points in the process of deterioration. Retirement is a danger for those who do not know how to play or learn or love. Retired people are at risk for becoming inactive, conservative, bored, and depressed. This certainly affects a marriage. Retirement is a much bigger change for the man than for the woman. If the retiree is male and his wife is not employed outside the home, her life is changed less than his. Her work has been expanded rather than contracted by his retirement. They have more time together, which may or may not be wonderful. Even if they get along well, he intrudes. He intrudes into her life, interrupts her schedule and activities, restricts her freedom of movement, and disrupts her pace of doing things. He is underfoot at home and has no headquarters of his own. A relationship that worked part-time may be stifling full-time. They may really begin to get on each other's nerves. One person recommended that the first thing a woman should do when her husband retires is to get a job outside the home. But, in fact, there is no such thing as retirement for a woman. There is just a change in the workplace. Many people think that they can move to Florida, and this will be the panacea. Unless the retirement and the move occur early in the aging process, it can be a disaster because they live in cramped quarters among strangers, and they may have to be far more interdependent than their marriage can tolerate.

Old people have a tendency to need one another more, but they begin to bore one another and themselves, and they begin to realize that their children and grandchildren visit them only out of duty and that the youngsters often make excuses to avoid them. They may enjoy their grandchildren's pictures more than they enjoy their grandchildren's visit. The grandchildren probably know this, too.

In every marriage that lasts into this stage, one partner begins to age before the other. They go out less. They talk to one another less and fuss at one another more. They do not seem to enjoy one another anymore or maybe they never did, but they nonetheless become inseparable. Often a crisis occurs, and one partner has to become a caretaker.

*Death*

The death of a spouse at age 90 is more expected than at age 30 but not as easy. It may be harder, as the chances of remarriage are minimal and the loneliness even more intense. The end of that intimacy becomes cruel and bitter. When death occurs, men often do not do very well alone. Some of the most interesting work a family therapist does is with families in this situation, trying to unravel custody battles over an old man who is trying to hold his own family together while starting a new one when he is past the point of maximum flexibility or sensitivity and when he may be sitting on an estate that all the vultures are eyeing. The family continues when Mom remarries. She sees to that. But the money is not secure when Dad remarries, and Dad's new marriage puts a buffer between him and his children because he will join the wife's new family. One of the advantages of being poor is that your children are usually delighted when you marry again in your dotage.

Children do not find it much easier when the aged parent is living alone. The family accuses the aging member of becoming irritable over minor changes, of trying to control things too rigidly, of never wanting to do things, of being hypochondriacal, of only talking about the past, of being stingy and conservative, of demanding attention. It is only after the person begins to get confused and to forget things that the family realizes that the brain is not hitting on all cylinders and the irritating habits were efforts at holding on. Then the old person begins to ignore personal hygiene, to lose things, to hide things. He or she may talk about people who are long dead, wander off during the conversation and leave the phone off the hook, forget that you just called and fuss about your not doing so. He or she may fail to cash checks, may put bills in the refrigerator, and may save old newspapers because they may contain something important but he or she cannot remember what. These habits can be understood and may irritate or worry the family only a little. Mostly, they are just sad.

*Role Reversal*

When the child becomes parent to the parent, there is some friction. The children may have to force the parent to make a will, to make decisions about funeral arrangements or division of property. These dreaded subjects may detonate explosions and may have to be negotiated by a therapist. One of the most awkward is the encounter during which the aging autocrat must be asked by his children to turn over the helm of the family business he had created and developed when he knows very well that none of his children is what he was, even though he cannot face that he is not what he was either. This also involves getting what is called power of attorney.

In therapy, neurological assessment is often necessary; it is very important to do an informal mental status exam. Families have often been known to panic over the subtle signs of intellectual decline. Often they feel that grandpa is crazy; yet the process he is going through is normal. A painful developmental crisis occurs when the old person can no longer live alone. Something has to be done, and therapy may be sought to determine what the family is to do. These are some of the most painful decisions a family must make, and most families have to make them. The expense and all the bother have to be considered. The matter of what to do with Mom or Dad who is now old and feeble can also produce conflict among the siblings. Either all the children want custody or none does, and they fight about who gets the pleasure or the pain of Mom's or Dad's presence in their household. Sometimes they even set up split custody.

No one ever fully grows up, and it is helpful to keep some principles in mind in dealing with the elderly. First, they are perfectly capable of change. Old people must change and probably do so more rapidly and wrenchingly than in any time since their own adolescence. Second, this is a frightening period for most people. They fear their death, their disability, loss of their faculties, loss of bladder control, loss of memory, loss of money, loss of love. Third, they face the same crises that everyone else does.

## ALCOHOL AND OTHER SUBSTANCE ABUSE

In the DSM-III-R classification (American Psychiatric Association, 1987), there are five classes of substance abuse: barbiturates, amphetamines, opioids, cannabis, and alcohol. This section deals primarily with alcohol as it relates to marital problems because alcohol abuse is reported more often as a problem in marital cases and because the same basic treatment applies to all substances. Individuals or couples with nonalcohol substance abuse problems are more likely to contact a substance abuse professional than a marital/family therapist.

Alcohol as an issue in marriage may surface in terms of dependence, abuse, or problem drinking. Dependence is the most serious because it indicates that there is a physiological need for the alcohol and the body is dependent on it. Dependence also means that there is likely to be physical withdrawal when alcohol is stopped. The criteria for alcohol abuse are somewhat less specific and have been a source of ongoing professional debate. Generally it means that alcohol is affecting the individual, either socially or occupationally. The usage may be intermittent or regular. The problem drinker refers to any individual who may not fulfill the DSM-III-R requirements for abuse or dependence but whose drinking creates problems in the marriage. Although the problem may not cause an occupational or social impairment, it may be used as a way to keep distance from the partner. The drinking may not be frequent or heavy enough, but it may be just enough to help the person avoid some of the responsibilities necessary to create a successful relationship—for example, the woman who has a glass or two of wine each night with dinner, the man who drinks only once per month but usually heavily, or the husband and wife who seldom drink but when they do it is heavy and a major conflict results.

Often couples with these problems have the self-efficacy (Bandura, 1987) necessary to stop upon suggestion from a counselor. Likewise, the marital system can effectively change to accommodate this shift. It is important to note that these changes are not made by the counselor. The control of drinking rests in the hands of the individual and his or her marital system.

According to Nichols (1988), there is a reciprocal relationship between marital problems and difficulties with alcohol. Marital discord can certainly contribute to an increased use of alcohol, even to the appearance of alcoholism, but this does not appear to happen very often. Alcoholism, however, frequently results in marital discord, and once problem drinking has made its appearance, it tends to become the major focus of the life of the marital partners (pp. 207–208).

### Assessment

According to Nichols (1988), there are two broad categories that need to be assessed. One pertains to the patterns, role, and meaning of alcohol use within the marriage, and the other is concerned with marital problems, including those related to the use of alcohol. It is important to assess when the drinking problem originated, whether it was before or after the marriage began. Was the spouse aware of drinking problems prior to marriage, and did the drinking become problematic after the marriage? It is also helpful to assess the family history and to see if a similar marital relationship is being created. According to Paolino and McCrady (1977), it is important to understand what system the problem drinker was involved with when the problematic drinking began. It is important to assess whether the couple has ever functioned without the presence of problematic drinking. It is likely that if drinking is a recent problem, the appropriate relational patterns have already been established. The therapist's job is to help the couple return to a previous level of functioning. Otherwise, a more educational approach will have to be utilized to teach the couple to function at a new skill level. It is also important to assess the current status of the marital relationship and its use of alcohol. Is it possible for the individual to stop on his or her own, or will it be necessary to provide support?

### Treatment

We have found it helpful in treating alcohol problems to utilize the existing Alcoholics Anonymous and Alanon programs. We use this as an adjunct to treatment, and we encourage drinkers to work the 12-step program. But we also view drinking as a problem of the marital system.

According to Paolino and McCrady (1977), changing a drinking problem involves three distinct stages: an acknowledgment that a problem exists and that the individual is willing to make a commitment to change; an actual change process in which problematic drinking is stopped and the marriage is stabilized for several months; and maintenance of this change for a longer period.

There does not appear to be any one acceptable method to help the problem drinker arrive at a decision to stop drinking. Many authors feel that it is necessary to have the problem drinker bottom out or to experience severe consequences if he or she continues drinking. Many therapists need to develop their own creative methods to secure this decision. We feel that it is important to have the problem drinker stop drinking, not just to moderate or to drink in controlled amounts. Moderating of drinking is usually something the problem drinker cannot do and actually tends to involve the therapist in an alcoholic game. Systems therapists also know that once this decision has been reached, it is necessary to assist the nondrinking partner to stop engaging in actions that maintain the problem drinking and to deal with his or her own codependent issues. This often involves the cessation of nagging and helping the partner to acknowledge the positive changes that are occurring. The longer-term goal is to help the couple to develop a new marital system with changed attitudes, values, and behaviors.

Working with the couple in the conjoint fashion is the usual strategy employed. Nevertheless, a variety of formats may be needed in order to break up the impact of alcohol on the marriage. The intervention strategies depend on the particular problem, as well as the stage of treatment. It is not unusual to see each partner separately in order to change the marital system by helping the dry partner to be less enabling or the drinker to stop drinking. Therapists have also found it useful to augment treatment with family therapy, couples group therapy, Alcoholics Anonymous, and Alanon, as well as inpatient and day hospital stays. Therapists also need to utilize behavioral contracts, possibly Antabuse, and to develop procedures necessary to prepare the couple for possible relapses. Further information on these approaches and their use may be obtained from Lewis, Dana, and Blevins (1988).

## SPOUSE ABUSE

Spouse abuse is the physical maltreatment of a husband or wife by his or her mate. According to Straus and Gelles (1986), wife abuse is much more common than husband abuse. Women are violent about as often as men in a family, but a great deal of their aggression against their husbands is self-defensive or retaliatory. Straus, Gelles, and Steinmetz (1980) found that younger couples were the most violent and that spouse abuse was higher among lower income families and in situations in which there was unemployment and economic stress, although middle-class violence is common and marital therapists should be alert to its presence. Conflict over children is the form of husband-wife disagreement most likely to lead to physical violence.

### Cycles of Violence

According to Walker (1979), there appears to be a predictable cycle of violence with three phases that vary in length and intensity. The first, or tension-building, phase, may be marked by constant arguing or the escalation of conflict. It may last from days to years and frequently leads to a battering episode. The second phase, the violent incident, often results in police intervention, the woman's voluntary departure from the home, or hospitalization. The final, or conciliation, phase finds the battering man typically remorseful, contrite, and begging for forgiveness. He may buy his wife gifts, promise her it will never happen again, and in some cases may seek treatment on his own.

According to Bandura (1973), violence is a learned response to stress, it is reinforced by the reduction in stress following a battering incident, and men are typically socialized from a very early age to inhibit their emotions and to act out physically instead of verbally. Elbow (1977) collected data that indicated that battering men were strong externalizers, projecting blame and responsibility for problems or conflict onto their spouses. Furthermore, pathological jealousy characterizes many of these men and is often a leading emotional precipitant of violence. Underlying this jealousy are deep-seated feelings of inferiority, insecurity around intimacy, social isolation, and general low self-esteem that may predispose the batterer to periods of depression. The impulsive nature of many of these men further accounts for their inability to control or appropriately express their anger. Alcohol and drug abuse are common, as is a tendency to hold demeaning attitudes toward women. Perhaps the most unifying characteristic is a history of violence as children and in other intimate adult relationships.

Abused women also tend to subscribe to traditional sex roles and values. They have often been abused as children, and many suffer low self-esteem and believe in the myth that they somehow create the beatings and are responsible for the batterer's actions. We once encountered a woman who was so used to abuse that once we were able to intervene and stop her partner from abusing her, she went into a depression because she felt that he no longer cared for her.

## Treatment Assumptions

The following treatment assumptions are helpful to the understanding and development of an approach to work with couple violence (Nichols, 1986).

1. Violence in the family is common and falls into predictable patterns.
2. Social causes, rather than individual psychological factors, account for the majority of family violence.
3. The most useful approach for comprehending and treating family violence (including spouse abuse) is one based on understandings derived from systems theory.
4. The recognition and treatment of spouse abuse are appropriate concerns for all marital therapists.

Cook and Frantz-Cook (1984) have developed a comprehensive treatment approach based upon the following components:

1. Assessment of the problem and extensive history taking
2. An explicit protection plan
3. A written agreement to be nonviolent
4. Differentiation of roles
5. Identification of coalitions and triangles
6. Identification of conflict themes and sequences
7. Facilitation of alternative patterns of communication and behavior

An assessment model developed by Rosenbaum and O'Leary (1986) is helpful in assessing the severity and lethality of the violence. If there appears to be imminent or continuing danger, it is important to refer the wife to a shelter and possibly secure police involvement. The therapist also needs to assess whether the couple wishes to remain together and whether remediation is a reasonable possibility.

If a change is desired, the first step is to stop the abusive and violent behavior. The therapist often has a difficult time keeping a balance in dealing with abusiveness. This process involves rejecting the rationalizations of an abusive spouse, pointing the spousal system toward more productive ways of relating and problem solving, and supporting the needs and feelings of both parties simultaneously (Nichols, 1988).

The therapist needs to clearly understand the following five concepts when responding to a couple in which marital violence has occurred.

1. The abuser alone is responsible for the violence. The victim cannot cause or eliminate the violence.

2. Violence is learned. The abuser learned to be violent, primarily in his family of origin. If the abuser learned to be violent, he can also learn to be non-violent.

3. Provocation does not equal justification. There are always alternatives to violence. There are no circumstances under which violence between spouses is legitimate.

4. Violence is harmful to all family members including the abuser. Damage to the victim may be obvious. Effects on the children may be less obvious but equally serious. Violence is illegal, and the abuser can be arrested, tried, and jailed if convicted.

5. Once violence has occurred in a relationship, it will most likely continue unless changes are made. (Rosenbaum & O'Leary, 1986, pp. 393–394)

## CONCLUDING NOTE

A variety of common problems and issues of marriage have been discussed. This sampling of challenges to the marital therapist makes the rigors of this profession clear. The effective marital therapist needs to have a clear idea of marital systems and how to intervene effectively.

## REFERENCES

Albert, L., & Einstein, E. (1986). *Strengthening stepfamilies.* Circle Pines, MN: American Guidance Service.

American Psychiatric Association (1987). *Diagnostic and statistical manual of mental disorders* (3d ed.). Washington, DC: American Psychiatric Association.

Annon, J. S. (1974). *The behavioral treatment of sexual problems. Volume I: Brief therapy.* Honolulu, HI: Enabling Systems.

Bandura, A. (1973). *A social learning analysis.* Englewood Cliffs, NJ: Prentice-Hall.

Bandura, A. (1987, May). Self-efficacy. *University of California-Berkeley Wellness Letter,* pp. 1–2.

Comfort, A. (1988). *The joy of sex.* New York: Pocket Books.

Coogler, O. J. (1978). *Structured mediation in divorce settlement.* Lexington, MA: D. C. Heath.

Cook, D. R., & Frantz-Cook, A. (1984). A systematic treatment approach to wife battering. *Journal of Marital and Family Therapy, 10,* 83–93.

Dinkmeyer, D., McKay, G. M., & McKay, J. (1987). *New beginnings.* Champaign, IL: Research Press.

Elbow, M. (1977). Theoretical considerations of violent marriages. *Social Casework, 63,* 515–526.

Erickson, S. K., & McKnight-Erickson, M. S. (1988). *Family mediation casebook: Theory and process.* New York: Brunner/Mazel.

Folberg, J., & Milne, A. (1988). *Divorce mediation: Theory and practice.* New York: Guilford Press.

Glick, I. D., Clarkin, J. F., & Kessler, D. R. (1987). *Marital and family therapy* (3d ed.). Orlando, FL: Grune & Stratton.

Greene, B. L. (1970). *A clinical approach to marital problems: Evaluation and management.* Springfield, IL: Charles C Thomas.

Heiman, J., LoPiccolo, L., & LoPiccolo, J. (1981). The treatment of sexual dysfunction. In A. Gurman & D. Kniskern (Eds.), *Handbook of family therapy.* New York: Brunner/Mazel.

Kaslow, F. W., & Ridenour, R. I. (1984). *The military family: Dynamics, structure, and treatment.* New York: Guilford Press.

Kaslow, F. W., & Schwartz, L. L. (1987). *The dynamics of divorce: A life cycle perspective.* New York: Brunner/Mazel.

Kübler-Ross, E. (1969). *On death and dying.* New York: Macmillan.

Lewis, J. A., Dana, R. Q., & Blevins, G. A. (1988). *Substance abuse counseling: An individualized approach.* Pacific Grove, CA: Brooks/Cole.

Masters, W., & Johnson, V. (1966). *Human sexual response.* Boston: Little, Brown.

McGoldrick, M., Pearce, J. K., & Giordano, J. (Eds.). (1982). *Ethnicity and family therapy.* New York: Guilford Press.

Mendola, M. (1980). *The Mendola report: A look at gay couples.* New York: Crown.

Nichols, W. C. (1986). Understanding family violence: An orientation for family therapists. *Contemporary Family Therapy, 8,* 188–207.

Nichols, W. C. (1988). *Marital therapy: An integrative approach.* New York: Guilford Press.

Paolino, T. J., & McCrady, B. S. (1977). *The alcoholic marriage.* New York: Grune and Stratton.

Pearsall, P. (1987). *Super marital sex.* New York: Doubleday.

Rosenbaum, A., & O'Leary, K. D. (1986). The treatment of marital violence. In N. S. Jacobson & A. S. Gurman (Eds.), *Clinical handbook of marital therapy.* New York: Guilford Press.

Sager, C. J. (1974). Sexual dysfunction and marital discord. In H. S. Kaplan, *The new sex therapy.* New York: Brunner/Mazel.

Sager, C., Brown, H., Crohn, H., Engel, T., Rodstein, E., and Walker, L. (1983). *Treating the remarried family.* New York: Brunner/Mazel.

Straus, M. A., and Gelles, R. J. (1986). Change in family violence from 1975 to 1985. *Journal of Marriage and the Family, 48,* 465–479.

Straus, M. A., Gelles, R. J., & Steinmetz, S. K. (Eds.). (1980). *Behind closed doors: Violence in the American family.* New York: Doubleday/Anchor.

Walker, L. (1979). *The battered woman.* New York: Harper & Row.

Wallerstein, J. S., & Blakeslee, S. (1989). *Second chances: Men, women, and children a decade after divorce.* New York: Ticknor and Fields.

Wallerstein, J. S., & Kelly, J. B. (1980). *Surviving the break-up: How children and parents cope with divorce.* New York: Basic Books.

# 12

# *Research*

M ost persons involved in the training of marital therapists believe that marital therapists need to continue developing their professional skills and understanding of couples after training is completed. There are basically three sources of such learning. The most obvious is course work, workshops, and professional reading about marital dynamics and couple interventions. But as helpful as these secondary sources of learning are, they are no substitute for learning through the experience and observation of clinical work. Through supervision, consultation, and review of his or her own videotapes, the therapist can profit tremendously from review of his or her treatment successes and failures. A third major source of learning is the empirical research of others.

Research efforts in the area of marital and family therapy have so burgeoned in the past 10 years that it is nearly impossible for a researcher, much less a trainee or practicing clinician, to keep abreast of this research. There now are nearly 40 reviews of outcome research in marital therapy alone. The purpose of this chapter is to survey research findings that have immediate implications for the day-to-day practice of marital therapy. It is not possible to present an exhaustive review of process and outcome research studies. There are numerous commentaries, and the reader is referred to the excellent research reviews of Gurman and Kniskern (1978b, 1981), Gurman, Kniskern, and Pinsof (1986), and Baucom and Hoffman (1986). This chapter begins by listing the research resources readily available to trainees and practicing clinicians and by reporting research findings on the effectiveness of marital therapy. The chapter then focuses on research findings pertinent to four areas of marital therapy: the therapist's role functioning and skills, the couple's capacity for treatment, treatment format, and differential therapeutics.

## RESEARCH RESOURCES

The major publications in marital therapy that contain current research and theoretical updating are the *Journal of Marriage and Family* and *Family Relations*. Other important journals on marriage and family therapy are *Family Process, Journal of Marital and Family Therapy, American Journal of Family Therapy, Contemporary Family Therapy, Journal of Sex and Marital Therapy, Journal of Psychotherapy and the Family,* and *The Journal of Divorce*. These journals all provide empirical and clinical research studies as well as theoretical and clinical practice. Abstracts of significant studies reported in these journals are presented quarterly in the *Sage Family Studies Abstracts* as well as in the *Inventory of Marriage and Family Literature*. These last two publications are available in most college and university libraries.

## THE EFFECTIVENESS OF MARITAL THERAPY

Two generalizations can be made about the effectiveness of marital therapy: improvement rates in marital therapy are similar to improvement rates in individual psychotherapy, and deterioration rates in marital therapy are similar to deterioration rates in individual psychotherapy. Smith, Glass, and Miller (1980) reported on their meta-analysis of 475 outcome studies and concluded that psychotherapy is indeed an effective treatment. They noted that there was an 80% improvement rate for those needing psychotherapy and receiving it as compared to those who needed psychotherapy but who remained untreated. Gurman and Kniskern (1981) noted a 65% improvement rate for marital therapy and a 73% improvement rate for those in family therapy. These improvement rates held for behavioral therapies and nonbehavioral marital therapies.

Marital therapies have also been associated with both individual spouse and couples deterioration. Apparent frequency of such negative effects is approximately 5 to 10%. These figures are similar to those documented in the practice of individual psychotherapy and group psychotherapy.

There is some evidence to suggest that marital therapy may be the preferred treatment intervention strategy. Comparative outcome studies do favor the marital treatment format in three areas: marital problems and conflicts, sexual dysfunction that involves the marital interaction, and depressive symptoms in one spouse (Glick, Clarkin, and Kessler, 1987).

## THERAPIST'S ROLE FUNCTIONING AND SKILLS

This section details some of the research relating therapists' experience, level and mastery of technical skills, relationship skills, and personal life to the outcomes of marital therapy. This section also indicates some research findings relating treatment failure to inadequate assessment and referral factors.

The level of therapist experience in marital therapy does not have a consistent relationship to treatment outcomes. There are some data, however, that suggest that experience-level differences between co-therapists may weaken their therapeutic effectiveness. Gurman and Kniskern (1981) suggested that therapists who possess a reasonable mastery of technical skills are likely to produce positive outcomes in marital therapy. Such a level of skills can prevent deterioration or maintain pretreatment functioning with very-difficult-to-treat spouses.

Therapist relationship skills have a significant impact on the outcome of therapy. Good relationship skills tend to produce positive treatment outcomes, whereas poor relationship skills tend to produce deterioration. The research suggests that positive treatment outcomes follow when the therapist is active, is encouraging, and provides some measure of structure in the early interviews. Deterioration and negative outcomes are associated with the following:

1. The therapist provides little structure or guidance in the early sessions.
2. The therapist confronts sensitive affective issues early in treatment.
3. The therapist labels and interprets unconscious motivations in the early stage of treatment rather than providing support, gathering information, or promoting interaction.
4. The therapist permits, without challenge, references that accept or promote sex-role stereotypes (Gurman & Kniskern, 1978a, 1981).

Therapist relationship skills have a significant impact on the outcome of marital therapy regardless of the theoretical orientation of the clinician. In other words, the impact of therapist relationship skills is not limited to the more psychodynamic and experientially oriented therapies; the impact is equally relevant in behavioral therapies. Unfortunately, research has yet to articulate the specific therapist relationship skills that work positively or negatively across different kinds of therapy as well as different types of couples.

There is enough evidence to conclude, however, that training programs need to focus not only on the conceptual and technical skills, but also on relationship skills for marital therapists in training.

Coleman (1985) has reviewed several factors involved with failures in marital and family therapy. He suggested that treatment failure is in part a function of the therapist's own life circumstances. Coleman suggested that therapists need to consider questions such as: What is happening in a therapist's own life and experience—including the therapist's own marital-family experiences—and how these may impact on the treatment approach taken with the couple? What are the therapist's attitudes, values, and countertransferences, and how do these impact on the couple in treatment? Does therapist burnout impact treatment outcome?

Coleman asserted that a startling 83% of treatment failures in marital therapy were due to inadequate assessments and referral factors. That the therapist has not collected and elicited sufficient information to know and understand the couple's predicament, needs, and expectation for treatment is unforgivable and may even constitute malpractice. A couple who does not feel understood by the therapist is unlikely to engage and commit to the treatment process and thus may prematurely terminate. Furthermore, Coleman noted that certain kinds of referrals had limited chances for successful treatment outcome. For instance, the referring source can contaminate treatment outcomes by inducing expectations that are unrealistic for treatment. Or one or both of the spouses may have previously been involved in a psychodynamic treatment with an individual intrapsychic focus. They may find it difficult to make the transition to a systems and interactional focus unless the therapist spends sufficient time to resocialize the couple or the spouse to an alternative mode of treatment. Too often, therapists do not elicit information about the previous treatment and expectations for the present treatment or elicit this information and fail to incorporate it in their efforts to engage the spouse or the couple in the present therapy.

## THE COUPLE'S CAPACITY FOR TREATMENT

This section focuses on factors that promote positive treatment outcomes, factors that result in premature termination and defection from treatment, and factors that are predictive of poor prognosis.

The research on spouse and couple factors that promote positive treatment outcomes is quite limited. According to Gurman and Kniskern (1981), when spouses are involved in conjoint therapy, there is a greater chance of positive outcome than when only one spouse is involved in treatment. Other couple factors favoring positive outcomes are compliance with sessions and compliance intersession tasks or homework. Missed appointments and repeated requests to reschedule appointments are generally predictive of limited or poor outcomes. According to Wood and Jacobson (1985), noncompliance with homework is the most common problem arising during marital therapy. Positive outcomes are dependent on the ability of the couple and therapist to negotiate and resolve this matter. Many therapists contend that the greater the couple's commitment to their marriage, the better the likelihood of positive outcomes (Nichols, 1988). When marital therapy expands to include other family members in therapy sessions, participation of the father increases the probability of successful outcomes. Finally, marital type, marital interaction styles, and marital demographic factors have not been demonstrated to be related to the outcome of marital therapy (Gurman & Kniskern, 1981).

The issues of dropout and premature termination are extremely important issues for clinicians. But these issues are seldom discussed in the marital therapy literature. The general psychotherapy literature indicates that approximately 50% of clients or patients do not return to treatment following the initial interview. For those returning, the average length of treatment is only eight sessions. These data are relatively consistent across various types of treatment settings, patient diagnosis, and therapist orientation (Koss & Butcher, 1986; Phillips, 1985). Biglan et al. (1985) reported one of the few studies on defection and premature termination in marital and family therapy. They reported that 30% of cases referred for treatment failed to appear for the first session. These were labeled as "defectors." The researchers found that 30% terminated within the first three sessions, and these were labeled "premature terminators." Thus, only 40% of those initially referred to treatment continued after three sessions. The main reason the "defectors" gave for not initiating treatment was a "change of heart" and a denial that any problem existed. The main reason that premature terminators gave for stopping treatment was a lack of activity on the part of the therapist.

Coleman (1985) noted four variables associated with poor treatment prognosis.

1. A long history of problems and a persistent major symptom.
2. A previous history of individually-focused rather than system-focused therapy.
3. The diagnosis of a relatively severe psychiatric disorder.
4. External referral source and indications of limited motivation for therapy.

## TREATMENT FORMAT

This section focuses on factors in the treatment setting itself that can influence the process and outcome of treatment. These factors include length of treatment, conjoint and co-therapy format, treatment focus, and factors arising in the course of treatment.

Among the psychotherapeutic modalities, marital therapy appears to be one of the briefest. Positive results of both behavioral and nonbehavioral marital therapy occur in treatments of short duration, that is, between 1 and 20 sessions. This brief, limited therapy appears to be as effective as open-ended marital therapy.

Basically, movement and change appear to occur more quickly in marital therapy than in individual psychotherapy. Marital therapy tends to be more action-oriented, more geared to the present than the past, and more focused on problem solving than on insight, as may be the case in individual psychotherapy. In addition, marital therapy tends to deal more with the couple's interactional issues and is based more on the here-and-now and on directly observed behaviors and interactions than is possible in individual psychotherapy. Although many treatment changes are noted immediately, some changes take considerably longer than 20 sessions to manifest themselves.

In general, it can be stated that couples tend to benefit the most from treatment when both spouses are involved conjointly in the therapy. This statement is not to discount the efficacy of individual marital therapy. Recently, Gurman and Kniskern (1986) revised their 1978 position about the relative efficacy of individual marital therapy as compared with conjoint marital therapy. They conceded that in some circumstances, individual marital therapy may be preferable, but, generally speaking, conjoint marital therapy is the treatment of choice for marital problems. Indeed, conjoint marital therapy is the preferred mode of treatment for the majority of those practicing marital therapy. Co-therapy—that is, when two therapists are present and sometimes called multiple-conjoint marital therapy or parallel-conjoint marital therapy—has not been shown to be superior to marital therapy conducted by a single therapist.

The only treatments that consistently correlate with positive process and treatment outcomes are those treatment strategies that increase couples' communication skills. According to Gurman and Kniskern (1981), communication skills are the sine qua non of effective marital therapy. Others have argued that treatment that focuses on increasing communication skills may be a necessary condition for effective marital therapy but cannot be considered the sufficient condition for positive treatment of discord (Nichols, 1988).

A number of factors arising during the course of marital therapy itself may induce negative effects. Glick, Clarkin, and Kessler (1987) listed five such process factors. First, there is an exacerbation of presenting symptoms. In the course of most marital therapies there is a phase in which problems or symptoms may worsen. Second, new symptoms appear. Commonly these symptoms occur in the previously nonsymptomatic spouse. Third, the couple may abuse or misuse therapy. Often one spouse engages in one-upmanship. The husband may say, "The doctor said I seem to have better judgment than you" and then proceed to verbally undermine his spouse. Other times couples refuse to terminate treatment even though the therapist believes they are capable of functioning without it. Fourth, the couple's capacity for change is overextended. Some therapists may overreach the couple's capacities and attempt to make changes that are clearly beyond the couple's reach. The end result is often disastrous. Fifth, disillusion with the therapy or the therapist may ensue. The couple may be trying therapy as a last resort, and when it does not produce beneficial effects, the couple may be even more demoralized. As indicated earlier, the precise incidence of negative effects resulting from marital therapy is not known but is estimated to be between 5 and 10%.

## DIFFERENTIAL THERAPEUTICS

Well-controlled comparisons of different psychotherapeutic approaches that were reviewed from 1970 through 1985 suggested that there was no evidence of differential effectiveness among the various types of psychotherapy. In other words, no one approach seemed to be any better than any other approach. But in their 1986 review, Gurman, Kniskern, and Pinsof (1986) were able to suggest that there were some differential effects as a result of treatment. They noted that the effectiveness of behavioral marital therapy had been clearly established with such treatment conditions as marital discord, anxiety disorders, affective disorders (particularly depression), and conduct disorders. They also noted that psychoeducational interventions were shown to be clearly superior to other methods when schizophrenia was present in a spouse or a family member.

But Beutler and Crago (1987) found that only three disorders—panic disorder, premature ejaculation, and primary orgasmic dysfunction—were indisputably better treated by one intervention (behavioral therapy) than any other. Beutler and Crago commented that treatment specification based on psychiatric diagnosis was not a particularly effective means for planning treatment interventions. Even though the majority of clinicians and researchers think in such "diagnosis suggests treatment" terms, Beutler and Crago maintained that it was more appropriate to think in terms of nondiagnostic factors, such as spousal characteristics, need, and expectations, as the basis for matching treatment. Although the various marital therapy orientations often claimed or implied superiority, there was very little controlled research on the effectiveness of these various approaches. Baucom and

Hoffman (1986) compared six major orientations to marital therapy: behavioral, communications, systems, psychodynamic, cognitive, and experiential. They determined that the majority of controlled outcome research involved behavioral marital therapy, which was found to be more effective than nonspecific treatments in changing communication and other specific behaviors of concern to couples. But these specific changes did not consistently result in a greater increase in marital adjustment and happiness than did nonspecific treatments.

Baucom and Hoffman were also able to evaluate five outcome studies on the communication therapy approaches. They concluded that when compared to no treatment, communications therapy did result in improved communication but had little overall effect on marital adjustment. Communication therapy did teach couples specific skills that led to change in the relationship, but there was no significant difference between the treatment and increased marital adjustment.

Baucom and Hoffman then reviewed five well-controlled studies that compared the systems approach, the psychodynamic approach, and the cognitive-behavioral approach to the behavioral and the communications approaches. (Apparently, there were no well-controlled studies comparing the efficacy of the experiential approaches.) Because of the extremely limited amount of data available in these studies, the authors were unable to draw any definitive conclusions about the effectiveness of the systems, the psychodynamic, or the cognitive approaches.

A word of caution is offered in evaluating the results of Baucom and Hoffman's study. Because distressed married couples were randomly assigned to treatment conditions regardless of the type of presenting complaints and without regard to the individual spouse's and the couple's capacities for treatment, it is not possible to specify what type or orientation of treatment would have been most effective for any particular couple. In clinical practice, the therapist takes into account the unique characteristics of a couple and then attempts to tailor treatment accordingly. In the past, research designs that allowed for this specification of individual differences in the couples were not utilized. Only when such individual differences can be included in the research design will clinical research have more immediate applicability to practicing clinicians.

## CONCLUDING NOTE

When a marital therapist recommends a specific treatment technique or modality, he or she has consciously or intuitively matched the couple's needs and styles with his or her own experience of, or fantasies about, various treatments. The preceding section concluded that clinical research showed that no one therapeutic orientation or technique was clearly superior for particular couples or particular presenting problems. It remains for future research to clarify the differential application and effectiveness of the various techniques. For now, differential therapeutics remains primarily an art. For further information about ways in which the art of making decisions about differential therapeutics or tailoring treatment to individual cases can be done, the reader is directed to Frances, Clarkin, and Perry (1984) and Glick, Clarkin, and Kessler (1987).

# REFERENCES

Baucom, D., & Hoffman, J. (1986). The effectiveness of marital therapy: Current status and application to the clinical setting. In N. Jacobson & A. Gurman (Eds.), *Clinical handbook of marital therapy.* New York: Guilford Press.

Biglan, A., Hops, H., Sherman, L., Friedman, L., Arthur, J., & Ostee, V. (1985). Problem-solving interactions of depressed women and their spouses. *Behavior Therapy, 16,* 431–451.

Beutler, L., & Crago, M. (1987). Strategies and techniques of prescriptive psychotherapeutic intervention. In R. Hales & A. Frances (Eds.), *Psychiatric updates: APA annual review* (Vol. 6). Washington, DC: American Psychiatric Press.

Coleman, S. (Ed.). (1985). *Failures in family therapy.* New York: Guilford Press.

Frances, A., Clarkin, J., & Perry, S. (1984). *Differential therapeutics in psychiatry.* New York: Brunner/Mazel.

Glick, I., Clarkin, J., & Kessler, D. (1987). *Marital and family therapy,* 3rd ed. New York: Grune and Stratton.

Gurman, A., & Kniskern, D. (1978a). Deterioration in marital and family therapy: Empirical, clinical and conceptual issues. *Family Process, 17,* 3–20.

Gurman, A., & Kniskern, D. (1978b). Research on marital and family therapy: Progress, perspective and prospect. In S. Garfield & A. Bergin (Eds.), *Handbook of psychotherapy and behavior change* (2d ed.). New York: Wiley.

Gurman, A., & Kniskern, D. (1981). Family therapy outcome research: Knowns and unknowns. In A. Gurman & D. Kniskern (Eds.), *Handbook of family therapy.* New York: Brunner/Mazel.

Gurman, A., & Kniskern, D. (1986). Individual marital therapy: Have reports of your death been somewhat exaggerated? *Family Process, 25,* 112–117.

Gurman, A., Kniskern, D., & Pinsof, W. (1986). Research on the process and outcome of marital and family therapy. In S. Garfield and A. Bergin (Eds.), *Handbook of psychotherapy and behavior change* (3d ed.). New York: Wiley.

Koss, M., & Butcher, J. (1986). Research on brief psychotherapy. In S. Garfield & A. Bergin (Eds.), *Handbook of psychotherapy and behavior change* (3d ed.). New York: Wiley.

Nichols, W. (1988). *Marital therapy: An integrated approach.* New York: Guilford Press.

Phillips, E. (1985). *Psychotherapy revised: New frontiers in research and practice.* Hillsdale, NJ: Lawrence Erlbaum.

Smith, M., Glass, G., & Miller, T. (1980). *The benefits of psychotherapy.* Baltimore, MD: Johns Hopkins University Press.

Wood, L., & Jacobson, N. (1985). Marital distress. In D. Barlow (Ed.), *Clinical handbook of psychological disorders.* New York: Guilford Press.

# 13
# *Professional and Ethical Issues*

A number of specific ethical concerns are involved in the work of marital therapy. Which partner is the therapist ethically bound to serve? Should the therapist begin working with one partner and try to involve his or her spouse? What is done in the case of a reluctant partner? Should the therapist lie to a couple in order to help solve its problems? Should the spouses attempt to reveal all secrets, even to the extent that they may suffer embarrassment, great anxiety, and loss of respect? These are some of the many thorny and complicated ethical issues that impinge upon the work of a marital therapist. In this chapter we touch on some of these and present the current code of ethics.

## ETHICAL ISSUES

### Orientation to Therapy

According to Hare-Mustin (1978, 1980) and Everstine et al. (1980), couples need to be oriented to therapy in an ethically responsible fashion, and the following five points should be covered:

1. A full explanation of the procedures of therapy and their purposes.
2. A clear discussion about the qualifications of the therapist and the role to be taken by the therapist in the session.
3. A disclosure of anticipated discomforts and risks as well as benefits of treatment.

223

4. Alternative treatments and available referral sources that may be better suited to the needs of the couple.

5. A firm understanding that each individual and the couple as a whole may discontinue treatment whenever they wish.

The requirement that a therapist provide accurate, honest descriptions or informed consent can be overwhelming, if not impossible. This becomes especially difficult for therapists using strategic or systemic approaches or paradoxical interventions (Doherty, 1989). To forecast such intervention strategies is actually to doom the possibility of their effectiveness. Therapists who practice according to such principles naturally want to present their procedures in a less conscious, more general fashion.

## Unwanted Outcomes

Another dilemma is that marital therapy can lead to outcomes not desired by one partner. Rarely is each person equally enthusiastic about the prospect of treatment. Some are bound to be more reluctant than others. Sometimes a therapeutic action or suggestion may be helpful for one individual but not helpful or even temporarily harmful to another individual, at least on a short-term basis. The ethical issue, however, is who should make this decision? Should it be the therapist, or should it be the couple?

## Lack of a Common Purpose

A common challenge to the marriage therapist occurs when partners do not have a common purpose for seeking therapy. An interesting question is raised when one person wants divorce counseling and the other is coming to the sessions under the expectations of saving the marriage or improving the relationship. In this situation, who is the primary client? How does the therapist carry out his or her ethical responsibility when the two people in the relationship have differing expectations? Attempts to balance therapeutic responsibilities toward individual members and toward the couple as a whole involve intricate judgments. Because neither of these responsibilities cancels out the importance of the other, the marriage therapist cannot afford blind pursuit of either extreme (Margolin, 1982).

In marriage therapy, it may not be clear who the patient is. Often the troubled partner is viewed as the patient by the couple, but it is important to designate the couple as the patient. The marital therapist needs to be aware of the ethical issue involved in implying that a nonsymptomatic partner is the patient when he or she originally did not think so or even need to contract for treatment. Many come to therapy hoping to help their partners.

A basic issue is that of equitability—everyone is entitled to have his or her welfare and interest considered in a way that is fair to the related interest of the others. In essence, the therapist "chooses sides" and is often the advocate for the weaker partner (Glick, Clarkin, & Kessler, 1988).

## Extramarital Affairs

One commonly encountered dilemma for therapists is the confiding by one spouse of involvement in an extramarital affair. The disclosure is often made to the therapist alone, and the partner asks the therapist not to divulge it. In fact, the client often demands secrecy. Even though the therapist may believe that dealing openly with the issue of the affair could have long-term benefit for both spouses, revealing it may not be done without violating confidentiality unless the therapist has openly taken the position, as an increasing number apparently do, that he or she will not assure confidentiality regarding matters that vitally affect the marriage unit or where there is evidence of criminal behavior and intent. A therapist who does assure confidentiality is obligated to maintain it for each partner and to be consistent so as to discourage repeated attempts to reveal what was told. If the policy is full sharing, the couple should be informed.

Often therapists are confused about how to handle an ongoing sexual relationship outside of the marriage that the partner does not wish the therapist to reveal. It is helpful if therapists do not get involved in doing couple therapy in this situation. The therapist must be trustworthy and therefore cannot keep secrets. If the other spouse knows of this relationship, the couple can perhaps proceed toward the goal of mutual satisfaction and trust. This applies only to current extramarital sexual relationships. Past events are the property of the individuals involved, and whether they are shared is the decision of the owners of the memory, not the therapist. Generally a therapist will need to say something like, "I don't think I can help you develop intimacy with your spouse if you are seeking a similar goal with your lover. You may wish to continue this unsatisfying marriage because of power, position, children, or other reasons and find what intimacy you can elsewhere. That is surely a respectable and perhaps viable choice, but if you wish to promote growth in your life with your spouse, letting go of your lover will be necessary in order not to become entrapped in unresolved ambivalence." The therapist may agree to work with either or both on an individual basis, but not conjointly.

## CODES OF ETHICS

Several professional association ethics committees have published casebooks of recommendations and interpretations of their respective codes of ethics as well as of how the committee dealt with selected cases. Codes of ethics are by nature generalizable and often debatable. They are helpful with the issues they address, but they are clearly incomplete (Green & Hansen, 1989). Such case-books represent a consensus from reputable professionals to assist practitioners in understanding and applying the principles the codes represent. Nevertheless, ethical codes are in a sense temporary because they require timely revisions that reflect changes in the culture, society, and developments within the field (Hobbs, 1965).

The primary professional affiliation for marriage and family therapists is the American Association for Marriage and Family Therapy. This organization has promulgated a code of ethical principles (American Association of Marriage and Family Therapy, 1988). The association maintains a committee on ethics and professional practices. Operating under the AAMFT by-laws, the ethics committee interprets the code of ethical principles, considers allegations of violations of this code made against AAMFT members, and if the case is heard by judicial counsel, adjudicates the charges against the member (Engelberg, 1985).

The AAMFT has not yet published a casebook to offer additional guidance to its members in adhering to the code of ethical principles. Neither has the American Psychological Association nor American Association for Counseling and Development published a casebook specifically on marital and family issues.

Ethical codes are changing instruments, just as the laws of a society change with the passage of time and with alterations in the social and cultural orders. Ethical principles are broader than the code and hence are subject to lesser degrees of change. The AAMFT's code contains seven major ethical principles, which are as follows:*

1. *Responsibility to Clients*
Marriage and family therapists are dedicated to advancing the welfare of families and individuals, including respecting the rights of those persons seeking their assistance, and making reasonable efforts to ensure that their services are used appropriately.

1.1 Marriage and family therapists do not discriminate against or refuse professional service to anyone on the basis of race, sex, religion, or national origin.

1.2 Marriage and family therapists are cognizant of their potentially influential position with respect to clients, and they avoid exploiting the trust and depen-

---

*Reprinted by permission of the AAMFT Committee on Ethics and Professional Practices, AAMFT, 1717 K Street, N.W., Suite 407, Washington, DC 20006.

dency of such persons. Marriage and family therapists therefore make every effort to avoid dual relationships with clients that could impair their professional judgement or increase the risk of exploitation. Examples of such dual relationships include, but are not limited to, business or close personal relationships with clients. Sexual intimacy with clients is prohibited. Sexual intimacy with former clients for two years following the termination of therapy is prohibited.

1.3 Marriage and family therapists do not use their professional relationship with clients to further their own interests.

1.4 Marriage and family therapists respect the right of clients to make decisions and help them to understand the consequences of these decisions. Marriage and family therapists clearly advise a client that a decision on marital status is the responsibility of the client.

1.5 Marriage and family therapists continue therapeutic relationships only so long as it is reasonably clear that clients are benefiting from the relationship.

1.6 Marriage and family therapists assist persons in obtaining other therapeutic services if a marriage and family therapist is unable or unwilling, for appropriate reasons, to see a person who has requested professional help.

1.7 Marriage and family therapists do not abandon or neglect clients in treatment without making reasonable arrangements for the continuation of such treatment.

1.8 Marriage and family therapists obtain informed consent of clients before taping, recording, or permitting third party observation of their activities.

### 2. *Confidentiality*

Marriage and family therapists have unique confidentiality problems because the "client" in a therapeutic relationship may be more than one person. The overriding principle is that marriage and family therapists respect the confidence of their client(s).

2.1 Marriage and family therapists cannot disclose client confidences to anyone, except: (1) as mandated by law; (2) to prevent a clear and immediate danger to a person or persons; (3) where the marriage and family therapist is a defendant in a civil, criminal or disciplinary action arising from the therapy (in which case client confidences may only be disclosed in the course of that action); or (4) if there is a waiver previously obtained in writing, and then such information may only be revealed in accordance with the terms of the waiver. In circumstances where more than one person in a family is receiving therapy, each such family member who is legally competent to execute a waiver must agree to the waiver required by subparagraph (4). Absent such a waiver from each family member legally competent to execute a waiver, a marriage and family therapist cannot disclose information received from any family member.

2.2 Marriage and family therapists use client and/or clinical materials in teaching, writing, and public presentations only if a written waiver has been received in accordance with sub-principle 2.1(4), or when appropriate steps have been taken to protect client identity.

2.3 Marriage and family therapists store or dispose of client records in ways that maintain confidentiality.

### 3. *Professional Competence and Integrity*

Marriage and family therapists are dedicated to maintaining high standards of professional competence and integrity.

3.1 Marriage and family therapists who (a) are convicted of felonies, (b) are convicted of misdemeanors (related to their qualifications or functions), (c) engage in conduct which could lead to conviction of felonies, or misdemeanors related to their qualifications or functions, (d) are expelled from other professional organizations, (e) have their licenses or certificates suspended or revoked, (f) are no longer competent to practice marriage and family therapy because they are impaired due to physical or mental causes or the abuse of alcohol or other substances, or (g) fail to cooperate with the Association at any stage of an investigation of an ethical complaint of his/her conduct by the AAMFT Ethics Committee or Judicial Council, are subject to termination of membership or other appropriate action.

3.2 Marriage and family therapists seek appropriate professional assistance for their own personal problems or conflicts that are likely to impair their work performance and their clinical judgement.

3.3 Marriage and family therapists, as teachers, are dedicated to maintaining high standards of scholarship and presenting information that is accurate.

3.4 Marriage and family therapists seek to remain abreast of new developments in family therapy knowledge and practice through both educational activities and clinical experiences.

3.5 Marriage and family therapists do not engage in sexual or other harassment or exploitation of clients, students, trainees, employees, colleagues, research subjects, or actual or potential witnesses or complainants in ethical proceedings.

3.6 Marriage and family therapists do not attempt to diagnose, treat, or advise on problems outside the recognized boundaries of their competence.

3.7 Marriage and family therapists attempt to prevent the distortion or misuse of their clinical and research findings.

3.8 Marriage and family therapists are aware that, because of their ability to influence and alter the lives of others, they must exercise special care when making public their professional recommendations and opinions through testimony or other public statements.

### 4. *Responsibility to Students, Employees, and Supervisees*

Marriage and family therapists do not exploit the trust and dependency of students, employees, and supervisees.

4.1 Marriage and family therapists are cognizant of their potentially influential position with respect to students, employees, and supervisees, and they avoid exploiting the trust and dependency of such persons. Marriage and family therapists, therefore, make every effort to avoid dual relationships that could impair their professional judgement or increase the risk of exploitation. Examples of such dual relationships include, but are not limited to, provision of therapy to students, employees, or supervisees, and business or close personal relationships with students, employees, or supervisees. Sexual intimacy with students or supervisees is prohibited.

4.2 Marriage and family therapists do not permit students, employees, or supervisees to perform or hold themselves out as competent to perform professional services beyond their training, level of experience, and competence.

### 5. *Responsibility to the Profession*

Marriage and family therapists respect the rights and responsibilities of professional colleagues; carry out research in an ethical manner; and participate in activities which advance the goals of the profession.

5.1 Marriage and family therapists remain accountable to the standards of the profession when acting as members or employees of organizations.

5.2 Marriage and family therapists assign publication credit to those who have contributed to a publication in proportion to their contributions and in accordance with customary professional publication practices.

5.3 Marriage and family therapists who are the authors of books or other materials that are published or distributed should cite appropriately persons to whom credit for original ideas is due.

5.4 Marriage and family therapists who are the authors of books or other materials published or distributed by an organization take reasonable precautions to ensure that the organization promotes and advertises the materials accurately and factually.

5.5 Marriage and family therapists, as researchers, must be adequately informed of and abide by relevant laws and regulations regarding the conduct of research with human participants.

5.6 Marriage and family therapists recognize a responsibility to participate in activities that contribute to a better community and society, including devoting a portion of their professional activity to services for which there is little or no financial return.

5.7 Marriage and family therapists are concerned with developing laws and regulations pertaining to marriage and family therapy that serve the public interest, and with altering such laws and regulations that are not in the public interest.

5.8 Marriage and family therapists encourage public participation in the designing and delivery of services and in the regulation of practitioners.

### 6. *Financial Arrangements*

Marriage and family therapists make financial arrangements with clients and third party payors that conform to accepted professional practices and that are reasonably understandable.

6.1 Marriage and family therapists do not offer or accept payment for referrals.

6.2 Marriage and family therapists do not charge excessive fees for services.

6.3 Marriage and family therapists disclose their fee structure to clients at the onset of treatment.

6.4 Marriage and family therapists are careful to represent facts truthfully to clients and third party payors regarding services rendered.

### 7. *Advertising*

Marriage and family therapists engage in appropriate informational activities, including those that enable laypersons to choose marriage and family services on an informed basis.

7.1 Marriage and family therapists accurately represent their competence, education, training, and experience relevant to their practice of marriage and family therapy.

7.2 Marriage and family therapists claim as evidence of educational qualifications in conjunction with their AAMFT membership only those degrees (a) from regionally-accredited institutions or (b) from institutions recognized by states which license or certify marriage and family therapists, but only if such regulation is accepted by AAMFT.

7.3 Marriage and family therapists assure that advertisements and publications, whether in directories, announcement cards, newspapers, or on radio or television, are formulated to convey information that is necessary for the public to make an appropriate selection. Information could include: (1) office information, such as name, address, telephone number, credit card acceptability, fee structure, languages spoken, and office hours; (2) appropriate degrees, state licensure and/or certification, and AAMFT Clinical Member status; and (3) description of practice.

7.4 Marriage and family therapists do not use a name which could mislead the public concerning the identity, responsibility, source, and status of those practicing under that name and do not hold themselves out as being partners or associates of a firm if they are not.

7.5 Marriage and family therapists do not use any professional identification (such as a professional card, office sign, letterhead, or telephone or association directory listing) if it includes a statement or claim that is false, fraudulent, misleading, or deceptive. A statement is false, fraudulent, misleading, or deceptive if it (a) contains a material misrepresentation of fact; (b) fails to state any material fact necessary to make the statement, in light of all circumstances, not misleading; or (c) is intended to or is likely to create an unjustified expectation.

7.6 Marriage and family therapists correct, wherever possible, false, misleading, or inaccurate information and representations made by others concerning the marriage and family therapist's qualifications, services, or products.

7.7 Marriage and family therapists make certain that the qualifications of persons in their employ are represented in a manner that is not false, misleading, or deceptive.

7.8 Marriage and family therapists may represent themselves as specializing within a limited area of marriage and family therapy, but may not hold themselves out as specialists without being able to provide evidence of training, education, and supervised experience in settings which meed recognized professional standards.

7.9 Only marriage and family therapist Clinical Members, Approved Supervisors, and Fellows—*not* Associate Members, Student Members, or organizations—may identify these AAMFT designations in public information or advertising materials.

7.10 Marriage and family therapists may not use the initials AAMFT following their name in the manner of an academic degree.

7.11 Marriage and family therapists may not use the AAMFT name, logo, and the abbreviated initials AAMFT. The Association (which is the sole owner of its name, logo, and the abbreviated initials AAMFT) and its committees and regional divisions, operating as such, may use the name, logo, and the abbreviated initials AAMFT. A regional division of AAMFT may use the AAMFT insignia to list its individual Clinical Members as a group (e.g., in the Yellow Pages); when all Clinical Members practicing within a directory district have been invited to list themselves in the directory, any one or more members may do so.

7.12 Marriage and family therapists use their membership in AAMFT only in connection with their clinical and professional activities.

Violations of this Code should be brought in writing to the attention of the AAMFT Committee on Ethics and Professional Practices at the central office of AAMFT, 1717 K Street, N.W., Suite 407, Washington, D.C. 20006.

Effective August 1, 1988.

# CONCLUDING NOTE

The complicated professional and ethical issues of marital therapy, along with a code of ethics, have been presented. This area will receive great attention in the upcoming years as marital therapy and interventions become more commonplace. It is likely that this code of ethics and ethical problems will continue to evolve, just as the laws of society will change with the passage of time. It is important for the professional to be continually aware of changes in what is the appropriate ethical/professional posture.

# REFERENCES

American Association of Marriage and Family Therapy. (1988). *AAMFT code of ethical principles for marriage and family therapists.* Washington, DC: AAMFT.

Doherty, W. J. (1989). Unmasking family therapy. *The Family Therapy Networker, 13*(2), 35–39.

Engelberg, S. L. (1985). General counsel's report: Ethics committee procedures outlined. *Family Therapy News, 16*(2), 16.

Everstine, L., Everstine, D. S., Heymann, G. M., True, R. H., Frey, D. H., Johnson, H. G., & Seiden, R. H. (1980). Privacy and confidentiality in psychotherapy. *American Psychologist, 35*(9), 828–840.

Glick, I. D., Clarkin, J. F., & Kessler, D. R. (1988). *Marital and family therapy* (3d ed.). Orlando, FL: Grune & Stratton.

Green, S. L., & Hansen, J. C. (1989). Ethical dilemmas faced by family therapists. *Journal of Marital and Family Therapy, 15*(2), 149–158.

Hare-Mustin, R. T. (1978). A feminist approach to family therapy. *Family Process, 17*, 181–194.

Hare-Mustin, R. T. (1980). Family therapy may be dangerous to your health. *Professional Psychology, 11*, 935–938.

Hobbs, N. (1965). Ethics in clinical psychology. In B. Wolman (Ed.), *Handbook of clinical psychology*. New York: McGraw-Hill.

Margolin, G. (1982). Ethical and legal considerations in marriage and family therapy. *American Psychologist, 7*, 788–801.

# 14

# *Marital Therapy Case*

T he following case illustrates an integrated approach with one couple. Marital therapy is intended to treat both the marital partners and the marital system. As we believe treatment has to be tailored, the most important aspect of this case is to become aware of how this process works.

Our own approach is much in line with the position taken by Francis, Clarkin, and Perry (1984): In making a decision to use marital therapy, we have to consider the couple, the relationship, the marital situations and problems; the limitations and potential of the modality of treatment; and the therapist's own preferences, attitudes toward marital difficulties, and competence to perform marital therapy. The important component of the tailoring process is determining which therapeutic procedure is most appropriate in intervention.

Bob and Betty have been married for 14 years and have known each other for more than 22 years (see Figure 14.1), having grown up in the same suburban neighborhood. They are each 34 years of age and have three children, ages 6, 11, and 12. The 12-year-old child has been placed in a classroom for children with emotional disturbances. Both indicate that marital affairs occurred after the seventh year of marriage. Betty got involved with another man out of boredom, and Bob thought his involvement was for revenge. Bob has had no stable employment for the last year and a half. He previously had a high-ranking job in city government; however, he lost his position when political parties changed. Presently he is seeking employment but is unwilling "to take just anything." Betty works fulltime as a nurse to support the family of five.

Bob is the youngest of three children. His father was a real estate broker and his mother a legal secretary. Bob's father died at age 45 of a heart attack. He

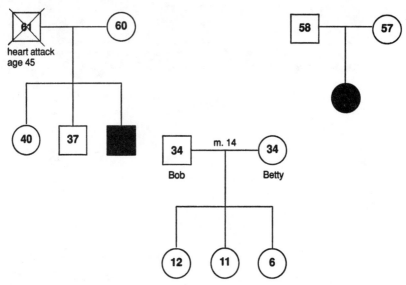

**Figure 14.1 Genogram**

was described as an ambivalent man who had a difficult time being a bread-winner. The marriage was highly conflictual, with frequent arguing and a variety of sexual concerns. His mother was a caregiver who never remarried and continues to spoil her son. Both older siblings have professional careers and stable marriages. Betty is an only child. Her father is a manager in a local discount store and her mother a clerk.

They have stated as the reason for attending treatment that they would like to get a divorce, but they believe they owe it to the kids to try marriage counseling. The stated reasons for wanting to divorce are that:

1. They have no fun with each other,
2. The kids are real problems and Bob and Betty cannot see eye-to-eye on discipline,
3. Bob doesn't support the family financially.
4. Betty isn't available for Bob emotionally.

## FIRST SESSION

The intent of the first session is to get the best picture possible of what the partners are having problems with and what the therapist and couple may be able to accomplish together. Is this a crisis situation or is it a chronic set of problems and difficulties that finally have reached the point of intolerance? Whose idea was it to come to therapy? What do the two desire from the therapist? How do they interact? How committed are they to each other and to doing anything constructive about whatever problems may be present? How willing and able are they to change? What is the prognosis for them and for the marriage? The prognosis may not be as easily answered as some of the other questions. Several weeks or months may be required before the therapist has a clear picture of what the future holds for the marital relationship.

Perhaps the most pressing task for the therapist at the outset is to engage the couple in the process of therapy. We believe, as did Rudolf Dreikurs (1950) and Harry Stack Sullivan (1954), that clients should leave each session with a sense of having derived some benefit. It is often important to leave the couple at the initial interview with a feeling of hope, but this should not be false hope. By providing hope, the therapist often can help them to settle down so they can benefit from the therapeutic process. The therapist accomplishes this through careful attention to the couple's feelings and behaviors, as well as his or her own feelings and behaviors and the ways in which they mix. The therapist must try to monitor not only the content of the sessions but also the process factors. Therapists must keep in mind and view how each partner is responding and how the therapeutic relationship and endeavor are proceeding so that necessary alterations can be made in order to continue effectively and sensitively with the couple.

Bob and Betty were referred for treatment by their family physician. Both arrived early for the first interview, but they did come in separate vehicles. Bob initiated contact with the receptionist and seemed to carry on the majority of the conversation; however, he seemed to look at Betty for confirmation and validation that what he was saying was indeed the truth. The opening statement with couples is a simple and stereotyped one. After having the two seat themselves and exchanging a pleasantry or two, the therapist says, "I know what you have sketched out for me on the telephone and your intake forms, but let's start out as if I know nothing at all about you. What brings you in?" If only one of the partners has made the phone contact, the therapist may wish to go over the information that already has exchanged and follow up with an inquiry, "Is that about it?" which will allow the other partner to catch up.

A question such as "What brings you in?" is a focused projective question aimed at both partners. In this, the therapist will be looking at the answer as well as at how the couple responds. Do the two agree? Have they come for the same reasons, at least insofar as they verbalize their reasons for being present? What are the presenting reasons? Do they fit in one of the following categories: to change the spouse, to dump their mate on the therapist, to leave the marriage, to find out what the difficulties are, to get marital therapy, to get divorce therapy, or what?

After this initial introduction, Bob and Betty were each asked to describe what they saw as the major conflicts in their relationship. Additionally, each was asked to identify the major strengths. Finally, each was asked to respond on a 10-point scale, with 1 being "limited" and 10 being "very committed," to how committed they were to maintaining the relationship. Bob responded with a 10 and Betty with a 1. Through this method, both partners were engaged in the process of participating, sharing their views, and taking a position on how they are experiencing the marital relationship.

As part of the engagement process, an assessment procedure, "Taking the Temperature of Marriage" (Dinkmeyer, Dinkmeyer, & Sperry, 1987) was utilized. In this procedure both partners are asked to independently rank on a 10-point scale how they think they are doing in a particular area, with 0 being a weakness and 10 a strength. In the area of alcohol, no differences were noted. Both ranked the area of entertainment low. The only area that the couple could identify that was mutually fun was "possibly" movies; however, Bob and Betty had different basic tastes in video.

Religion was given high points for both. Both were brought up in the Catholic faith and believe that attending church services regularly is important, as well as having their children grow up in the faith. In-laws was an area in which the couple reported in the mid range or as okay, although Betty did not care much for Bob's family. Work was a problem area, as she resented Bob's not working, and he was discouraged and emasculated as a result of his wife being the breadwinner. Household chores posed another problem area. Although Bob did not work outside the home, he also did not work (or think that he should) within the home. The couple reported different levels of motivation, with Betty having considerable motivation and Bob none. But he is motivated to continue the relationship, whereas she is not.

Sex seemed to be the barometer of their relationship. She was not interested but able, and he reported being somewhat interested but not able. Both rated their health status as good; however, he had sustained a mild heart attack 9 months prior to treatment. Although his recovery has been uneventful, he has been preoccupied with the thought that any exertion might precipitate another heart attack. Consequently, he has become increasingly sedentary, despite reassurance from his physician that he can safely resume his previous active lifestyle. Health was the reason given for his low motivation, failure to share household responsibilities, lack of interest in sex, and restricted efforts toward employment. Neither Bob nor Betty reported having friends or a social life, but they did not seem to be concerned about this situation.

To interrupt the destructive communication pattern between Bob and Betty, the therapist had to be firm. Although a formal history was not taken, many of the important elements in each partner's history are filled in as the therapy moves along. The focus in most sessions is on the here and now, although brief time is spent discussing the respective families of origin. The therapist works hard at this initial session to help them hear what the other is saying, as well as to enable them to acknowledge their own hurts and the hurtfulness of their words and behaviors. This involves a considerable amount of time spent dealing with disagreements, particularly emphasizing implicitly and explicitly the possibilities for problem solving that could be found in their dealings with each other. The therapist endeavors to provide an atmosphere in which dialogue and growth can occur. Once this happens, exploration of individual issues and more in-depth therapeutic topics can be explored. The therapy hour becomes somewhat of a modeling process in which both have opportunities to witness and experience different ways to communicate with one another. This process encourages new ways of relating and behaving.

A formal assessment was completed prior to intake, in which the couple took the Marital Inventory (Dinkmeyer & Dinkmeyer, 1983) and a Millon Clinical Multiaxial Inventory (Millon, 1983). The marital self-inventory confirmed the information that was presented via the "Taking Temperature of Marriage." The Millon scales confirmed the therapist's clinical impressions of dysthymia, a passive-aggressive personality disorder and dependent traits in Bob, and dependent personality disorder and histrionic personality features in Betty.

## COUPLE-CENTERED ASSESSMENT PROFILE

Assessment involves not only evaluating problems and dysfunctions but also strengths and coping abilities. We believe that assessment continues throughout the course of therapy. At the time of the initial assessment, a tension frequently exists between assessment and intervention. Although obtaining a firm grasp of the problems being presented is important, as is understanding the nature and meaning of the presenting symptoms, equally important are establishing the beginning of a working relationship with the couple and making early interventions needed to continue the course of the treatment. Unlike the high-functioning and minimally distressed individual client, for whom an extended in-depth evaluation precedes treatment intervention, the acute distress and dysfunction of a couple may require immediate intervention.

In our approach, assessment and intervention/treatment go hand in hand. Treatment proceeds by phases; consequently, to establish the detailed treatment plans that many clinicians develop for individual therapy is difficult, if not impossible. But developing a clear approach to working with the couple is important.

Effective assessment must deal with both the marital/interactive subsystems and the individual/personal subsystems. As Framo (1980) has pointed out, the relationship between the intrapsychic world and the interpersonal world provides the greatest understanding and therapeutic leverage available to us. By this he means, "how internalized family conflicts from past family relationships are being lived through the spouse and children in the present" (p. 58).

The therapist will have to spend time exploring the background of each of the partners. When possible, we prefer to see the couple together for the initial interview and then to see each partner separately for an individual session, followed up by ongoing conjoint sessions. Individual interviews are concerned not only with the past, such as the childhood and developmental experiences of the partner being interviewed, but also with the present active and live relationships with family members and other carried-over issues from the past that have yet to be resolved but could be impacting the present relationship. To identify the models of relationships that existed in each partner's past is also important. This involves assessing how the parents in the family of origin dealt with each other and their children, and how the children interacted with each other.

## Situation

The couple presented with many problem areas including difficulties with the children, work, motivation, and sources of entertainment. Additionally the couple has financial pressures, and an acting-out child with emotional disturbance. Financially (as well as sexually) Bob feels impotent, and Betty feels resentful. These difficulties have led to a marital stand-off, each living parallel lives with decreasing closeness and increasing resentment.

## System

The couple has many cultural similarities, having grown up in the same suburb and having many mutual childhood friends. Following the "seven year itch," both partners had affairs. This breakdown likely could be part of a relationship cycle that hits the bottom every seven years. Further, the couple is experiencing considerable stress as a result of the change in Bob's health status, having had a recent heart attack. The couple seems to have no clear boundaries in terms of roles or rules, and limited relating ability. Communication involves Betty being over-emotional and over-reactive, whereas Bob communicates in a limited manner and only when he deems it appropriate.

## Spouse

Both spouses have diagnosable personality disorders, per DSM-III-R criteria. He has a passive-aggressive personality disorder with dependent features, and she has a dependent personality disorder with histrionic features. The dependent characteristics are a problem for the couple in that neither seems willing to take charge or to make decisions, which results in family tension, confusion, and conflict and leaves their relationship directionless. Betty gets upset and Bob agrees to change but develops a myriad of explanations as to why he cannot.

Further problems revolve around Bob's health status and the recent heart attack experience, which left both shaken. He also seems reluctant to participate in physical activities, and she resents the cost of the medical problem and the way he utilizes this as a further excuse for underfunctioning.

## Formulation

Bob and Betty have been married for 14 years. He is a passive-aggressive husband who has been using his recent heart attack to avoid returning to work and relating with his wife and family. She is more histrionic and dependent—meaning that she indirectly demands attention from him—but is frustrated by his ambivalence and physical and emotional impotence. The couple has significant deficits in relational skills, particularly assertiveness, as well as a transgenerational history that predisposes both to function minimally. In addition, biological factors (i.e., her caffeinism and his recent heart attack) seem to exacerbate the couple's symptoms and concerns. They are adequately motivated for treatment and appear to have a positive prognosis. A therapeutic mixture of dynamic, systemic, and cognitive-behavioral strategies will be utilized for general relational issues and psychoeducational interventions for specific problems. (Some of the psychoeducational strategies have been highlighted in Table 14.1.)

## Suitability for Treatment

In terms of level of marital functioning, the couple seems to be between Guerin's (Guerin, Fay, Burden, & Kautto, 1987) stage 2 and stage 3. The expectations between the couple appear to be polar—she being doubtful about whether therapy will work or if she wants it to, and he reportedly being overly optimistic and willing to do whatever it takes. Neither has been involved in therapy in the past, and therefore both are unsure about what to expect.

**Table 14.1**   Treatment Plan for Bob and Betty

| Assessment | Goal | Treatment Intervention |
|---|---|---|
| *Biological* | | |
| overstressed; limited coping skills (Bob) | increase coping skills, especially relaxation | bibliotherapy and relaxation cassette, using hypnosis and Basics of Stress Management (Carlson, 1982) |
| anxiety/panic-like symptoms (Betty) | reduce caffeine consumption | follow guidelines on caffeine reduction handout |
| depression/low motivation (Bob) | increase physical energy level | refer to local YMCA for assessment and development of fitness program |
| decreased sexual desire/ fear of intercourse (Bob) | increase frequency of sexual intercourse | explore purposes of dysfunction |
| *Psychological* | | |
| high on perfectionism; demanding (Betty) | develop courage to be imperfect | complete David Burns' (1985) perfection versus satisfaction exercise |
| difficulty with direct expression of feelings (Bob) | learn to directly communicate angry/resentful feelings to partner | written and verbal anger processing exercises from TIME program (Dinkmeyer & Carlson, 1984) |
| non-assertive; dependent; difficulty saying "no" and making requests (couple) | learn assertiveness behaviors | assertiveness skill module (Alberti & Emmons, 1978) |
| discouragement at not working (Bob) | develop meaningful employment | refer to Division of Vocational Rehabilitation |
| resentment toward husband not working (Betty) | increase emotional support; reduce negative feelings | complete "Encouraging Days" exercise (Dinkmeyer & Carlson, 1989), pp. 58–61 |
| *Social* | | |
| limited caring; giving/ receiving of affection (couple) | develop methods to care for partner in appropriate manner | "Encouragement Meeting" and "Encouragement Days" exercise as outlined in TIME program (Dinkmeyer & Carlson, 1984) |
| minimal skills in communication (couple) | increase quantity and quality of daily communication (change balance of communication) | complete daily dialogue exercise/ model and stress attending behavior |
| limited problem solving (couple) | learn four-step problem-solving process | read chapters 8 and 9 Dinkmeyer and Carlson's (1984) *Time for a Better Marriage*, hold weekly marriage meeting |
| no fun time together (couple) | increase couple fun time to a once-per-week basis | alternate dates on a biweekly basis |
| no mutual social contacts (couple) | develop couple friends | each to identify four possible couple friends and invite to fish fry on consecutive Friday nights |
| minimal skills in childrearing (couple) | develop skills of effective parenting | complete nine-session STEP class (Dinkmeyer & McKay, 1989) |
| inequality in household chores (couple) | develop sharing in household tasks | conduct marriage meeting (Dinkmeyer & Carlson, 1989), pp. 97–99 |

Nevertheless, both appeared at the session and neither seemed to be interested in terminating the relationship, despite her verbal statements. If push came to shove, both likely would continue in the relationship. With this in mind, the couple was seen conjointly for treatment.

## Diagnosis (DSM–III–R)

*Bob*

| | |
|---|---|
| Axis I | 300.40 Dysthymic disorder |
| | V61.10 Marital problems |
| | 302.71 Hypoactive sexual desire disorder |
| Axis II | 301.84 Passive-aggressive personality disorder with dependent features |
| Axis III | recent heart attack |
| Axis IV | 3: marital discord, unemployment, worries about health |
| Axis V | current GAF: 50, highest GAF past year: 68 |

*Betty*

| | |
|---|---|
| Axis I | 305.90 Caffeine intoxication |
| | V61.10 Marital problems |
| Axis II | 301.60 Dependent personality disorder with histrionic features |
| Axis III | none |
| Axis IV | 3: marital discord |
| Axis V | current GAF: 58, highest GAF past year: 72 |

## Treatment

At the conclusion of the initial assessment process, after the partners have been seen separately, they are seen together for taking stock, recommendations, and decisions about where to go with their difficulties. At this point the treatment plan is presented. An experienced therapist may do both the initial assessment and what we call the recommendations during the same session. Often, however, the process has to be spread out for a total of four interviews: an initial conjoint meeting, individual sessions with each of the partners, and another conjoint appointment. (This is provided that the couple is not in a state of crisis that demands immediate intervention.)

During the recommendation stage the clinician goes over the treatment plan with the couple. The therapist must provide his or her impressions of what the couple's needs are and then discuss what, in his or her best professional judgment, has to take place to help them. Finally, an attempt is made to clarify expectations and agreements regarding therapy. We believe the therapist must act in accordance with professional ethics and social responsibility and provide the couple as much "truth in packaging" as possible. This means presenting and discussing the recommendations and procedures in an honest, realistic fashion.

Sometimes a couple needs time to consider the therapist's recommendations; other couples are willing to go right ahead and engage in the therapeutic process. The therapist must respect the couple's wishes. The couple is encouraged to discuss the treatment suggestions privately and to raise any additional questions with the therapist, either at the next consultation or via phone contact.

Gerald Zuk (1969) believes that a major goal of treatment is achieved when the therapist is able to obtain a commitment from the couple to be treated on the therapist's terms. He thinks that settling the terms of the commitment to be treated is a major determinant in the outcome of successful marital therapy. It is not simply a precondition as has been thought previously.

The treatment plan (Table 14.1) identifies some of the biological, psychological, and social target areas for treatment. Some areas are directly identified for intervention at this time; others may have to be added. We have found that problems in one area often "take care of themselves" as interventions are made in other areas. As more adaptive behaviors, attitudes, and feelings occur, they tend to generalize throughout the marital system and impact areas that have not been directly targeted.

After assessment and the commitment to treatment were reached, Bob and Betty returned. Both seemed discouraged after a weekend battle with their 12-year-old son, Frank.

Betty:      Frank talked back to me, so I sent him to his room and he refused to go. He (looking at Bob) just sat there and didn't say or do anything to help me.

Bob:       Well, I didn't think you need to freak out over something so simple.

Betty:      You always think it's me. You always back the kids and never support me.

This dialogue seemed representative of the impasse the couple seemed to be experiencing. Betty's over-reacting to Bob's subtle (almost surgical) methods of passive punishment creates further feelings of discouragement, unhappiness, and entitlement. As the partners begin their sparring and dialoging, the therapist attempts to adhere to a position that supports adequate exposure and encourages adequate restraint. This is an art that is developed with experience rather than a precise science.

Therapist:  It seems like you both put a lot of energy into making your family life better.

Betty:      What are you talking about? (Bob nods in support.)
Therapist:  Betty seems to be working on the front line of discipline, while Bob works hard as a "color commentator," evaluating the play-by-play events from the press box.
Bob:        I guess I never saw it that way.
Therapist:  I wonder what would happen if you were to switch roles and have Bob discipline and Betty observe.
Betty:      I'd like that. Whenever Frank would say something, I could say, "Ask your father."
Therapist:  Exactly. You would each be involved with the children differently. Are you up for this, Bob?
Bob:        I guess, but I'm not sure what to do when. . . .

The therapist was effectively able to utilize paradox and reframing to help the couple continue to do what had to be done. The art of reframing it as constructive, rather than destructive, however, changes the pattern of interaction and the method in which Bob and Betty relate with one another. The therapist initiated efforts to reverse their pattern of nonproductive dialogue. The session continued with both Betty and Bob learning to appreciate the other's parenting strengths (i.e., Bob's patience, Betty's firmness). The couple was instructed to obtain the *STEP: Parent's Manual* (Dinkmeyer & McKay, 1989) and to each read chapter 1 before the next session. In addition, they were to enroll in a local STEP class.

Early stages of marital intervention involve reducing stress, disrupting ineffective patterns of interaction, and offering encouragement. During these initial sessions reluctant clients are able to hide behind their more overt defenses, throwing up a smoke screen of words and behaviors that often cloud the issues. Similarly, these sessions provide an outlet to vent some of their more pressing concerns. This has a tendency to alleviate anxiety and stress and may allow clients to feel better. Once the anxiety has been lowered, they often have little or no desire to continue with therapy. That is, with some couples, once the immediate tension has been eased, there is not enough residual pain or conflict to motivate clients toward continuing with therapy. Often the case involves the couple becoming exposed to interactions and feelings that are too threatening to deal with, which causes the couple to want to avoid this and, therefore, to terminate treatment.

In many cases a significant change occurs between the sixth and tenth sessions. With the passage of time and with continued contact with the therapist and involvement in the therapeutic process, the couple begins to have some attachment to the therapist. A crisis occurs in that a decision point is reached. The most simple explanation is that the partners may begin to care about the therapeutic relationship and what it brings them, as well as to move back to the conflict that originally brought them in and the ensuing anxiety, so they are faced with the question of really committing themselves to a process of change or of stopping treatment. Many couples stop by the tenth to fifteenth session, especially in cases in which the immediate problem-solving approaches in crisis intervention are all that are desired. Those who continue beyond this point often move into longer treatment for one to two years.

As treatment progresses, direct intervention of the presenting marital issues becomes a principal focus. The relative importance of issues change over time. Betty, for example, was still discouraged about Bob's lack of employment but was not resentful, because he was meeting with the DVR (Division of Vocational Rehabilitation) counselor. The problem of no meaningful (fun) time together persisted.

Betty:      Why can't we ever do anything together?
Therapist:  You would like to be involved with Bob differently.
Betty:      Heck, yes. We never go out and he always just sits around watching TV like his family.
Therapist:  You're angry and want to see this change. How about you, Bob?
Bob:        I like to do things with Betty, but who would watch the kids. . . .
Betty:      He doesn't believe in babysitters other than relatives.
Bob:        Kids need to be with their families.
Therapist:  What would happen if Frank were to be hired as the sitter?
Bob:        It would be family, and he could use the money.
Betty:      It would also make him feel that we trust him.

The couple continued to describe the mechanics of going out together. The therapist worked at getting the couple to develop solutions that took into account each person's needs.

During the middle stage of treatment, a therapist is seeking to repair, restore, and establish adequate communication between the partners. Therapists can use a variety of procedures to help the couple develop effective communication: clarify, offer feedback, make observations, and interrupt not only the message that one partner is beaming to the other but also partners' intentions as one can understand them. The therapist also can serve as a mediator who persuades them to reinterpret the intentions of their partner, thus removing barriers and permitting the flow of effective communication.

As Bob and Betty began to communicate more clearly, it became more evident that communication was not the panacea to their problems. They began to communicate clearly and found that as they understood the other, they had many profound disagreements. They also understood that they had conflicts in terms of basic needs and wishes. As the communication uncovered the differences between Bob and Betty, the issue became one of how to help the partners deal with those differences. Once these disagreements and differences came into the open, the therapist observed how they dealt with them. Bob and Betty both acted as though they were independent and quite willing and able to handle their own problems; however, they both are largely dependent and wished the other, as well as the therapist, to resolve their difficulties.

The therapist avoided a dependent relationship by not responding to direct questions and by facilitating Bob and Betty to talk directly with each other.

Bob: What should we do when that occurs, Dr. C?
Therapist: What do you think?

Another example:

Betty: Well, I'm not sure about this plan. How do you think I'm doing, Dr. C?
Therapist: *You* seem pleased.

The couple worked collaboratively to create a system of having more fun and involvement with each other. The two decided to take turns asking each other for dates on a weekly basis.

As the therapy progressed, the couple learned to communicate directly with the other, to create boundaries, and to resolve problems as they occurred. The most important event was the increase in respect for one another.

Throughout the marital therapy the therapist was observing and better understanding how Bob and Betty were responding to conflict. They seemed to enjoy conflict as long as it did not get too far out of hand. When this occurred, Bob tended to shut down, whereas Betty tended to increase her speaking volume and rapidity. To help them deal more effectively with conflict, the therapist had to obtain the compromises necessary to secure accommodation and, eventually, resolution. Through the ongoing marital therapy, major amounts of fear and anxiety were removed. The couple needed to clearly understand how the problem might be solved and, specifically, what each of their roles has to be for effective resolution.

In marital therapy the couple often has to take three steps forward and then one step backward, and so forth. The growth pattern is not consistent, and relapses occur periodically. Once Bob and Betty were solidly into working on issues such as communication and conflict resolution, the therapy had moved into the middle phase of treatment. Once this occurs, smoother sailing happens, as the couple has decided to work together and has the skills to do so. Many of the patterns that occur in the relationship are now being identified.

Betty:      I sure would like to start walking after work each evening. Would you be willing to go along with me, Bob?

Bob:        Well, I really would like to very much, but I'm afraid the cool air won't be good for my heart. I have to be careful. We just can't afford any more financial problems.

Therapist:  Bob, it's interesting to note that each time Betty suggests something new to do, you claim it's going to be bad for your heart. Could it be that you use this for an excuse?

Betty:      Yeah, I was wondering the same thing myself. I felt that for a long time but have never been able to verbalize just what it is.

Bob:        I guess it's possible. I don't do it intentionally. I'm not very interested in walking. I would prefer more indoor activity.

Therapist:  Have you got any ideas, then, how you could respond differently to Betty's request?

Bob:        I guess I could say I'm not interested in walking, but I'd be more than happy to do something indoors with you, such as bowling or watching aerobics videos together.

In this dialogue the therapist was able to bring into awareness an ongoing pattern in which Bob utilizes his health problems to hide behind.

Two sessions later a breakthrough occurred when Bob discussed his "fear" of sexual intercourse. As he was indicating a belief that physical exertion would bring on a second heart attack, the therapist facilitated a discussion about the consequences and purpose of this belief. Betty described deep hurt and resentment, which led Bob to understand how this belief safeguarded him from relating to her and was actually withholding. He was able to clearly see how this was in line with his passive-aggressive personality. He agreed to begin to initiate and participate in sexual relations and to commit to fulfilling more of Betty's expectations.

At this phase of therapy, the therapist also is accentuating the positive. The therapist helps the couple recognize the positive thing or things that either or both of them have done, rather than to permit them to seize on or magnify their failures.

Betty:      I just hate to go home after work and find the house in turmoil. The kids don't seem to listen to either of us, especially you.

Therapist:  It's interesting to note that your original problems dealt with physical abuse between your son and your oldest daughter. But now it seems like the problems are much less severe.

Betty:      Wow! I hadn't realized the changes that had occurred.

Bob:        Me neither.

Therapist:  What do you think you did to create these changes?

At this point, the couple began to look at the kinds of movement that had taken place in the relationship. Bob and Betty realized that they had resolved many of the issues that they had requested help with. The success they had achieved in dealing with difficult situations created a history of success experiences that gives them confidence in their own ability to face and deal with problems in the future. They both felt confident that they would like to try to deal with their marital relationship alone.

A follow-up visit was suggested, to occur in one month, to monitor how things were going. It is likely that individual therapy with Bob would be prescribed should his passive-aggressive pattern unbalance the marital system. Occasional couples sessions also may be needed, as they deal with some of the normal life transitions that often throw couples off track and cause them to regress to previous behaviors.

# REFERENCES

Alberti, R., & Emmons, M. (1978) *Your perfect right* (3d ed.). San Luis Obispo, CA: Impact Publishers.

Burns, D. (1985) *Intimate connections*. New York: William Morrow.

Carlson, J. (1982) *Basics of stress management*. Coral Springs, FL: CMTI Press.

Dinkmeyer, D., & Carlson, J. (1984) *Training in marriage enrichment*. Circle Pines, MN: American Guidance Service.

Dinkmeyer, D., & Carlson, J. (1989) *Taking time for love*. New York: Prentice-Hall.

Dinkmeyer, D., & Dinkmeyer, J. (1983) *Marital inventory*. Coral Springs, FL: CMTI Press.

Dinkmeyer, D., Dinkmeyer, J., & Sperry, L. (1987) *Adlerian counseling and psychotherapy* (2d ed.). Columbus, OH: Charles Merrill.

Dinkmeyer, D., & McKay, G. (1989). *Systematic training for effective parenting*. Circle Pines, MN: American Guidance Service.

Dreikurs, R. R. (1950). *Fundamentals of Adlerian psychology*. Chicago: Greenberg Publisher.

Framo, J. L. (1980) Marriage and marital therapy: Issues and initial interview techniques. In M. Andolfi & I. Zwerling (Eds.), *Dimensions of family therapy* pp. 49–71. New York: Guilford Press.

Francis, A., Clarkin, J., & Perry, S. (1984) *Differential therapeutics in psychiatry: The art and science of treatment selection*. New York: Brunner/Mazel.

Guerin, P. J., Fay, L. F., Burden, S. L., & Kautto, J. G. (1987). *The evolution and treatnent of marital conflict*. New York: Basic Books.

Millon, T. (1983) *Millon clinical multiaxial inventory*. Minneapolis: National Computer Service.

Sullivan, H. S. (1954). *The psychiatric interview*. New York: W. W. Norton.

Zuk, G. H. (1969) Triadic-based family therapy. *International Journal of Psychiatry, 8,* 539–548.

# Index